GENDERED CITIZENSHIP

Gendered Citizenship
HISTORICAL AND CONCEPTUAL EXPLORATIONS

Anupama Roy

Orient Longman

ORIENT LONGMAN PRIVATE LIMITED

Registered Office
3-6-752 Himayatnagar, Hyderabad 500 029 (A.P.), India
e-mail: hyd2_orlongco@sancharnet.in

Other Offices
Bangalore, Bhopal, Bhubaneshwar, Chennai, Ernakulam,
Guwahati, Hyderabad, Jaipur, Kolkata, Lucknow,
Mumbai, New Delhi, Patna

ISBN 81 250 2797 1

Typeset in 11/13 pt. Adobe Garamond

Typeset by
Scribe Consultants
New Delhi

Printed in India at:
Sai Printopack Pvt. Ltd.
New Delhi

Published by
Orient Longman Private Limited
1/24 Asaf Ali Road
New Delhi 110 002
e-mail: olldel@del6.vsnl.net.in

Contents

Acknowledgements

Evolving from my doctoral research at the State University of New York, Binghamton, this work was substantiated and completed in the course of the Sir Ratan Tata Fellowship at the Institute of Economic Growth, Delhi. I am indebted to both institutions for providing the space for a convergence of scholarship cutting across disciplinary boundaries. I learnt much from Professor Kelvin Santiago-Valles as his student and teaching assistant. Professor Caglar Keyder's course on peripheral societies was responsible for concentrating my interests in the present field of study. I express my gratitude to both of them for helping me develop the concepts and methodological tools for exploring issues within a framework of sociohistorical transformations. I read and re-read with great interest Professor Gladys Jimenez Munoz's works, deriving useful insights and analytical frameworks for understanding issues of shared concern. Late Professor Terry Hopkins was always a source of inspiration and his memory continues to motivate me. I acknowledge also the support I received from Professor Ana Davin and Professor Juanita Diaz. I am also obliged to Dr David Taylor for his valuable suggestions during the course of my research. For Professor Manoranjan Mohanty and Professor Patricia Uberoi, I have deep respect. In their distinctive ways, at different moments, both of them have encouraged me to know my capacities and to have faith in myself. I thank Biswamoy Pati for showing me the way and Nivedita for her comments and suggestions, which helped me weave together the arguments that lay scattered across the book. I thank my friends and colleagues at Binghamton University, Punjab University, Institute of Economic Growth, and the Centre for Women's Development Studies for their support and for many memorable moments of companionship and collegiality. I thank the library staff at the Glenn Bartle Library, Binghamton, Cornell University Library, Cornell, India Office Library, London, School of Oriental and African Studies Library, London, Hindi Sahitya Sammelan Library, Allahabad, Nehru Memorial Museum and Library, New Delhi, Ratan Tata Library, Delhi University, Parliament Library, New Delhi, the A.C. Joshi Library, Chandigarh, and the libraries at the Institute of Economic Growth and Centre for Women's Development Studies for giving me access to their facilities. The Sir Ratan Tata Trust I thank for the postdoctoral fellowship which gave me space and freedom to continue my research and complete my manuscript. I also acknowledge the financial support I received from the Charles Wallace Trust for my stay and research in London. The Dissertation Year Fellowship awarded by the Binghamton University enabled me to complete my degree at Binghamton University. The comments and suggestions that came from the anonymous referee were extremely helpful in sharpening some arguments and removing ambivalence in others.

My family—ma and papaji, Ujjwal and Anatya, sisters Anamika and Aparna, Bhaiya and Bhabhiji—have always been a source of strength, love and affection. I dedicate this work to my parents Usha and Siddeshwari who simply gave without expectations of return.

1

Citizenship: Conceptual Exploration

More than twenty years after the concept of citizenship had gone 'out of fashion' among political theorists, its return was announced in 1994 in an article titled 'Return of the Citizen: A Survey of Recent works on Citizenship Theory' in the journal *Ethics* (Kymlicka and Norman 1994, 352).[1] The decade of the nineties, indeed, saw a renewed and hitherto unprecedented interest in the notion, manifested in a deluge of writings on citizenship. A common strand running through almost all these writings, however, is that the concept of citizenship has transformed under conditions specific to the late twentieth century.[2] Although there have been other ages of 'heightened consciousness of citizenship', the writings argue that the present time is different. While the earlier periods of increased interest in citizenship were associated with specific states, in the present

---

[1]Will Kymlicka and Wayne Norman propose that citizenship has become the 'buzz word' among thinkers on all points of the political spectrum.

[2]An exploration of recent writings on citizenship will be taken up in chapter six.

context it is not confined to a single state; *it is virtually global in its extent.*[3]

One is left bewildered by this sudden burst of energy among scholars to redefine the frontiers of citizenship in a supposedly 'new' context of globalisation. The assumption on which the redefinition of citizenship is proposed as well as the terms of redefinition appear fraught with contradictions. The present work engages with this scholarship to unravel these contradictions. It proposes that the 'newness' of the circumstances described as 'specifically' late twentieth century were present at least a century before and may be seen as persisting from the nineteenth century. It was largely in the context of 'globalisation', that is, the expansion and consolidation of Europe, a feature of the modern world system from the sixteenth century onwards, the slave trade, imperial domination, competition among states and political and social groups within states, and the production of the 'West' and 'the colonies' or the 'third world' as sociohistorical realities that mutually though hierarchically constituted each other, that the discursive formulation of the 'universal citizen' took place. The notion of 'man' and 'citizen' was part of the same discursive formulation, one augmenting the other. The exclusionary domain of citizenship was very much conditioned in this context by the way women, slaves, workers, and subject peoples as social categories and as lived experiences were simultaneously incorporated within and omitted from national-cultural and juridico-political identities as citizens.

Spread over six chapters, this work seeks to draw attention to citizenship as a terrain of conflict and struggle, where a multitude of social and political forces and ideological formulations exist in unequal and often conflicting relationships. It argues that in specific historical contexts, the 'citizen' is an exclusive category, epitomising the hegemonic socioeconomic forces. At the same time, it also seeks to show that the idea of citizenship is

---

[3]The earlier periods were, fifth to fourth century BC Athens, first century BC to first century AD Rome, late medieval Florence, late eighteenth-century America and France (Heater 1999, 1).

potentially emancipatory, so that at different moments in history 'becoming a citizen' has involved either an extension of the status to more persons or a liberatory dismantling of hitherto existing structures of oppression, which were replaced by more egalitarian and inclusive structures. This work hopes to bring out this paradox in the nature of citizenship by stressing its liberatory potential as a 'momentum concept'[4] as well as the limits of the concept that immediately come into play when citizenship unfolds in practice. While delineating citizenship's paradoxical nature, this work also points out that as an analytical category, its constituent elements are uncertain and often contradictory, making it difficult to outline a precise notion of citizenship. There would be divergent responses, for example, to questions pertaining to whether rights or duties are the defining elements of citizenship, or whether the arena of politics or state activities is its rightful domain as opposed to the spheres of culture, economy, and society. Again, there would be also no consensus on whether citizenship is only a status or a measure of activity, on what is of primary significance for citizenship—the autonomy of the individual or the community and the societal contexts which shape the needs of the individual—and on questions pertaining to the unit of membership, viz., the nation-state, or the global civil society.

This work proposes that the divergences and uncertainties in the theory of citizenship have emerged historically as diachronous strands. In order to fully comprehend the idea, it is important to explore these various strands in their specific historical contexts, keeping in mind, however, that at each historical moment the earlier strands coexist, which keep alive the tensions and uncertainties over the form and content of citizenship. A historical-conceptual perspective has, therefore,

---

[4]J.Hoffman used the expression to refer to citizenship's internal logic that demands that its benefits necessarily become progressively more universal and egalitarian. See 'Citizenship and the State', paper presented at the Conference on Citizenship for the Twenty-first Century, University of Central Lancashire, October 1997, cited in Keith Faulks (2000, 3).

been adopted in the present work. Since the form and substance of citizenship reflect the dominant configuration of socioeconomic and political forces, the specificity of citizenship in each historical period can be understood by seeking answers to questions such as: Who are the citizens? Who are excluded from citizenship and what is the process/basis of exclusion? What is the nature of citizenship? Is it a legal status indicating entitlements or does it also involve active participation in political life? What kind of relationship between the individual and religious-cultural community is envisaged in the rights and responsibilities of citizenship? What are the avenues of participation towards building responsible citizenship? Answers to such questions would give an insight into the manner in which the notion of citizenship has evolved historically and the complexities of contemporary debates.

Historical Development of the Concept of Citizenship[5]

As an idea inspiring struggle and as an 'instituted process' whereby in specific historical settings citizenship rights are engendered through the interaction of 'social practices' with 'institutional ideals and rules of legal power' (Margaret Somers 1993, 589, 610–11), citizenship has remained an enduring link between political thought and practice in ancient and present times. The word citizenship itself is derived from the Latin *civis* and its Greek equivalent *polites* that means member of the *polis* or city. The manner in which citizenship is understood today as a system of equal rights as opposed to privileges ascribed by conditions of birth took root in the French Revolution (1789). With the development of capitalism and liberalism, the idea of the citizen as an individual bearing rights irrespective of her/his class, race, gender, ethnicity, etc., became further entrenched.

---

[5]For details of the historical development of citizenship see Derek Heater, *Citizenship: The Civic Ideal in World History, Politics and Education* (1990), *What is Citizenship?* (1999), Michael Walzer, 'Citizenship', in *Political Innovation,* eds. Ball, Farr and Hanson (1989) and Gershon Shafir, ed., *The Citizenship Debates: A Reader* (1998).

Since the 1980s, globalisation and multiculturalism have provided the contexts within which this notion of citizenship has been challenged. Thus, the development of the ideas which surround the concept of citizenship can be attributed to four broad historical periods: (i) classical Graeco-Roman periods (fourth century B.C. onwards), (ii) late medieval and early modern periods including the period of the French and American Revolutions, (iii) the developments in the nineteenth century corresponding to the growing influence of liberalism and capitalism, and, (iv) the contests over the form and substance of citizenship in the late twentieth century with increasing preoccupation with multiculturalism and community rights. Two dominant strands or traditions of rights and citizenship can be seen to have developed over these periods: (i) civic republicanism characterised by the ideas of common good, public spirit, political participation, and civic virtue, and, (ii) liberal citizenship with an emphasis on individual rights and private interests. The Marxists and feminists have criticised both these traditions as exclusionary and have suggested radical changes in the theory and practice of citizenship. Similarly, cultural pluralists, radical pluralists, and civil society theorists have offered alternative ways of thinking about citizenship and rights.

The classical period and republican citizenship

In its earliest forms, in the Greek republics or city-states, citizenship was an expression of the inherent centrality of the political element in human nature and remained the primary organising principle of human life. Greek republics, such as Athens and Sparta, were closely knit, self-governing political communities characterised by small populations and minimum social differentiation. The organisation of the republic was based on familiarity and trust, principles of active political participation, the prioritisation of the public and political aspects of life, and the primacy of the identity of man [sic] as citizen. The idea of citizenship around which the city-states were organised may be seen as manifesting the conditions in which human beings may, following the Aristotelian dictum, realise their natural selves. In its classical formation, therefore,—as a binding force in the community and as the means by which human beings could be consonant with their true nature—citizenship emerged as 'a framework for securing freedom for citizens'. This notion of citizenship as the means as well as the state or condition of freedom has been an enduring element of citizenship since classical times.[6]

An important element of citizenship as a means and condition of freedom was the idea of citizenship as participation in civic life. The Greek citizens were described by Aristotle as 'all who share in the civic life of ruling and being ruled in turn'. While the idea of citizenship as participation continues to be a significant component of active citizenship, zealously cherished by those who espouse citizenship as a civic ideal, in the context of classical Greece, not everyone could share in the civic life of ruling and being ruled. Citizenship was limited to those having the *capacity* to participate in the process of governance and was confined to 'free native-born men', excluding women, children, slaves, and resident aliens. In the ultimate analysis, therefore, citizens constituted only a small part of the population whose participation in public life was made possible by the exclusion and subordination of the private sphere of family and economic life, and by the existence of slaves, who were responsible for performing the principal economic function. Thus, the classical notion of citizenship while handing down the legacy of

---

[6]The idea of citizenship as a state of freedom is also seen in its formulation as transcendence of the instrumental sphere of necessity, in which we toil to satisfy our material wants, into the sphere of freedom in collective rational and moral deliberation over a common destiny. This contrast has been conceptualised in multiple forms, for example, as emancipation from the private sphere of the household (*oikos*) into the public sphere of political life (*polis*) or, as Pocock chooses to designate it, from the world of things into the world of persons and actions. This definition of freedom as an aim sought after for its own sake shows, in his words, that 'citizenship is not just a means to being free it is the way of being free itself' (Shafir 1998, 3).

citizenship as a 'realm' of freedom and participation, also spelt its association with privileges and exclusion.

The Greek idea of citizenship as active participation was modified during the time of Roman imperialism, dictated by the need to hold together a large and heterogeneous empire. As fresh grounds of inclusion were added to meet the need of integrating a diverse population into the Roman Empire, a gradation within the framework of citizenship was introduced. While within the *polis* there existed only one kind of citizenship, whereby all citizens enjoyed equal privileges of participation and governance, in the Roman Empire, the idea of citizenship was modified by the introduction of a passive notion of citizenship as legal status. The introduction of this element brought large numbers of people, ethnically different from Romans, within the purview of Roman influence by extending to them the protection of a uniform set of laws. Subsequently, citizenship could now be imagined not solely as participation in the making and implementing of laws (as in the Greek tradition), but also as a legal status involving certain rights and equal protection of the law. The new element of citizenship as legal status, while making possible a degree of inclusiveness (that is, including non-Romans into Roman citizenship), added also a hierarchy of status by introducing the second-class category of *civitas sine suffragio* (citizenship without franchise, that is, legal but not political rights). Moreover, women and the lowest classes (chiefly rural) continued to be denied the status of citizens.

The nature of citizenship was modified in yet another way in the transition from the Greek self-governing city-states to the massive Roman Empire. The conception of freedom was altered from an enabling state of freedom deriving from participation in political decision making to a legal status that merely provided protection from arbitrary rule. The increase in the scale of administration (the empire as different from the city-state) also meant that it was not possible for all who had the status of citizens to participate in the affairs of governance. The characteristics of a citizen, however, continued to be marked in a way so that, ideally, citizenship denoted activity or manifested the potential or capacity for activity. Citizens were required thus to develop qualities of 'civic virtue', a term derived from the Latin word *virtus* which meant 'manliness' in the sense of performing military duty, patriotism, and devotion to duty and the law.

The late medieval and early modern periods

About the sixteenth century, the notion of citizenship as a legal status, which was, as discussed earlier, a strand in the notion of citizenship in the Roman tradition, became dominant. The concerns of absolutist states with imposing their authority over heterogeneous populations provided the context in which a citizen came to be defined by Jean Bodin, the sixteenth century jurist, as 'one who enjoys the common liberty and protection of authority'. The citizen, in this view, was, unlike the Greek citizen, not himself an authority, but, following the Roman tradition, someone who was under the protection of the state. Unlike the Greek and Roman traditions, however, this view of citizenship was primarily a passive idea. Citizenship in this period did not stand for common (shared) public responsibilities and civic virtues. Instead, the notion of 'common (shared) liberty' became the primary concern of citizenship. This concern embodied a 'passive' or 'negative' notion of citizenship. It indicated claims for 'security' or protection which was to be provided by the authorities. For the early liberals, what was to be protected was one's physical life (as in Hobbes), the family and home (as in Bodin and Montesquieu), or conscience and property (as in Locke). The principle of liberty thus established the primacy of the private and the familial world. The protection of authority was needed primarily to preserve this domain. Citizens were, thus, not political people, the political community was not the predominant core of their lives, but rather the outer framework in which each citizen enjoyed the liberty of private pleasures and pursuits of happiness and, as mentioned earlier, the protection and security of the private/familial domain in which these pleasures were realised.

Thus, the principle of imperial inclusiveness can be seen to have brought about, in this period, a passive notion of citizenship as a legal status.[7] A nostalgia for citizenship as activity, as in classical Greece and Rome, with an emphasis on civic virtue and public duty, however, persisted. Alongside the notion of citizenship as a status that guaranteed the enjoyment of liberty, the emphasis on public responsibilities and civic virtue remained influential as an ideal. Machiavelli, for example, praised the ideal of 'civic virtue' in classical republicanism. He firmly believed that men [sic] had to be kept constantly alert to their performance of civic obligations, which could be achieved by education, religion, and a fear of consequences in case of dereliction of citizenship duties. Montesquieu, likewise, argued that a state based on the principle of popular participation, as distinct from other forms of government, depends for its stability on the civic virtue of its citizens. For Rousseau, civic virtue and participation were the necessary elements of citizenship. He saw the 'General Will' as citizens contributing without thought of personal advantage to political decisions. It may be pointed out that all the thinkers of this period looked at 'civic virtue' as an ideal to be pursued and lamented the lack of citizenship qualities in their own social-political contexts. Machiavelli, for example, lamented the fact that few of the Italian states of the sixteenth century

---

[7]Finer points out that after a millennium of breakdown, then near-anarchy and then feudalism, when the Europeans did *reinvent* the state, what they reinvented was in many respects unlike any antecedent. Legalism was one such characteristic. The individual was not a mere subject but a citizen in the following sense: Athenian citizenship involved active and direct participation in public policy making and administration, while Roman citizenship conferred the active right to choose one's magistrates. These forms of citizenship are what the French revolutionaries came to call *active* citizenship. In these newly emergent European states, c.1500, only a few enjoyed such active citizenship; but all free men enjoyed certain traditional inherent rights to, notably, life, liberty, and above all, property. In this sense they were not just subjects (that is, mere objects to be administered) but *passive* citizens. S.E.Finer, *The History of Government III: Empires, Monarchies and the Modern State* (1999, 1298).

displayed the qualities of the ancient republics and few men the qualities of virtue. Most thinkers of this period (sixteenth to eighteenth centuries), including Rousseau and Montesquieu whose ideas influenced the American and French Revolutions, favoured the revival of the civic ideals of the classical republican tradition, which had been sidetracked by pursuits of private pleasures and personal interests.

It was this strand of civic republicanism, which was a feature of classical tradition and which remained an elusive ideal in the medieval and early modern periods, that was resurrected by the French Revolution in 1789. As mentioned before, the period from the sixteenth to the eighteenth centuries saw the principle of imperial inclusiveness bring in a passive notion of citizenship as a legal status. Alongside this legal imperative for citizenship as status, however, was a growing nostalgia for the civic republicanism of classical Greece and Rome that had emphasised civic virtue. The French Revolution was a revolt against the passive citizenship of the early modern times. It attempted to resurrect the republican ideals of participation against the claims of empire and the monarchical or liberal state. Apart from attempting to change the apolitical lives of the citizens, the French revolutionary tradition introduced an important element to citizenship, which changed the way in which rights were incorporated into the notion of citizenship. In fact the manner in which citizenship is understood today, as a system of horizontal (equal) rights as against the hierarchical (feudal) system of privileges, has its roots in the doctrines of the French Revolution. The French Revolution and the 'Declaration of the Rights of Man and Citizens' gave rise to the notion of the citizen as a 'free and autonomous individual' participating in making decisions which all had agreed to obey. Thus, the conception of the citizen established by the French Revolution combined the classical connotation of citizenship as civic participation with modern liberal individualism.

The revival of civic republicanism, and its association with the idea of the citizen as an autonomous and rational individual, owed its emergence to nationalism as a powerful force that redefined the form of sociopolitical solidarity and paved the way for a more democratic notion of citizenship. Generally understood, nationalism refers to the self-definition and self-consciousness of the 'nation' or 'a people' as a unified entity. An expression of solidarity or interconnections among people as well as recognition by others of this solidarity is integral to nationalism. In other words, nationalism involves the self-definition by a people that they constitute a nation, the consciousness that there is something about them as a nation that makes them different from other nations, and that there is a larger imperative from which the self-definition as nation derives. The definition of nationalism by Anthony Smith as 'an ideological movement, for the attainment and maintenance of self-government and independence on behalf of a group, some of whose members conceive it to constitute an actual or potential nation like others', captures the core content of nationalism, which he sums up in the phrase 'ideal of independence' (Smith 1983, 171). The aspiration for solidarity and sovereignty implies that the group should be free from external interference and internal divisions to frame its own rules and set up its own institutions in accordance with its needs and 'character'. The group is self-determining because its individuality gives it laws that are peculiar to it. Only the assembly of all the citizens of the community acting in concert can make laws for the community; no section, no individual, and no outsider can legislate (Smith 1983, 171).

It is significant that the idea of the 'nation' rooted in identity and sovereignty was remarkably different from its earlier usages. In ancient Rome, the Latin word *natio*, meaning 'a group of outsiders', referred *to the communities of foreigners* who lived in Rome as aliens and did not have the privilege of Roman citizenship. Moreover, the term *nation* had a derogatory connotation insofar as being a 'national' placed one below Romans in terms of status. In its modern usage, notably in the sixteenth century, reflecting the transformations in the socioeconomic contexts of modernity, 'nation' came to be understood as a synonym for 'people' and acquired its modern political meaning as a 'sovereign people'.[8] This modern meaning of nation as connoting a sovereign people or a community of equals made nationhood a desirable status. Moreover, the concept also assumed an unprecedented universality. The concept 'nation' became the overarching identity embracing every member of the political community, each one of whom had a national identity. It must be noted that with the new meaning and widened scope of nation, a dramatic change occurred in the meaning of 'people' itself. Before it came to be associated with the nation, the term 'people' was generally used to refer to the 'masses', the 'rabble', or the lower class, and the nation referred to the elite. The equation of the two concepts—'nation' which meant 'elite' and 'people' which meant 'plebs'—implied a reconceptualisation of both the concepts. The 'people' as 'nation' acquired immense prestige and far from being the depoliticised rabble and masses were redefined as an object of loyalty and the basis of political solidarity. With the new association, when one talked of the English, French, German, or Russian people, one referred to all the constituent members, the free and equal members constituting the citizenry. This was accompanied by a major transformation in the social order. Defined as a nation, the community, inclusive of all classes, had to be imagined as sovereign, and as a community of equals (Greenfeld 2001).

The nineteenth and twentieth centuries and the modern notion of citizenship

With the development of capitalist market relations and the growing influence of liberalism in the nineteenth century, the combination of the two traditions—civic republicanism and liberal individualism—proved tenuous. The idea of citizens as individuals with private and conflicting rather than a

---

[8]For a study of the changing meanings of 'nation' see Liah Greenfeld, 'Etymology, Definitions, Types', in *Encyclopedia of Nationalism* (2001, 251–65).

commonality of interests gradually gained precedence. The classical connotations of citizenship as civic activity, public spiritedness, and active political participation were relegated to a vestigial past. In its place a much less demanding liberal citizenship involving a loosely committed relationship to the state, held in place by a set of civic rights honoured by the state, which in turn interfered as little as possible in the citizen's life, took over. The emergence of a market economy and an influential bourgeoisie was accompanied by the dismantling of the existing (feudal and quasi-feudal) socioeconomic structures, which with their emphasis on personal subservience and entrenched social and economic hierarchies had fettered individual initiative and profit making, which were the core elements of capitalism ((Heater 1999, 4).

Heater (1999, 8) has delineated the transformatory process from the precapitalist socioeconomic relations and political system to the modern form of citizenship in the following table.

Feudalism →	*Capitalism* →	*Citizenship*
Individual subservience	Individual initiative	Individual rights
Hierarchical society	Permeable class structure	Civic equality
Provincially fragmented society	Open access to markets	National identity

As the table shows, the idea of citizenship that emerged in the context of burgeoning capitalism was due largely to the replacement of the defining elements of the feudal society, viz., individual subservience by individual autonomy and initiative, accompanied by the extension of individual rights; a rigid hierarchised society restricting horizontal mobility by notions of individual mobility across social class, made possible by the idea of equality among citizens; and the replacement of a localised civil society by an all-encompassing national political community (Heater 1999, 7–8).

In his paradigmatic work on the development of citizenship in England, T.H.Marshall's influential account of the growth of citizenship in Britain over the last 250 years sees citizenship as having grown in a peculiar relationship of conflict and collusion with capitalism. His widely accepted definition of citizens as 'full and equal members of a political community' comes basically from the study of citizenship as a process of expanding equality against the inequality of social class, which is an element of capitalist society. In *Citizenship and Social Class* (1950), Marshall distinguishes three strands or bundles of rights constituting citizenship, viz., civil, political, and social. Civil rights defined by Marshall as 'rights necessary for individual freedom' include freedoms of speech, movement, conscience, the rights to equality before the law, and the right to own property. These were 'negative' rights in the sense that they limited or checked the exercise of government power. Political rights, viz., the right to vote, the right to stand for elections, and the right to hold public office, provided the individual with the opportunity to participate in political life. The provision of political rights required the development of universal suffrage, political equality, and democratic government. Social rights, argued Marshall, guaranteed the individual a minimum social status and provided the basis for the exercise of both civil and political rights. These were 'positive' rights 'to live the life of a civilised being according to the standards prevailing in society'. These standards of life and the social heritage of society are realised through active intervention by the state in the form of social services (the welfare state) and educational system. Each of these three strands identified by Marshall have, he suggests, a distinct history. The history of each, moreover, was specific to a particular century—civil rights in the eighteenth century, political rights in the nineteenth century, and social rights in the twentieth and corresponded with the development of the judiciary, the parliamentary institutions of governance, and the educational system and the welfare state, respectively (Marshall 1950, 8).

Marshall's evolutionary, simple threefold typology of citizenship rights, applied to the historical development of rights and duties in England since the eighteenth century, however, was not entirely true for other societies. Civil rights, for example, were not fully established in most European countries until the early nineteenth century. Even where they were generally achieved, some groups were omitted. Although the constitution granted such rights to Americans well before most European states had them, blacks were excluded. Even after the Civil War, when blacks were formally given these rights, they were not able to exercise them. While the legal and political rights were being won in Europe, colonisation was proceeding in many parts of the world. Almost without exception, colonised peoples were excluded from full citizenship of the parent states of the colonial regimes (and normally also within the colonial states themselves). The majority of the population acquired legal and political rights only with the disappearance of colonialism in the twentieth century.

Nonetheless, the idea that modern citizenship is inherently egalitarian—having the capacity to extend and deepen itself by bringing into its fold increasing numbers of people and changing its content to meet emergent needs—is proposed in Marshall's account. Bryan Turner too identifies this element of modern citizenship when he sees it as having an inherent impetus towards universality '…as a series of expanding circles which are pushed forward by the momentum of conflict and struggle' (Turner 1986, xii). The element of equality and universality are much emphasised by those espousing the virtues of liberal citizenship. The definition of citizenship given by Marshall as 'full and equal membership in a political community' (Marshall and Bottomore 1992, 50–51) encapsulates the two promises which modern citizenship makes: (i) a 'horizontal *camaraderie*' or equality as opposed to hierarchical inequalities among members of the 'political community', and, (ii) the promise of 'integration' whereby citizenship gradually brings into its fold various marginalised sections of the population. This membership is also then the expression of an identity, of a sense of belonging to a political community, which is the nation-state, and it assures a share in a common (national) culture and social heritage.

Both these promises of liberal citizenship, viz., of equality and universality are based on an acceptance of the freedom of the competitive market forces and the subsequent inequality of social class. It is here that Marshall's description of the growth of citizenship alongside capitalism in a relationship of collusion and conflict becomes most manifest. The development of citizenship's bundles of rights, for instance, while ameliorating some of the ill effects of capitalism, does not dismantle existing structures of inequality. Moreover, citizenship's promise of equality is premised on effacing ascriptive (hierarchical) inequalities and masking differences (of culture, caste, gender, ethnicity, etc.) to make them irrelevant for the exercise and enjoyment of the rights of citizenship. Thus, the equal citizens of the nation are seen as bearing rights and exercising their rights equally with others. This condition in which they exercise rights equally is achieved by making the conditions of difference irrelevant for the exercise of the rights of citizenship. The expansion of citizenship as seen in the above framework has been seen both as the basis of its achievements and as the source of its limitations. Whereas the generalisations of modern citizenship across the social structure mean that all persons as citizens are equal before the law and, therefore, no person or group is legally privileged, the provision of citizenship across the lines dividing unequal classes is, however, also likely to mean that the practical ability to exercise the rights or legal capacities which constitute the status of citizen will not be equally available to all. Those disadvantaged by exploitative systems, of class, caste, race, gender, etc., are, for example, unable to participate in the community of citizenship in which they have legal membership. The disability is a double one because in these circumstances, citizenship rights that are only formal cannot influence the conditions which render the possession of citizenship ineffective, if not worthless.

Critics of liberal citizenship including those on the Left, the feminists, communitarians, multiculturalists, etc., have pointed at the contradictions and ambivalences that surround citizenship's relationship with capitalism. While Marxist and feminist critiques will be taken up at length in subsequent sections, it is important to point out that even within liberalism these ambivalences and the limits they put on citizenship's potential as a 'momentum concept' have been visited at various points in time. Marshall himself located the roots of this contradiction and its potential for conflict in future. He sought the alleviation of this contradiction in social citizenship that assumed for each citizen 'equal social worth, not merely of equal rights' (Marshall 1950, 24). The promise of equal social worth was seen as important for building a sense of community membership through bonds of responsibility and loyalty to a 'civilisation which was a common possession' (Marshall 1950, 24). This promise, though imperative for sociopolitical solidarity was, however, dependent on a set of conditions that would guarantee to citizens an equality of status—'a minimum supply of certain essential goods and services':

> The extension of the social services is not primarily a means of equalizing incomes...What matters is that there is a general enrichment of the concrete substance of civilized life, a general reduction of risk and insecurity, an equalisation between the more and the less fortunate at all levels...Equalisation is not so much between classes as between individuals within a population which is now treated for this purpose as though it were one class. Equality of status is more important than equality of income (Marshall 1950, 33).

Thus, the egalitarian promise of citizenship, in order to envelope every single individual, has to be consummated also in the social domain. In this domain each individual, despite the raging inequality of a capitalist society, ought to feel secure as a member of a political community, which values equality and a state that takes it upon itself to supply such securities to the citizens. It is in this domain of social rights that Marshall also saw an imminent conflict brewing between the imperative of the market economy to make profit and the demand of citizenship for equality in the social domain. The contradictory impulses of capitalism and citizenship, he pointed out, are more than evident in the development of social rights in the twentieth century: '…it is clear that in the twentieth century, citizenship and the capitalist class system have been at war' (Marshall and Bottomore 1992, 18).

These contradictory impulses were addressed by John Rawls in the 1970s (*A Theory of Justice* 1971) and then again in the 1990s (*Political Liberalism* 1993). Generally speaking, Rawls's citizens are free and equal members of a constitutional democracy, each with his/her distinctive conception of the good. In order to pursue these goods, they need the same primary goods, that is, the same basic rights, liberties, and opportunities as well as the same all-purpose means such as income and wealth and some social basis of self-respect. In order to ensure that the same primary goods are available to all, they agree on a conception of justice that states that 'all social primary goods— liberty and opportunity, income and wealth and the bases of self-respect—are to be distributed equally, unless an unequal distribution of any or all of these goods is to the advantage of the least favoured'.

At the basis of this society is the idea of social cooperation and the notion of *justice as fairness* which lays down the conditions of a free and fair society. In such a society, cooperation among individuals is not primarily for self-interest, but for a mutually beneficial association whereby the enhancement and redistribution of some of the *primary goods* takes place, altering in meaningful ways the manner in which an individual is situated in his or her social context. The idea of cooperation and justice as the basis of cooperation does not deny that there exists in society multiple notions and understandings of what constitutes good for a person. These multiple notions can be, however, accommodated and attained in a cooperative and just society without traversing a path of conflict. A conflict-free path of attainment of good is possible in a *well-ordered society* that reflects a contract or agreement on certain *structures* and *norms* that make way for social justice. Fairness is built into the structures of such a society through the assumption that the contracting individuals, at the time of entering into the agreement to constitute a just society, agree to *an original position* where each contracting individual is behind *a veil of ignorance*. This veil of ignorance masks their social contexts so that they enter the political community as free and equal members. As rational and moral individuals, having agreed on the basic principles of fairness in society, they show a capacity for social justice and a conception of what is of value to human society. Rawls's two principles of justice provide the framework within which a liberal democratic citizenship could now unfold, viz., (i) 'a fully adequate scheme of equal basic rights and liberties', and, (ii) equal opportunity combined with the most clearly distinguishable feature of Rawls's approach of justice as fairness, *'the difference principle'*, namely, that 'social and economic inequalities' would be acceptable only insofar as they operate 'to the greatest benefit of the least advantaged members of society' (Shafir 1998, 7).

New Contexts and Changing Concerns: Globalisation and Multiculturalism[9]

For most of the twentieth century the dominant understanding of citizenship continued to place the individual at its core, and citizenship was seen as a legal status indicating the possession of rights. This dominant liberal model of citizenship has, however, been criticised precisely on these grounds. The liberatory content of citizenship rights, seen in the achievement of a 'sameness' or 'equality' among different sections of the population by making the various contexts of birth and power accruing from it irrelevant for the exercise of one's rights, has been questioned. In practice, the power to dissociate from one's context is only differentially available to large masses of citizens and in almost all cases the forging of sameness serves only to mask the repression of those who do not belong to the dominant culture. The specific circumstances of one's birth/life form the

---

[9]The themes introduced in this section will be explored in detail in chapter six.

(debilitating/enabling) contexts, which determine the extent to which one can enjoy one's citizenship rights. Contemporary debates on citizenship and rights have questioned the idea that the citizen can enjoy rights independent of the contexts to which she/he belongs. A significant terrain of contestation opened up in the 1980s in citizenship theory, with multiculturalism, plurality, diversity, and difference having become significant terms of reference for retheorising citizenship. This contest pertains in effect to the unmasking of those differences that were seen earlier as irrelevant to citizenship. Given that modern societies are multicultural, the specific contexts, cultural, religious, ethnic, linguistic, etc., of citizens are being seen as determining citizenship in significant ways. In most societies ethnic, religious, and racial communities have pressed for rights which would look at their special needs and would thereby substantiate the formal equality of citizenship. There is a growing effort to redefine citizenship by giving due importance to cultural differences among individuals and to strike a balance between the numerous religious, ethnic, linguistic identities while constructing a common political identity of the citizen of the nation. The notion of 'differentiated citizenship' was therefore advanced by some theorists who felt that the common rights of citizenship, originally defined by (and for) white men in a class-differentiated society could not accommodate the needs of specific cultural groups.[10] This notion has gained currency to accommodate the needs of specific cultural groups. A substantial bulk of the present debate on the nature and scope of citizenship concerns itself with the so-called 'universalism' (of Western constitutional democracies) vs. 'particularism' (claims of specific communities to preserve their ways of life) debate—issues of

---

[10]The term 'differentiated citizenship' was used by Iris Marion Young in 1989. The concept advocates the incorporation of members of certain (cultural) groups not only as individuals but also as members of groups, their rights depending in part on this group membership catering to their special needs. Iris Marion Young, 'Polity and Group Difference: A Critique of the Ideal of Universal Citizenship' (1989).

individual entitlement vs. attachment to a particular community —issues, in other words, critical to the debate between the liberals and the communitarians. There is also, however, a growing impulse to find a meeting ground between the two, seeking to make cultural rights relevant and admissible in societies where a 'universal' culture of 'liberal' values (respect for individual rights, a rule of law, etc.) already exists.[11]

While these concerns have largely been expressed in the context of 'multicultural' societies of the West, the frames of reference may not be entirely new. The centrality of 'difference' in rationalising the suspension/deferral of modernity in colonial societies has been talked about by several scholars and will be discussed in the next chapter. The domain of citizenship since its inception had in fact been fashioned on a series of exclusions, whereby sometimes entire societies (for example, the colonised) or large sections of them (slaves, women, and immigrant workers) were considered inadequate for citizenship.

Thus, in the changing contexts of the late twentieth century, viz., globalisation, transnational migration, multicultural national populations, etc., the manner in which citizenship has been understood so far has been redefined. In this context it has become acceptable to talk of the ideas of (i) global/world citizenship with its basis in human rights that delink the relationship between citizenship and the nation-state, the hitherto uncontested unit of membership, and, (ii) differential rights and differentiated citizenship for members of cultural groups which gives them rights not only as individuals but also

---

[11]While reiterating the liberal faith in individual choices, Will Kymlicka, for example, emphasises the importance of the 'contexts' which fashion such choices, especially what he calls 'societal culture', referring to 'practices and institutions' that are territorially and linguistically concentrated and provide individuals with 'meaningful ways of life across the full range of human activities, including social, educational, religious, recreational and economic life, encompassing both public and private spheres'. See Will Kymlicka, *Multicultural Citizenship: A Liberal Theory of Minority Rights* (1996). See also for this discussion, Gurpreet Mahajan, *Identities and Rights* (1998, 173).

as members of groups, their rights depending also on this group membership and catering to their special needs.

Search for Alternatives

Marxist critique of 'modern citizenship': from political emancipation to human emancipation

It is generally pointed out that for Marx the claims of citizenship to equality and freedom were incompatible with capitalism. Simply put, Marx's explanation of this incompatibility was grounded in his interpretation of the modern state as a bourgeois state, a manifestation of and guardian of bourgeois interests. The fact that the modern state was embedded in the structures of capitalism made it incapable of delivering the promises of citizenship, which is why, in the context of capitalism, citizenship as a status and a value was mere fiction, a cloak for the citizen's impotence: 'political man is only the abstract fictional man' (McLellan 1977, 56). Marx's criticism of abstract, equal rights in *Critique of the Gotha Programme* is often taken to be one of the most important indications of this. The formulation of 'equal rights' is nothing but the application of an equal/uniform standard which becomes 'a right of inequality in its content', since with the application of an equal standard, people are 'taken from one definite side only', while other attributes, needs, social contexts, relationships, etc., are ignored.

Marxist criticisms of citizenship, as evident in McLellan's interpretation, have focussed on the failure of citizenship to address itself to transform an inherently unequal capitalist structure. It may be recalled that the idea of citizenship grew alongside capitalism in what Marshall calls a curious relationship of complicity and resistance. In the ultimate analysis it strove to alleviate the effects of capitalism by integrating more and more groups of people into its system of rights, including industrial workers, and stabilised thereby the essentially unequal structures of capitalism. Exhibiting distrust for the idea of bourgeois rights, the Marxist critics call for a rectification of the social and economic subordination of the disadvantaged. The civil and political rights in this analysis are, therefore, only superficial trappings of equality while the dominant classes retain their privileges, and the working class remains subjugated. Modern citizenship, according to such critics, does not breed citizens, but rather, in Marx's philosophical terminology, 'self alienated, natural and spiritual individuality', men and women who occasionally imagine themselves as citizens but whose everyday actions are governed by the imperatives of the market.[12]

The discomfort of Marxists with citizenship as a framework of equality has made several writers sceptical of Marxism's capacity and inclination to 'take rights seriously'. Rights, according to these scholars, are not supported in the Marxist tradition.[13] Steven Lukes, for example, argues that a Marxist cannot believe in rights because Marxism views rights as 'expressive of the egoism of bourgeois society' and approaches rights as 'unwarrantably abstract and decontextualised' (Lukes 1987, 60–70). Both Lukes and Buchanan argue that Marx was 'scornful' of rights, and he rejected them. Others such as Samuel Bowles and Herbert Gintis argue that there is little sustenance to be had in Marx's treatment of rights, choice, and freedom. Marxism's discursive structure, they point out, lacks the fundamental theoretical vocabulary to represent the conditions of choice, individual liberty and dignity, and the Marxian theoretical lexicon does not include such terms as freedom, personal rights, liberty, choice, or even democracy (Bowles and Gintis 1986, 18–20). Those who do not see any theory of rights in Marx, base their conclusions on Marx's criticism in *On the*

---

[12]See Michael Walzer, 'Citizenship' in *Political Innovation*, eds. Ball, Farr and Hanson (1989), and 'The Civil Society Argument' in *Dimensions of Radical Democracy*, ed. Chantal Mouffe (1992).

[13]Steven Lukes, 'Can a Marxist Believe in Rights', *Praxis International* (1982); *Marxism and Morality* (1987); Drucilla Cornell, 'Should a Marxist Believe in Rights', *Praxis International* (1984); William McBride, 'Rights in the Marxian Tradition', *Praxis International* (1984); Allen Buchanan, *Marx and Justice: The Radical Critique of Liberalism* (1989).

Jewish Question of the 'so-called rights of man', which he calls merely the 'rights of egoist man', the 'right of the circumscribed individual', of the 'isolated monad'. Again, they point out that in the *Critique of the Gotha Programme*, Marx criticises the Eisenach faction of the German Social Democratic movement for focussing on 'such pretty little gewgaws' as 'bourgeois rights' and argued that the party should abandon such 'ideological nonsense'. Finally, insofar as Marx is read as suggesting that communism would be a society beyond rights (because it would eradicate the conditions which make rights necessary), it is taken as a rejection of rights.

The criticism of modern democratic citizenship was clearly outlined in the 1840s by Karl Marx in his study of the Constitutions of the American and French Revolutions, through which modern citizenship first arose. Marx summarises his objections to modern democratic or bourgeois citizenship when he says that:

> The state in its own way abolishes distinctions based on birth, rank, education and occupation when it declares birth, rank, education and occupation to be non-political distinctions, when it proclaims that every member of the people is an equal participant in popular sovereignty regardless of these distinctions, when it treats all those elements which go to make up the actual life of the people from the point of view of the state. Nevertheless, the state allows private property, education and occupation to act and assert their particular nature in their own way, i.e., as private property, education and occupation. Far from abolishing these factual distinctions the state presupposes them in order to exist.[14]

An ambivalence or inconsistency, however, may be detected in Marx insofar as he also describes modern citizenship as 'a big step forward' and, significantly, as the best that could be achieved 'within the prevailing scheme of things'. He insists, however, that mere political emancipation in citizenship is inadequate and

---

[14]Karl Marx, 'On the Jewish Question' in his *Early Writings* (1975, 219).

advocates a general human emancipation in which persons are freed from the determining power of private property and its associated institutions. According to Marx, then, the limitations of citizenship which arises through political transformation can be overcome only through a social revolution in which the class basis of inequalities in social conditions and power is overthrown. Scholars such as Amy Bartholomew, therefore, dispute that Marx was scornful of rights and rejected them.[15] Bartholomew proposes that Marx was in fact critical of and unevenly committed to them. At the most, she suggests, it may be said that Marx's treatment of rights is critical, differentiated, underdeveloped and, in more than a few instances, ambiguous. She puts forward a case to argue that Marxism can be rethought in a way as to weave rights commitment more firmly into its theoretical lexicon, without moving away from Marx. Bartholomew builds her argument by relying on Marx's understanding of and commitment to the development of 'rich individuality' and 'self-development' entailed in his notion of 'human emancipation'. She derives Marx's commitment to rights from his other commitments as well, that is, to the development of working-class capacities and socialist political strategy. Bartholomew argues that Marx's criticism of rights is basically directed towards the 'rights of man', the so-called natural rights. She points out that in *On the Jewish Question*, Marx distinguishes between the 'rights of man' and the 'rights of citizen'. He criticises the former which were embodied in the French and American declarations of rights. According to Marx's distinction, the rights of man include freedom of religion, equality, liberty, security, and private property. He argued that none of these rights 'go beyond the egoistic man, man as he is,...that is as an individual separated from the community...'. The only 'bond that they admit between people is natural necessity, need and private interest', and they both reflect and are (re)constitutive of competitive, egoistic, atomistic individuals who view the community and

---

[15]See Amy Bartholomew, 'Should a Marxist Believe in Marx on Rights?' in *Socialist Register*, eds. Ralph Miliband and Leo Panitch (1990, 244–64).

others as potential enemies. Correspondingly, Marx complains that none of the rights of man address or embrace communal or social concerns, human sociality, or species being.

Marx, Bartholomew argues, provided a different view of citizens' or political rights and political participation in general. As distinct from the rights of man, citizens' rights in Marx's schema included political liberty, civil rights, and democratic participation rights. His criticisms of political rights focussed, among other things, on their not touching the real distinctions of status, wealth and ownership in civil society and for being subordinate to the 'rights of man' so that the 'political community' became 'a mere means' to maintain these so-called rights of man. Yet, he praises citizens' rights, because they could be exercised only if one was a member of a community. Their content was 'participation in the community life', in the 'political life of the community', the 'life of the state'. He argued that despite being severely limited, political emancipation, which entails the realisation of political and civil rights, 'certainly represents a great progress'. One year before writing *On the Jewish Question*, Marx argued that the importance of those 'liberals…who have assumed the thankless and painful task of conquering liberty step by step, within the limits imposed by the constitution should be recognised'.

Following Bartholomew's line of argument, it can be said that Marx was more than marginally supportive of citizens' or political rights, in terms of both restricting the freedom of the state and providing the participatory rights which encouraged some kind of collective action. He supported freedom of speech, dissent, and organisation as well as universal franchise because he admitted the possibility of achieving socialist transformation through the vote. Marx's criticisms of rights can therefore be better understood as pertaining to the actually existing rights of man, which he argued emerged from and contributed to a particular form of individualism—bourgeois individualism—and were 'wholly preoccupied with his private interest and acting in accordance with his private caprice'. Thus, the right to liberty as expressed in the French Declaration of 1793 as 'the power which man has to do everything which does not harm the rights of others', was not acceptable to Marx in this particular articulation. This, however, does not suggest that Marx was against the right to liberty that could also be expressed in a manner to provide a right to refuse exploitative and hierarchical work, etc. Rights articulated in the above manner, however, separated individuals and became 'boundary markers', rather than promoting human sociality. Marx distinguished between egoistic, atomistic individualism and 'rich individuality', which is connected individuality within community, aspiring for self-guidance, self-development, and creativity; a rich conceptualisation of the individual, the community, freedom, choice, and rights. His commitment to the individual can be seen in his remarkably individualistic vision of communism in the German Ideology: 'nobody has one exclusive sphere of activity, but each can become accomplished in any branch he wishes'. But, again, it was only in 'community with others' that each individual could actually possess the means of cultivating his gifts in all directions and only in the community, therefore, was personal freedom possible.[16]

Feminism and citizenship

While the idea of 'general' and 'uniform' citizenship has been criticised by both feminists and theorists on the Left for overlooking the inequalities that exist in real life, feminists have shown how the idea of citizenship has been especially inimical to women. The expansion of citizenship to women and the provision of conditions in which women could act as citizens has come as a result of a long struggle by women. The unsettling of the core elements of citizenship in the context of multiculturalism and the onslaught on social rights in the face of a rampant global market has posed fresh challenges to

---

[16]See Amy Bartholomew, 'Should a Marxist Believe in Marx on Rights', (244–65), for the complex nuances of these arguments.

feminists. In their response, feminists have put forth compelling reconceptualisations of the community as the basis of a feminist alternative to the theory and practice of 'new' citizenship. While the feminist alternative is examined in the last chapter, it is important that feminism's relationship with citizenship be studied, in order to outline the premises from which the present critique emanates.

Feminists of all strands have criticised the dominant conceptions of citizenship on two counts. They argue first of all, that citizenship is gender blind. By focussing on uniform and equal application, it fails to take cognisance of the fact that modern societies are steeped in patriarchal traditions, which make for male domination and privileges. Equality in such conditions remains a façade and the inequality of women is sustained by policies that work within the framework of formal equality. More significant, however, is the analysis that shows that most historical conceptualisations of citizenship have thrived on the division between members and nonmembers. The discursive practices surrounding the notion of citizenship have produced dichotomies where the space of citizenship became increasingly identified with male and public activities. The universality and generality of the public sphere required that all particularities be relegated to the private. While the public/private distinction was essential for the assertion of the liberal notion of citizen as the autonomous individual, it also led to the identification of the private with the domestic, which played an important role in the exclusion and subordination of women. Historically, it may be seen that events celebrated as marking 'universal emancipation', viz., the French Revolution and the Declaration of the Rights of Man and Citizen (1789), were also moments of subordination and exclusion of women. Thus, feminists have argued that both the ancient and modern concepts of citizenship have been inimical to women, either excluding them from citizenship altogether as in the classical tradition or integrating them indirectly as citizen-consorts, as in the French revolutionary tradition. Modern citizenship, while not entirely excluding women, incorporated them on the basis of their socially useful and dependent roles as mothers and wives, placing them, thereby, outside the sphere of politics and distancing them from resources and opportunities such as education, property, etc., which equip individuals for political participation (Pateman 1988, 1992). The gender blindness of citizenship theory has been so pervasive that most authoritative works on the evolution of democratic citizenship retain the 'main story' of the gradual unfolding and universalisation of rights, only by moving women to the margins as historical anomalies. Thus, Marshall's paradigm of the evolution of rights of citizenship could retain its coherence only by citing women as aberrations in the general trend.[17]

Feminists have taken different routes to overcome their exclusion from the political community. In the process they have subscribed to different views on politics and political community. One strand of feminists has approached citizenship as an aspect of public/political activity and as embodying the transformative potential of democracy. They have looked for women's inclusion in the public sphere as equals, laying emphasis on revitalising/democratising the public sphere through communication, speech, and action, which are seen as empowering, and through alliances for a shared common objective (Mouffe 1992). A second major strand of feminism is, however, skeptical of what they feel is merely 'add women' approach, which while looking for avenues of inclusion into the public sphere does not question its 'maleness'. This view approaches citizenship from the vantage point of what women do in the private realm. Questioning the patriarchal state, it argues for the inclusion of women's specific functions into the public realm of citizenship, hoping thereby to promote the

---

[17]Thus, when Marshall says that by the early eighteenth century, citizenship in the form of civil rights had become universal since the status of personal freedom now pertained to all adult members, he qualifies this statement by adding 'or...to all male members, since the status of women, or at least married women, was in some important respects, peculiar' (Vogel 1991, 58–85).

suppressed private side of the public/private divide, into the realm of democratic politics (Prokhovnik 1998). This has led to two distinct lines of argument: (i) the private is political, which implies a continuity of power between the state and the so-called private domains and submits both of them to the norms of justice and equality of the public realm; and, (ii) maternalist citizenship, which advocates that women should value their particular skills and interests instead of merely entering the bastions of male-defined politics on its terms. This route is in a way a continuation of a kind of suffragette campaign to re-imagine citizenship and the public sphere to encompass 'feminine' values. Maternalists such as Carol Gilligan, Jean Elshtain, and Sara Ruddick feel that in the emphasis on the 'public' role, the degradation of the 'private' role and the domestic becomes unavoidable. They would prefer to see the dismantling of citizenship based on male personalities, and the development of new notions of citizenship based on female characteristics of love and compassion. Stressing the superiority of maternal qualities of caring, responsibility, and compassion as the key elements of citizenship, the maternalists dissolve, in the process, the distinction between male/public and female/private facets of life (Elshtain 1981; Gilligan 1982). While feminist politics continues to be debated from within, augmenting critical reflexivity, there has been, at the same time, greater recognition of differences of race, sexuality, ethnicity, religion, class, etc., as constituting significant contexts determining women's access to the political community. The recognition of different contexts has also brought to light the differences that exist among women and that derive from their different social positioning. At the same time there is also a great deal of unease with ideologies which while asserting 'difference', reify women's central and atavistic roles in preserving differences. Thus, theories of multiculturalism are treated with suspicion as are abstract notions of human rights, which fail to take into account the specific nature of women's deprivation.

In this work, as mentioned at the outset, an attempt will be made to explore the various themes and debates thrown up in the course of the historical unfolding of citizenship in the Indian context. This chapter has raised some conceptual issues that have continued to inform recent debates on citizenship, in particular, the main historical currents in the debates and the complexities of citizenship's relationship with class, caste, gender, ethnicity, national identity, etc. Chapters two, three, and four explore the emergence of citizenship in the historical context of late colonial India. In exploring the nationalist ideology of citizenship as it took shape in a contestary relationship with the colonial, it is proposed that the national movement may well be seen as having arisen as the struggle for self-determination against multilayered oppressive structures of brahmanic-feudal and colonial domination. The assumptions of equality and self-determination, which underlay citizenship, provided the moving force for the assertion of a 'national' self-identity counterposed in a conflicting (equal) relationship with the coloniser. It has been proposed in these chapters that the synchronisation of national identity and citizenship as the measure of equality with the coloniser, while providing a resisting identity and a liberatory promise, was, however, itself based on a series of marginalisations and exclusions. To explore this in greater detail, the manner in which women were implicated in the assertion of a national identity has been investigated. Discussing the formation and gendering of Indian nationalist ideologies of citizenship during the early twentieth century to highlight the manner in which 'women' were simultaneously incorporated within and excluded from citizenship, they attempt to map the gendered inclusions and exclusions that seemed to have informed, mediated, and regulated the enactment of Indian nationalism.

The late colonial period in India refers to the 1900s. The period is marked by what may be seen as the beginning of a process of significant changes in the context of a growing crisis of legitimacy for the colonial state in the face of a rising wave of 'popular' struggle for national self-determination. Colonial rule continued to unfold within the framework of 'colonial difference', which, while espousing the 'universality' of democratic principles of liberty, equality, and self-determination, was bound by the logic of colonial difference, which dictated that the elimination of difference would also mean the end of colonial rule. Discursive constructions of racial and civilisational superiority were invoked to mark out the difference between the colony and the metropole on a hierarchised scale of social/ civilisational conditions. Though the Ilbert Bill controversy over the removal of disqualification faced by Indian judicial officers in trying cases involving Europeans had ended more than thirty years ago, the core principle of racial superiority, around which colonial rule was organised, persisted. The incapability of Indians for self-rule, self-determination, and citizenship was seen to lie in their history and their religion, in the 'deep stream of tradition which had been flowing for thousands of years', as Vincent Smith put it in 1919, even while constitutional proposals assuring a measure of 'responsible' government to (a small section of) Indians were afoot (Smith 1919, 21).

In many significant ways, women were made the markers of the civilisational difference between the colonisers and the colonised and were the principal discursive sites where the contest between the colonial state and the nationalist elite was made manifest. Chapter two, *Anti-Colonial Nationalisms, the Women's Question and Citizenship*, surveys writings on nationalism(s) to explore how women were by and large excluded from such writings and to examine critically women's relationship to the 'national' project and its implication for the citizenship rights for women. Examining the positioning of women at the interface of colonial and nationalist discourses, the chapter explores the manner in which both these discourses, in a display of masculinist imaginary, discursively constructed women as images of purity and symbols of domesticity. While the British *memsahib*, oscillating between a dominant position of race and subordinate one of gender, figured in the colonial discourse in perpetual need of protection from native men, the colonised woman figured as her subaltern shadow, a passive object of colonial gaze, a victim to be saved from the barbarity of tradition. While both the figurations afforded the moral imperatives of colonial rule, they simultaneously emasculated the colonised male and implicated the colonised women as accomplices in the colonial project. The nationalists responded by 'recovering' the 'traditional woman', whose fate was henceforth made non-negotiable with the colonial masters. The manner in which the 'women's question' was constituted and defined by male nationalists and enmeshed within the construction of a national identity had important implications for determining women's simultaneous inclusion and exclusion from the body politic. Struggles by women to articulate their subjectivities within and outside these confines, however, have made such categories contested ones and shattered the legitimacy of the nationalist 'resolution of the women's question'.

Chapter three, *The Domestic, Domesticity and Women Citizens*, interrogates the nature of the 'inner domain' where the nationalists sought to 'reconstitute' and 'reaffirm' a 'national tradition' around the figure of the reformed 'Indian' woman. The chapter proposes that the meaning and contours of the 'domestic' took shape in the course of the contest between the colonial state and the nationalist elite over the demarcation of the domestic as the space for the assertion of 'legitimate' authority. For the coloniser the 'domestic' presented the challenge of reordering the normative codes of an 'imperfect' society and opened up avenues of 'negotiation' and 'communication' with the ruled. On the other hand, the idea of the 'domestic' also came to signify the domain of nationalist resistance to colonial domination. While the contest of the nature and meaning of the domestic was largely a male discourse, it demarcated the limits of women's behaviour and specified and legitimised her unequal position within the hierarchised structure of the family, nation, and state. The chapter examines a cross-section of domestic writings in Hindi—didactic/prescriptive conduct books/pamphlets of the period—to explore the 'ideal of domesticity' as encoded in these manuals of household duties. While the ideal of domesticity came to be glorified in terms of cultural/national codes, these codes, the chapter proposes, were reflective rather of the daily drudgery and domestic toil involved in the lives of upper caste/middle-class women and a differential positioning of women within the emergent political community. While women were constituted as atavistic members of the political community, the nature of male membership is construed as forward looking, active citizens, capable of effecting change in their surroundings.

It has often been asserted that the nationalist 'resolution' of the women's question and the ensuing silence enveloping it in this phase of nationalist politics was contingent on the sanctity that was awarded to the 'home'. The terms of the 'resolution', it is suggested, saw the 'disappearance' and edging out of 'issue(s) of female emancipation' from the political domain onto the inner domain of culture that was considered non-negotiable with the colonial state. The 'rapid' changes in the lives of middle-class women have been seen as taking place mostly outside the arena of political agitation, that is, at home. The 'home' is thus conceived as the 'terrain' where the 'real history' of the 'women's question' could be identified. It was the principal site where the 'hegemonic construct of the new nationalist patriarchy was being normalised' and thus also the site where, amidst a web of coercion, persuasion, and resistance, the meaning of 'Indian womanhood' was being worked out (Chatterjee 1994, 131–33). Chapter four, *The 'Womanly Vote' and Women Citizens: Debates on Women's Franchise in Late colonial India*, would, however, show how a section of the same demographic group, the middle class, interrupted this 'silence', and public debates on self-determination and equality were riddled by organised struggles by women for political rights on an equal footing with men. The 'vote' at this historical juncture not only signified a claim to the exercise of political rights of citizenship which were being denied to the colonised subjects, it also symbolised a terrain where various sociopolitical forces existed in a curious blend of conflict and camaraderie. The chapter looks at the debates surrounding suffrage as a terrain where a complex of relations of domination and subordination, colonial, nationalist, masculinist, and conservative, locked horns and attributed gendered meanings to the 'vote'. It unravels the meanings surrounding vote and women at the intersection of these contests, the social and political practices that informed these meanings, the manner in which these meanings changed in association with each other, and their implications for articulating women as citizens.

An important element which persists in all these chapters—in chapter two which takes into account the centrality of the figure of the Indian woman in the construction of a national identity, in chapter three which interrogates the domestic discourse, and chapter four which explores the social, political, and ideological forces which informed the struggle for the vote—is the manner in which national identity becomes equated with a dominant Hindu identity, and the tradition that garners this identity becomes invariably the Hindu religious-scriptural tradition. Chapter five, *The Nation and its 'Constitution': the Text and Context of Citizenship*, explores the circumstances in which citizenship rights were incorporated in the Constitution of India, viz., in the various contexts of struggles for self-determination against multilayered oppressive structures and discursive constructions of racial and caste superiority. While resistances against oppression spanned all the regions of India and manifested themselves in various forms, they may, it is argued, be broadly seen as aspiring to invert oppressive structures at two broad 'layers' of 'collective' bondage: against a hierarchically organised scheme of social relations marked by ascriptive inequalities and, second, the dominance-subordination relationship between the coloniser and colonised. At both these layers of collectively experienced oppression, attempts were made to articulate the nation/community as the organising principle of a resisting identity, as the basis of self-determination, sovereignty, and citizenship. Within this context the national/political community and the cultural/religious community acquired primacy, so much so that the individual citizen and disadvantaged and vulnerable sections remained in the background. The chapter explores the language of citizenship which arose at the historical juncture of the anticolonial movement in India, the forms in which it got ensconced within the emergent constitution, and the implication of the primacy of community rights on the rights of women as citizens, especially the carving out of a 'women's politics' in the context of ambivalently defined identities of citizenship.

Notions of multiculturalism and minority rights are frequently invoked as democratic values whereby cultural communities can lay claim to inherent rights and negotiate better terms of reference to the national culture. While the recognition of rights claims based on community membership is being recognised in liberal democratic theory in the form of differentiated citizenship, liberal philosophy has historically idealised the homogenous political community, even when such a philosophy was being generated within the confines of a large and multicultural empire. That some were citizens and others not good enough for this status has formed the basis of the theory of citizenship through much of modern times. Chapter six, *Rethinking Citizenship in an Age of Globalisation*, takes up the various contests and ambiguities that have informed recent writings on citizenship. A critical exploration of the idea of citizenship as it emerges in the recent writings is important since in so many ways it seeks to 'dissolve' the contests that have historically informed the notion. Arguing for the displacement of two categories that had hitherto been the core of citizenship theory, viz., the *individual* as the bearer of rights and the *nation-state* as the unit of citizenship identity, the writings claim that these displacements have made it necessary to talk of human rights and world citizenship in place of national citizenship, and cultural and community rights instead of individual rights. The chapter proposes that emphasis on human rights and cultural communities has brought into conflict existing ideological strands within the theory of citizenship. It further proposes that the arguments put forward to support the redefinition of citizenship are ambivalent and fraught with contradictions and that, quite like the dominant orthodoxy on citizenship, they work within the framework of exclusion and difference-deferral.

It is significant that recent attempts within Western sociopolitical theory to find a meeting ground between the abstract universal citizen and cultural-communities is more than counterbalanced by persisting doubts over the applicability of the Western and (therefore) modern notion of citizenship to the 'developing' world, where the so called 'premodern' (community-based) forms of social relations persist. This distancing is very much reminiscent of the colonial practices that rationalised imperial domination in terms of an inadequacy and incapacity on the part of the colonial to transcend the medieval (despotic) to the modern (rule of law). These contests are introduced in the following chapter and are revisited in the remaining chapters to show how they unfolded within the colonial context, especially in relation to women's citizenship. The chapter highlights the liberatory contents of national identity as the basis of citizenship, in certain contexts. The struggle for liberation against colonial rule, for example, entailed enunciations of shared bonds of common descent, history, and destiny. These shared bonds became powerful bases for the articulation of equality with the coloniser and was made manifest in self-rule, constitutional democracy, and citizenship. The 'dominant' national movements were thus movements for constitutional status as citizens, and at the particular juncture of anticolonial movements, citizenship and national identity thus tended to synchronise. The status of citizenship, as we know, did not accrue equally to all, and the benefactors were the leaders of the strand in the movement that took precedence over other expressions of citizenship at that moment in time. In the chapter that follows, we shall see how the resisting national identity formed in the course of the struggles against colonial rule is gendered and its implication on women's constitution as citizens.

2

Anticolonial Nationalisms, the Women's Question, and Citizenship

In the introductory essay to *Subaltern Studies*, Ranajit Guha comments on the 'unhistorical historiography' of colonial India, which left out the 'politics of the people' in favour of that of the nationalist elite (Guha 1982, 1–8). The process of recovering absences in history has come a long way since the task of rectification of 'unhistorical historiographies' began earnestly in the last two decades. The writing of women's history, in particular, has broken new theoretical grounds. The 'add gender and stir approach', which went no further than merely adding the extra/optional condiment of gender, while the other ingredients of the dish endured unchanged, has been edged out as irrelevant. This was accomplished after a long and arduous struggle that hammered persistently and persuasively at the encrusted cocoon of history to open it out for reexamination. The process involved the extrication of diachronous layers and synchronised strands, which were ironed out to produce a unified narrative, privileging one point of view, while obliterating others.

In picking out the strands that had been left hanging as so many threads extraneous and inconsequential to the main story, a multipronged process was involved. It entailed generating 'new knowledge about women' through means and sources that had hitherto found little or no validity in writing history; it involved looking for 'women' in spaces that had been squeezed out from the 'public' domain and memories; it involved looking for 'women' in 'public' spaces conceived as masculine; it also involved looking at the balance of socioeconomic and ideological forces and power relations that defined *women* and *womanhood* in ways that inscribed the prescriptive ideal-typical *woman* onto *women* and circumscribed their agency; it involved looking at these prescriptions and circumscriptions as a shroud that made invisible the contests and struggles informing the lives of women as they negotiated, questioned, rearticulated, readdressed, and generally made permeable the boundaries which enclosed their lives. Most importantly, however, this process involved rereading history in a manner so that women, who had hitherto been 'hidden from history', became historical subjects—the focus of historical inquiry—whether of political movements (as in the suffrage movement) or the unfolding of large-scale processes of sociopolitical change (as in anticolonial movements). These attempts involved a comprehensive 're-writing' of history, and entailed questioning and challenging the entrenched structures and practices of domination, including patriarchy.

While this chapter does not profess to reclaim the neglected subaltern by redefining the frontiers of history, it does seek to revisit and unravel from the seams of history the manner in which the 'women's question', as constituted and defined by male nationalists, was enmeshed in the construction of a national identity, which had important implications for determining the simultaneous inclusion and exclusion of women from the body politic. The purpose of such an exploration is to focus attention on the complex ways in which the categories 'woman', 'women', and 'womanhood' are discursively constructed by multifarious socioeconomic and ideological configurations, which traverse, shape, and determine the lived experiences of women. While drawing on the colonial experience elsewhere in the world, this chapter focusses especially on India and proposes that the category 'woman' was constructed ideologically through exclusionary cultural symbols in the course of the construction of a resisting, oppositional, national identity within the context of anticolonial movements. While the modular woman, produced in the minds of men and transmitted through cultural prescriptions, obliterated the inequality of lived experiences of women on account of their caste, class, race, etc., it invoked, at the same time, powerful and compelling images of liberation modelled on iconic heroines from the past. These images of liberation served to accentuate the tensions in the lives of nineteenth- and twentieth-century women between the promises held out to them as a result of political and economic change and the limitations that hedged them in through the hegemonic influences of the modular woman. The real lives of women did not, however, lie outside or in opposition to the ideal and the imagined, but exhibited an interactive relationship with the latter, reflected in the manner in which women interpreted and lived their lives in relation to the prescribed norms. Thus, at any given historical moment, the (anticolonial) national movement in this case, there may exist *a plurality of discourses on women*, which get constituted and reconstituted in an unequal yet dialogical relationship with each other. These discourses in turn reflect the balance of power relations and socioeconomic forces that provide the normative framework within which notions of womanhood get enmeshed. Alternatively, we can equally see the *idea[l]* of *woman* and *womanhood* running across the multitude of social and political forces and ideological formulations providing the cohesive bonds of national, religious, and, importantly, male identity, community, and camaraderie. The sections which follow will look at the manner in which the history of nationalism has largely been a history of male aspirations based on the exclusion of women.

Nationalism: A Gender Blind History?

Nationalism, Ernest Gellner notes, invents nations where they do not exist (Gellner 1964; 1983). Benedict Anderson, however, cautions against attributing any fallacy to such inventions and would rather see nations as 'imagined' (Anderson 1991). Irrespective of the debate over the origins, fecundity, or credibility of the idea, nationalism, suggests Anne McClintock, is 'radically constitutive of people's identities, through social contests that are frequently violent and always gendered' (McClintock 1993, 61). She contends that while the invented nature of nationalism has found wide theoretical currency, explorations of the gendering of the national imaginary has been conspicuously paltry, despite the latter's dependence on constructions of gender. Women are typically construed as the symbolic bearers of the nation, but are denied any direct relation to national agency or citizenship. The subsumption of women in the national body politic takes place as symbols of national honour, essence of the nation, as signifiers of differences or metaphorical boundaries between nations, and, by implication, the powers of men. The idea of unity, which forms the ideological foundation of nationalisms, has historically amounted to the sanctioned institutionalisation of (predominantly gender) *difference*. In an important intervention, Nira Yuval-Davis and Floya Anthiyas identify five major ways in which women have been implicated in nationalism: as *biological reproducers* of the members of national collectivities, as reproducers of the *boundaries* of national groups (through restrictions on sexual or marital relations), as active *transmitters* and producers of the national culture, as symbolic *signifiers* of national difference, and as *active participants* in national struggles.[1]

---

[1] A feminist rectification of nationalism would then involve, investigating the gendered formation of sanctioned male theories; bringing into historical visibility women's active cultural and political participation in national formations; bringing nationalist institutions into critical relation with other social structures and institutions, while at the same time paying scrupulous attention to the structures of racial, ethnic, and class power which continue to bedevil privileged forms of feminism (Yuval-Davis and Anthiyas 1989, 7).

Yet, the dominant and representative works on nations and nationalisms have seldom explored how nationalism is implicated in gender power. Theoretical formulations on nationalism have, as Cynthia Enloe remarks, 'typically sprung from masculinised memory, masculinised humiliation and masculinised hope' (Enloe 1989, 44). Not only are the needs of the nation identified with the frustrations and aspirations of men, the representation of national power is contingent on the construction of gender difference. In most works, national agency has been construed as male. Thus, for Gellner, the very definition of nationhood rests on the male recognition of identity and camaraderie: 'Men are the same nation if and only if they recognize each other as being from the same nation' (Gellner 1964). For Frantz Fanon both the coloniser and colonised are inadvertently male, and nations are figured through the iconography of familial and domestic space and the contest over its delineation. The struggle for decolonisation is waged over the (feminised) domestic body/space displaying a proprietary relationship of ownership, exchange, and conflict : 'The look that the native turns on the settler town is a look of lust...to sit at the settler's table, to sleep in the settler's bed, with his wife if possible. The colonised man is an envious man' (Fanon 1967, 30). In *Algeria Unveiled*, Fanon describes imperial intervention as taking the shape of a domestic rescue drama: 'Around the family life of the Algerian, the occupier piled up a whole mass of judgements...thus attempting to confine the Algerian within a circle of guilt' (Fanon 1965, 38). The dream of the 'total domestication of Algerian society' came to haunt colonial authority, and the domesticated female body became the terrain over which the military contest was fought (McClintock 1993, 65).

The recognition and construction of a national identity was not only structured around the confirmation of male power and pride in property (patrimony), it also aligned itself with the notion of race—of *white* patrimony. The latter almost inevitably asserted itself through violent (male) assertion and claims of property over (feminised) colonial land. Catherine Nash illustrates how in representations of the landscapes of Ireland in the early twentieth century, the nation's space (the land) was feminised, against 'masculine' colonial power (Nash 1993). Anne McClintock similarly refers to Afrikaner nationalism as synonymous with white male narratives of imperial conquest, the (Afrikaner) 'imperial journey' into 'empty' or 'virgin' lands. This imperial journey is also conceived as marking an inevitable march *forward* of (Western) civilisational values into geographical space. It also, however, marks a journey *backwards* in racial and gender time to a territory of (racial and gender) 'degeneration'. Ironically, the journey backward into civilisational time serves also as a justification for the imperial journey forward. The myth of the 'empty' and 'virgin land' within the colonial narrative effected, thus, a double erasure. While 'virgin land' signified passivity towards insemination of European reason, it also achieved an assurance of territorial appropriation. The symbolisation of colonial lands as virgin established colonial proprietary rights and assured at the same time that Africans could not claim having any prior, aboriginal territorial rights. White patrimony could be then be asserted through (violent) conquest and occupation (McClintock 1993, 69).

If colonial occupation signified a contradictory journey forward on geographical space and backwards in racial and gender time, nation itself has been characterised by theorists such as Tom Nairn as 'the modern Janus', as a contradictory figure of time (Nairn 1977). For Nairn, the nation takes shape as a contradictory figure of time, one face gazing back into the mists of the past, the other into an infinite future. This temporal contradiction is made manifest in the nationalist ideology which, as Deniz Kandiyoti expresses it, 'presents itself both as a modern project that melts and transforms traditional attachments in favour of new identities and as a reflection of authentic cultural values culled from the depths of a presumed communal past' (Kandiyoti 1992). The temporal anomaly within nationalism, the veering between nostalgia for the past and the progressive, purposive thrust towards the future, is resolved by explaining the contradiction as a 'natural' division of gender. Under such a division, women represent the atavistic and authentic 'body' of national tradition, inert, backward looking, and natural, embodying nationalism's conservative principle of continuity and eternity. Men by contrast represent the progressive agent of national modernity, forward thrusting, potent, and historic, embodying nationalism's progressive, or revolutionary principle of discontinuity and change. Nationalism's anomalous relation to time is thus 'resolved' in relation to gender, a paradox that lies at the heart of most national narratives.[2]

Physical violence on women's bodies and forceful impregnation provide further reaffirmation of the way the female body has become the allegory for the nation and its boundaries and the most gruesome reminder of how fundamentally nationalism is gendered. The partition and subsequent 'birth' of the two nations of Pakistan and India were accompanied by reclamation by the two governments of their lunatics, prisoners, and 'girls'. A historian of partition recalls, '[After independence] the Governments of India and Pakistan came to an agreement that any [abducted] girl [of any community] should be *forcibly*

---

[2]Anne McClintock points out that Britain's emerging national narratives gendered time by figuring women (much like the colonised and working class) as inherently atavistic, the conservative repository of the national archaic. Women, it was argued, did not inhabit history proper, but existed like colonised people in a permanently anterior time within the modern nation, as anachronistic humans, childlike, irrational and regressive, the living archive of the national archaic. White middle-class men were seen, in contrast, to embody the forward thrusting agency of national progress. Thus, citizenship as the universalist legal representation of a person's relationship to the rights and resources of the nation-state, became unstable when seen from the position of women. In post-French Revolution Europe, women were not incorporated directly into the nation-state as citizens, but only indirectly through men, as dependent members of the family in private and public law. The Code Napoleon was the first modern statute to decree that the wife's nationality should follow her husband's, an example other European countries briskly followed. A woman's political relation to the nation was submerged as a social relation to a man through marriage. For women, citizenship in the nation was mediated by the marriage relation within the family (McClintock 1993, 65).

recovered and returned to her relatives and, until such time as her relatives remain untraced, to the Government [of her country]' (Qidwai 1990, 151).[3] The next section will examine the ideology of nationalism as it emerged at the interface of colonial encounters and the manner in which women were implicated in it.

Colonialism, Nationalism, and the Discourse on Difference

The theme of difference permeated the colonial discourse as a legitimate basis for colonial domination. When a French or German scholar tried, for example, to identify the Chinese mind, the exercise was eventually intended to show how different the Chinese mind was from the German or the French mind. It also served to construct, on the basis of this difference, a unified entity which could be described and defined as French, German, or Chinese. Edward Said calls these differences 'invented essences' and 'constructed things' purporting to have a purity and persistence for eternity (Said 1978, 91). This ensured what Trinh Min-ha calls 'separate development', the attribution of certain natural features to an oppressed group to subsequently imprison this group within the boundaries of its so-called nature and essence (Minh-ha 1987). S.H.Alatas's book *The Myth of the Lazy Native* explores the function of this constructed essence (myth) in the ideology of colonialism, the way in which European colonialism created an object, the lazy native, who was fit only to be subjected to stringent rules and discipline and kept 'in an intellectual and moral state that despite their numerical superiority they may weigh less politically than a bar of gold'. This native was talked about, analysed, abused, and worked, fed with bad food and with opium, separated from his/her natural environment, sheathed with a discourse that kept him industrious and subordinate (Said 1990, 32).

[3]Anees Qidwai as cited in Gyanendra Pandey (1994, 189) (emphasis added).

The myth of the lazy native is synonymous with domination and domination is predicated on power. Ronald Inden, while criticising Indology, says that facts are produced by an episteme which presupposes a representational view of knowledge which the knower somehow transcends, producing a hierarchical relationship between the knower and known, privileging the one over the other (Inden 1986, 401). The construction of the categories of criminal tribes and dangerous species is symptomatic of the manner in which domination and disciplining unfolded. Shail Mayaram and Sanjay Nigam have pointed at the processes through which 'criminalisation' was effected to cope with problems of governance. In a study of the criminalisation of the *Mev* population, Mayaram mentions the 'systematic construction of a mythology of criminality' of the Mevs based on their regional contiguity with an *acknowledged* 'criminal tribe'. Apart from regional association, the mythical narrative *Darya khan* was taken as proof of blood relationship between the two populations, and criminality was confirmed through heredity (Mayaram 1991). In his study of 'a colonial stereotype' that is, 'criminal tribes and castes', Sanjay Nigam undertakes a detailed historical study of the Criminal Tribes Act XXVII of 1871 in colonial India, emphasising that the knowledge of criminal tribes was discursively produced, informed by Orientalist and Victorian ideas. Nigam proposes that stereotyping was 'a metaphor for Indian society' in that it signified not only attributes rooted in an unchanging past, but also a set of 'abnormal' native people who had to be disciplined and controlled by the colonial state. The disciplinary system that developed under the Act aimed ultimately at surveillance and control (Nigam 1987).

The nationalist discourse emerged within the space created by the colonial discourse, exhibiting peculiar symptoms of contest and collusion with the hegemonic discourse. The nationalist discourse made 'difference' as the logic of opposition and in the process created, like the former, an 'exclusive self' as an 'excluded other' (Donaldson 1992, 10). Edward Said sees mobilisations around difference in the anti-imperialist struggles as forming the 'resisting identity' of the revolutionary, which is exemplified by the concept of 'negritude' developed intellectually and poetically by Aime Cesaire (1972) and W.E.B.DuBois (1968). Said calls this resisting identity the 'acquired positive Being'. Where it had earlier been a mark of degradation and inferiority, it becomes now a matter of pride. Much the same 'revaluation of native particularity' occurred in India, where the denied or repressed native essence emerged as the focus of and even the basis for nationalist recovery and 'cultural reclamation' (Said 1991, 22). The creation of this 'exclusive self', sovereign and liberated from the oppressive strangleholds of colonialism, became the basis for the assertion of a resisting (national) identity. Thus, nationalism began its journey as a political movement after it had already proclaimed its sovereignty in the domain of culture and had inserted itself into a new public sphere constituted by the processes and forms of the modern (in this case colonial) state. In the beginning, nationalism's task was to overcome the subordination of the colonised middle class, that is, to challenge the 'rule of colonial difference' in the (political) domain of the state. The colonial state, we must remember, was not just the agency that brought the modular forms of the modern state to the colonies; it was also an agency that was destined never to fulfil the normalising mission of the modern state, because the premise of its power was a rule of colonial difference, namely, the preservation of the alienness of the ruling group.[4] As the institutions of the modern state were elaborated in the colony, especially in the second half of the nineteenth century, the ruling European groups found it necessary to lay down in law making, in the bureaucracy, in the administration of justice, and in the recognition by the state of a 'legitimate' domain of public opinion, the precise difference between the ruler and the ruled.[5]

---

[4]For a discussion on the notion of colonial difference and the paradox of colonial modernity in India, see Partha Chatterjee (1994).

[5]The Ilbert Bill controversy for example, and the questions raised by it— if Indians had to be admitted into the judiciary, could they be allowed to try Europeans? Was it right that Indians should enter the civil service by (*contd.*)

Ironically, it became the historical task of nationalism, which insisted on its own marks of colonial difference from the West, to demand that there be no rule of difference in the domain of the state. The rallying principle of anticolonial movements therefore was that of equality with the rulers.[6]

Women as Difference and the Colonial Project

Women featured in the colonial and nationalist discourses mainly as discursive constructions, as sites of struggle for power,

---

(*contd.*) taking the same examinations as British graduates? If European newspapers were given the right of free speech, could the same apply to native newspapers? See Partha Chatterjee (1994).

[6]Joanna De Groot in a study of the transformation of political culture and power structures in early twentieth-century Iran points out that the varied responses to European dominance exhibited what she calls defensive revivalism, projects of modernisation and resistance, or debates and conflicts with non-European societies. De Groot identifies comparable elements in the Arabi movement in Egypt and the founding of the Indian National Congress in 1885 to the Young Turk movement and the Iranian constitutional movement at the start of the twentieth century, and Indian, Moroccan, Turkish, Egyptian or Iranian nationalisms of the interwar years. She stresses that in this context concepts of 'nation', 'community', 'religion', and especially 'gender' became politically charged for participants. Examining the gender dimensions in the development of nationalist ideas and movements between 1890 and 1930, she points out that while there were visible tensions and divergences between trends in nationalist discourse which emphasised religion and those which did not, the fluidity and interaction of religious and secular approaches to the 'national question' was significant. She suggests that overlapping political concerns and alliances promoted the 'religious' concerns to save Islam and caused the 'secular' concerns regarding Iranian weakness faced with European intervention to interweave a rhetoric of 'nation in danger'. Constructions of 'social solidarity' to confront the danger revolved around the articulations of projects of reform and social change and gender was central to such enunciations. There was in Iran an influential cultural legacy linking images of sexual purity and modesty with the concept of public order, equating female sexual assertion with subversion and rebellion and breakdown of that order. Thus, at the core of the discussions on state, nation, or public good lay powerfully gendered and sexualised notion of the polity itself. Joanna De Groot, 'The Dialectics of Gender: Women, Men and Political Discourses in Iran c.1890-1930', *Gender and History* (1993, 256–68).

as objects of purity and symbols of domesticity and home. There appears to have been at least two main figurations of women within the colonial discourse, viz., the memsahib (bourgeois woman) in need of protection from potential sexual threat from native men and, in direct contrast, the sexually available colonised women. In her study of Anglo-Indian fiction, Jenny Sharpe shows that the English woman in India was part of the grand narrative of colonial legitimation. The image of native men sexually assaulting white women was in keeping with the idea of the colonial encounter as the battle between civilisation and barbarism and as affirming the moral and racial superiority of the mission. The moral imperatives of imperialism were also served by the figure of the 'native' woman waiting (passively) to be rescued from the cruelty of traditional practices. As seen in the official discourse on *sati*, saving the Hindu woman from the barbarity of customs became a significant point of intervention in the colonised society. The Indian and British women were, however, differentially positioned, insofar as the latter, owing to her dominant position of race, was relatively empowered. While the memsahib oscillated between a dominant position of race and subordinate one of gender in a state of precarious and unstable subjectivity, the Indian woman existed as her 'subaltern shadow' (Sharpe 1993, 12). The latter was positioned as an object of colonial 'gaze' and as a victim to be saved. Nowhere was this more evident than in the discourse on sati that located the sanctions behind women's bondage and passivity in the Hindu religion.

The official discourse on sati produced and affirmed these notions of servility and passivity of Hindu women. The official regulation of the practice was hinged on the criterion of women's will, and magistrates carefully monitored the burnings in order to ascertain whether Hindu widows went willingly to death or were coerced. In the process of determining what constituted women's will, the widow's subjectivity was effaced while others spoke for her. The woman who spoke in official records, for example, did so only at the command of the civil servant. Furthermore, her speech unfolded in a manner so as to confirm the colonial imperatives of introducing a new moral order—placing the civiliser as the agent of change, and the native woman as an object to be saved. The coloniser's 'gaze' on the act as a horrified onlooker in sympathy with the victim, but not identified with her, standing apart from and, more importantly, above the colonised, smacked of racial/moral superiority. In fixing the woman in an object position as a victim to be saved by the agency of a morally/racially superior white magistrate, the disempowerment of the colonised woman was effected (Mani 1985, 107–27; 1989). The process of disempowerment also attained in a more subtle way the emasculation of Indian men. At the same time, it created the impression of complicity of the colonised woman with the coloniser, so much so that women appear as collaborators with the colonisers in the mission of their liberation from their men, 'brown women saved by white men from brown men'.[7]

The aspect of complicity is also to be found in the slave narratives of antebellum America. The representations of black women in the abolitionist literature show that two different but interdependent codes of sexuality operated in the antebellum South. These codes produced opposing definitions of womanhood and motherhood for white and black women, which were incorporated in the figures of the slave and mistress, describing the parameters whereby women could be measured and declared to be or not to be women. Manifesting the effects of the dominant ideology of 'true womanhood', wifehood, and motherhood were glorified as the purpose of women's existence, and chastity was the prescribed virtue for white women. There appears a series of representations of female slave from victim to collaborator. The black woman is represented as overtly sexual, so much so that the white male is depicted as a victim of her sexuality, and there is a propensity to see her rape as an act of compliance. In the writings by black slave men, there exists a portrayal of mothers, sisters, and daughters as victims of brutality and sexual abuse. These writings, however, express an underlying blame on the women for being vulnerable and depriving black men of their status as male protectors (Carby 1987, 20–43).

---

[7]Gayatri Chakravarty Spivak cited in Malek Alloula (1986, xiii).

As mentioned earlier, the figure of the woman was important in the construction of oppositional identities by both the nationalists and the colonisers. The representations of women as the objects of male gaze or male protection within colonial texts were central to the process of constructing a male national identity in the colonial period. The aggressive masculinity of the colonial enterprise, intertwined with issues of the civilising mission and racial superiority, contributed towards framing the role of the white woman in the colonial enterprise. This construction, paradoxically, was based on the excising of women's involvement in colonialism (Mills 1991). The interest in the role of the white woman in colonial enterprise has, however, not been limited to such depictions and has ranged from popular romanticised depictions to more scholarly concerns regarding their complicity and resistance. The explosion of romantic images of Western women in the Empire is reminiscent of how juvenile literature of late nineteenth- and early twentieth-century Britain emphasised the theme of Empire to inculcate the ideas of imperialism and nationalism (Chaudhuri and Strobel 1992). The figure of the white woman either as the victim or as an accomplice of the coloniser was undoubtedly useful in attaining legitimacy for the colonial project among the metropolitan population. The 'raj revival' in the 1980s in a plethora of films on the Empire was replete with depictions of white women in a male space.[8] Recent works operating within this framework have drawn attention to the importance of studying Western women and imperialism beyond the romanticised frameworks offered within the colonial discourse.[9] These works point out that women were not just victims of patriarchy, they also colluded in it and often resisted and survived

---

[8]The expression 'raj revival' was coined by Salman Rushdie in his article of the same title in The *Observer* (1 April 1984).

[9]Some significant works which have thrown light on the complex role of the white woman in the colonial project are Joana Liddle and Rama Joshi (1985), Helen Callaway (1987), Anand Yang (1990) Chaudhuri and Strobel (1992), and Jane Haggis (1990).

it. The Ilbert Bill controversy in India illustrates the manner in which gender became central to the racial conflict informing the controversy.[10] Although the Bill mentioned nothing about women, it evoked vociferous criticisms from white women, who plunged into the controversy in a way 'hitherto unexampled in history' compelling the home member of the Viceroy's Council to remark that the female was 'far more unreasonable and active in opposition than the male'. Indeed, the native press expressed that it was the protest of the white women against being subjected to the jurisdiction of 'the Calibans lusting after the Mirandas of Anglo India' that eventually defeated the Bill. In their rhetoric against the Bill, white women resonated the dominant ideology of racial and cultural superiority over the colonised population. The motif of the colonised woman was invoked, her ignorance and decadence was reiterated as the proof of the effeteness of the native culture, and also of the incapability of native judges to make rational decisions (Sinha 1992).

Thus, the assumption among social historians that the white women constituted a subset of white men, either subsumed in the dominant male position or recuperated as strong and equal partners in the colonial mission, has been questioned for ignoring the specificity of the white woman within the colonial project. The 'new imperial woman', who emerged at the intersection of imperialism and patriarchy, marked the rupture of the ideological separation of the private and public. Imperial necessity required a reinvention of women as public actors, giving a distinctly public and imperial inflection to traditionally private activities. A study on the new imperial women in colonial India points out that the Anglo-Indian domestic sphere was made public because Anglo-Indians lived in their own compounds, a space separated from the Indians they ruled and also because the public sphere of governance extended to the

---

[10]The Ilbert Bill proposed, in 1883, an amendment in the Code of Criminal Procedure to remove a racially discriminatory clause whereby native civil servants were disabled from exercising criminal jurisdiction over European British subjects living outside the chief presidency towns.

private space of the domestic establishment and its social practices emphasising both the home nation and one's duty to it. The domestic establishment became, thus, a public forum, its life and policies public ones, and wives were not separated from colonial administration. Indeed, despite the ideology of separate spheres, the separation of the public and the private was rendered irrelevant in a domestic establishment whose purpose was to enshrine the notion of English civilisation, demonstrate its superiority, and underscore its strength, and whose social practices many of which, viz., the 'fabled hospitality' of the Anglo-Indian community, the dances, the dinners, the rounds of calling, a memsahib's relations with Indian servants, were as much rituals of government as the *durbar*. It is significant that the Anglo-Indian community as the ruling class in India was often placed in conflict with the middle-class domestic ideologies in England. This conflict was particularly evident in the context of the movement in England over the extension of suffrage rights to women. While imperialism was being centred in the domestic hearth by colonial administrative practices and Anglo-Indian writers on domestic practices, Curzon, the viceroy and one of the most vociferous opponents of women's suffrage, defended the natural extension of separate spheres in the colonial context (Sainsbury 1995).

The specific delineation of the white woman in the Empire was, however, ultimately contingent on the specific sociocultural and political space within which the white woman came to be located. The colonial space in India, for example, emerging in the immediate context of the 'mutiny', was fraught with anxieties and fears of sexual threat to the British memsahib, sustained by the 'racial memories' of 1857 with its 'hysterical myths of rape of white women'. At the same time, the colonial state as the extended arm of the metropolitan state in England was devolved with the responsibility of 're-presenting' and preserving 'English' civilization and culture amidst the polluting influences of the native civilisation. Significantly, the figure of the white women got foregrounded in both the narratives, as 'pure English womanhood', as the symbol of an Anglo-Indian identity distinct from as well as existing in an interactive relationship with both their 'English' identity and the 'native' culture that surrounded them. This identity was, however, premised on a series of exclusions based on both race and class and was traversed by contradictions and ambivalences on women's roles emerging from the imperatives of colonial rule. It is not surprising, then, that the writings of the period distanced the memsahib not only from 'native women', but also from 'women missionaries' who crossed the boundaries of 'imperial aloofness', and the lower-class English women—the 'barrack wives'—characterised by un-English demeanour. The preference from the 1860s for a 'self-contained' and 'aloof imperial lifestyle' not only meant that miscegenation was discredited, but that the 'Eurasian woman'—the hybrid—came to be seen as having a destabilising effect on the colonial hierarchy of race and class (Sen 2002).

Anticolonial Movements and Frameworks of Women's Participation

Colonialism was a significant historical experience in almost all territories of the Americas in the seventeenth and eighteenth centuries, and in Asia and Africa in the eighteenth, nineteenth, and part of the twentieth centuries.[11] It manifested itself in various forms and sustained itself through a powerful grid of exploitative and collaborative networks of relationships spanning the colonised population. The colonised population reacted to colonialism in diverse ways, viz., ignoring the dictates of colonial authority, cooperating and complying with it, or resisting it. Anticolonial movements present a broad range of struggles, which coalesced and made themselves manifest most prominently as national liberation struggle(s) for the recovery of the dignity of the people and the nation and the installation of popular sovereignty and democracy.

Our concern in this section, is to outline, within the historical

---

[11]It must be noted here that by the late eighteenth and early nineteenth century most of the colonies in the Americas had been liberated.

context of anticolonial movements, the responses of women to the significant material and ideological questions and perspectives about liberatory change that informed these movements, the manner in which women contributed to the course and contents of the movements, and the feminist issues which emerged and agitated the minds of women as the national liberation struggles unfolded. Two methodological propositions should, however, be made at this point. We will focus our attention on movements waged against colonial domination for national liberation as distinguished from movements that may have been waged against systems/structures of oppression rooted in other exploitative relationships, for example, feudal, caste, neocolonial, etc. It may, however, be pointed out that this distinction serves only the function of limiting the scope of and establishing the primacy for the purposes of this exploration of the issue of national liberation. Very often, the issues raised by the latter forms of exploitation, viz., feudal, caste, etc., were closely linked with the broad spectrum of national liberation struggles. The role and position of women in society or the so-called 'women's question', for example, was enmeshed in the contest for domination between the colonial state and the nationalist elite. On the other hand, women's struggles against oppressive practices took into account the socioeconomic and ideological forces that contributed towards the perpetuation of the subordination of women. As a statement from the *Association of African Women for Research and Development* (AAWORD) reveals, women were conscious of the futility of 'fighting against genital mutilation' without questioning 'the structures and social relations which perpetuated [it]' (Davies 1983, ii).

Secondly, in order to understand the nature and ramifications of women's participation in anticolonial struggles, one must bear in mind that women's roles were defined in terms of their specifically feminine roles in familial spaces and not in the context of the public/political where colonial domination was suffered and contested. More often than not, women's participation in or contribution to the national liberation movement was either wrapped in the folds of a masculinist history or conceived in terms of 'supportive' roles of nurses, cooks, harbourers, and couriers, or as 'passive resisters', and in some cases as guerrilla fighters in National Liberation Armies. It is important to note that in order to understand women's contribution, one has to steer clear of understanding it in terms of a 'womanly' contribution and redefine, instead, the manner in which 'meaningful' contribution is normally understood, that is, as public, decisive, etc. It is essential to point out, therefore, that the understanding of women's contribution in anticolonial movements should be understood not merely in terms of the nature and extent of their participation, but also with regard to the questions such struggles raised about 'women's roles', the ideological contests which informed the so-called 'women's question', the implications of such contests on the manner in which women's roles were envisaged in the emergent nation-state on feminist consciousness, organisation, and movement. In other words, it is important to understand how women themselves interpreted their struggles, viz., as directed primarily against colonial domination subsumed under the broad rubric of national liberation, or as struggles waged on multiple fronts— against dowry, against rape, against genital mutilation, against, in other words, their subordinate social, legal, and political positions.

Anticolonial nationalism emerged in the context of colonial rule and involved the crafting of a sense of nationhood and struggle(s) for national liberation and self-determination. Underlying the practices of colonial rule was a discursive framework that justified it in terms of a condition of tutelage, necessary to teach an inferior people the rules of governance and civilised living. The late nineteenth and early twentieth centuries saw, in most of the colonised Asian, African, and Latin American countries, mass movements to resist and eventually overthrow colonial domination. The dominant language or the idiom that gave meaning and strength to struggles against entrenched structures of domination was that of *equality*. Equality was aimed at both, (i) countering the ideological dimensions of domination viz., civilisational/caste/racial superiority and, (ii) its manifestation in practices of rule, viz., colonial/imperial, feudal domination and exploitation. Thus, anticolonial struggles witnessed an assertion of equality with the coloniser that would logically mean the end of colonial rule and assure political freedom and sovereignty for the colonised. The invocation of the idiom of equality was made also in resistance against other forms of exploitative relationships. Another significant element of anticolonial movements, especially in certain parts of Africa and Asia, was their adherence to some form of socialism. This was due primarily to the relationship that was beginning to be seen between political subordination and poverty in the colonies and the growth of capitalism in Europe and North America. The critique of economic exploitation at the hands of imperial capital became a vital part of the critique of colonialism. This critique provided the framework within which specific inequalities generated by capitalism could be understood and colonial rule and domination challenged. Moreover, this criticism provided the ideological tools determining some aspects of the struggle for liberatory change. Thus, struggles by industrial workers and peasants for economic and social equality against capitalist and feudal exploitation coalesced under the broad framework of national liberation struggles for social justice and economic freedom.

It was in the context of these struggles, which brought to the fore issues of oppression, resistance, and freedom, that notions of what constituted specifically women's oppression and emancipation and the definition of women's rights came to be identified and debated upon. It was also within the context of anticolonial struggles that women's organised struggle for rights and citizenship came to be articulated in a relationship of complicity and conflict with the national liberation struggles. Before we begin identifying women's 'participation' and their relationship with nationalism, it is important to recall the point made earlier that nationalism like colonialism was a masculinist project in which male agency was prioritised and female agency circumscribed. One can illustrate this perhaps with the help of Virginia Woolf's response to a question addressed to her in the context of the Second World War about how *she* would prevent war. Woolf's answer manifests the intricacies that inform women's relation to the nation. Women, who had historically been excluded from decisions to start war (or any political decisions for that matter) and had not decided to start *this* war, would ponder/wonder and raise a fundamental question, 'What does "*our* country" mean to *me* an "outsider"?'

> To decide this she will analyse the meaning of patriotism in her own case. She will inform herself of her sex and her class in the past. She will inform herself of the amount of land, wealth and property in the possession of her own sex and class in the present—how much of 'England' in fact belonged to her.... 'Our country', she will say, 'throughout the greater part of history has treated me as a slave; it has denied me education or any share of its possession...in fact, as a woman, I have no country. As a woman I want no country. As a woman my country is the whole world'. And if, when reason has its say, still some obstinate emotion remains, some love of England dropped into a child's ears by the cawing of the rooks in an elm tree, by the splash of waves on a beach, or by English voices murmuring nursery rhymes, this drop of pure, if irrational emotion she will make serve her to give to England first what she desires of peace and freedom for the whole world.[12]

Woolf presents here the dilemma of women who had not yet achieved full citizenship rights, yet were asked to support the nationalist cause in times of war. How could women be nationalists when they were not equal? How could women not be nationalists when they loved their country, people, and home? (West 1997, xi). Much the same delicate positioning of women between nation and citizenship, between circumscribed passivity and concerted activity, permeated anticolonial movements. A critical look at women and anticolonial movements would thus involve analysing the unequal ways in which men and women are incorporated in the national project, the gendered roles that define the inclusion of men and women on a differential basis,

---

[12]The extract is from Virginia Woolf (1938, 107–8), cited in Lois A. West (1997, xi).

and the manner in which women define their relationship to the anticolonial struggle and the national state (Yuval-Davis and Anthiyas 1989, 7).

Anticolonial Nationalisms and the Constitution of the Women's Question

We mentioned in the previous section that anticolonial movements coalesced together struggles for national liberation and struggles for democratising the existing structures of oppression. Thus, if one were to pick out some significant strands in anticolonial struggles, one would perhaps be able to identify three, viz., (i) the resistance that developed against imperialism and various forms of foreign domination, (ii) movements against feudalism, exploitative local rulers, and traditional patriarchal and religious structures, and, (iii) resistance against capitalist exploitation. These strands gave new and often irreconcilable dimensions to the notion of 'womanhood' and 'women's roles'.

Within the dominant paradigms of the nationalist discourse the 'women's question' was largely shaped by class concerns and concerns of a national identity and became enmeshed in the ongoing contests between the coloniser and the nationalist elite. The social reformers and nationalists purported to 'modernise' *their* women through a reformed system of education to add weight to their own claims of being equal to the coloniser. Working within the modernisation paradigm, social reformers attempted to 'emancipate women from a *savage* past', with the intervention of the colonial state. They identified certain areas of violence against women for eradication, such as sati in India, and veiling, polygamy, and seclusion in Egypt and Algeria. These movements for reforms, however, while attempting to eliminate 'social evils', did not involve any radical criticism of the existing structures of society and women's subordinate roles within it. They sought, rather, through reforms, to stabilise the social structure, which meant reforming the family and making secure, thereby, women's 'proper' (subordinate) role within it. In the context of the anticolonial movement in India, the women's question was the central issue in most debates over social reform in the early and mid-nineteenth century. Social reformers such as Raja Rammohan Roy, Vidyasagar, Jyotiba Phule, K.C. Sen, and Ranade campaigned against practices like sati, child marriage, conditions of widows, etc.[13] At the same time, however, in order to resurrect cultural pride, they asserted a faith in their ancient civilisations. Thus, very often the reformers idealised the civilisation of a distant past and spoke of the need to regain the lost freedom that women were seen as once possessing. Thus, social reformers in India constantly referred to a golden age of Vedic culture when women were said to have enjoyed equality with men, referring frequently to the goddesses of mythology, warrior queens, and famous historical figures among women to show that India had a tradition of according women a high status in society.[14]

What may be emphasised here is that the so-called women's question in the agenda of Indian social reform in the early

---

[13]The issues of women's emancipation formed a part of modernisation and 'nation-building' projects in other parts of the 'Third World'. Japanese intellectuals in the Meiji era such as Fukuzuwa and Soho condemned Confucian traditions of family life and advocated rights of women. In Turkey, the Young Turk reformers Ziya Gokalp and Ahmed Agagolu also advocated women's emancipation. Gokalp expressed the general current of opinion of male reformers when he wrote: 'In the future, Turkish ethics must be founded upon democracy and feminism, as well as nationalism, patriotism, work and the strength of the family'. In China, reformers of the later nineteenth century, such as Kang Yuwei and those of the early twentieth century, grouped around Sun Yat Sen and opposed the traditional constraints that bound women in Chinese society (Jayawardena 1982, 139).

[14]Egyptians expressed their pride in periods of ancient Egyptian history when women, it was claimed, had a high position and the country was ruled by famous Queens such as Nefertiti and Hatshpesut. In Turkey, Gokalp and Attaturk stressed a specific Turkish identity and ethnicity and referred to pre-Islamic Turkey where there was said to have been a tradition of freedom for women among the nomads of Central Asia. Similarly, Iranian reformers spoke of the early history of the country and its Zoroastrian traditions, which accorded a high status to women. The Japanese referred to their Sun Goddess and Empresses (Jayawardena 1982, 140).

nineteenth century was not so much about the specific condition of women within a definite set of social relations as it was about the political encounter between a colonial state and a supposed 'tradition' of a conquered people, a tradition that, as Lata Mani has shown in her study of *satidaha*, was being produced also by the colonial discourse (Mani 1985; 1989). It was the colonial discourse that by assuming the hegemony of Brahmanical religious texts defined *the tradition* that was to be criticised and reformed. Indian nationalism, in demarcating a political position opposed to colonial rule, took up the 'women's question' as a problem already constituted for it, namely, as a problem of Indian tradition (Chatterjee 1994, 119).

The contest over issues of Indian tradition appears, however, to have dissipated as an agenda of public debate towards the close of the nineteenth century. Questions regarding the position of women in society did not seem to arouse the same degree of public passion and acrimony as they did only a few decades earlier. The overwhelming issues now appear to be directly political ones, of self-determination and liberation. Scholars such as Ghulam Murshid see the mid-nineteenth century attempts in Bengal to 'modernise' the conditions of women, a result of the influence of Western ideas and the period of nationalism, that is, from the period late nineteenth century onwards, as a clear retrogression and even a stalling of the process of modernisation (Murshid). Others such as Sumit Sarkar argue, however, that the inability of nationalist ideology to push forward a campaign for liberal and egalitarian social change cannot be seen as retrogression from an earlier radical, reformist phase. The social reformers, he points out, were themselves highly selective in their acceptance of liberal ideas from Europe. Fundamental elements of social conservatism such as caste distinctions and patriarchal forms of authority in the family, acceptance of the sanctions of the *sastra* (scriptures), preference for symbolic rather than substantive changes in social practices, Sarkar points out, persisted conspicuously in the reform movements of the early and mid-nineteenth century (Sarkar 1985)

A different explanation pertaining to the apparent disappearance of the women's question and issues of social change from the nationalist agenda comes from Partha Chatterjee. Chatterjee argues that nationalism did in fact provide an answer to the new social and cultural problems concerning the position of women in 'modern' society, and that this answer was posited not on an identity, but on a difference with the perceived forms of cultural modernity in the West. The relative unimportance of the women's question in the last decades of the nineteenth century is explained by Chatterjee not in the fact that it had been censored out of the reform agenda or overtaken by the more pressing and emotive issues of political struggle, but rather in the relocation of the women's question in an inner domain of sovereignty, far removed from the arena of political contest with the colonial state. It was in this inner domain of national culture that 'tradition'/'women' was reconstituted and reaffirmed (Chatterjee 1994, 117).

The construction of a distinct national identity that was signified by difference based on gender was the basis for much of *national recovery* in anticolonial struggles the world over. Nationalism emerged in most parts of the colonised world as a doctrine of resistance to imperialism allied with an aroused sense of aggrieved religious, cultural, or existential identity, often taking the form of an assertion of the same practices that were sought to be reformed by the colonisers (Said 1990). Kenya in the 1920s, for example, experienced active campaigns by British missionaries against the tradition of female circumcision. In his novel *The River Between*, the Kenyan writer Ngugi wa Thiong'o describes the dilemma created by British interference and co-optation for those who wished to reform the society from within. In an assertion of their Kenyan identity against British imperialism, Kikuyu women in Kenya began demanding the right to womanhood through circumcision. In an analogous case, in Algeria, Fanon points at the 'reveiling' of women in Algeria, as symbolic of their resistance to French domination:

> The officials of the French administration in Algeria, committed to destroying the people's originality, and under instructions to

bring about the disintegration, at whatever costs, of forms of existence likely to evoke a national reality directly or indirectly, were to concentrate their efforts on the meaning of the veil, which was looked upon at this juncture as the symbol of the status of the Algerian woman—a symbolic and practical instrument in their resistance to French domination (Alloula 1986, xiii).

Much the same recovery of tradition occurred in India. Colonial texts condemned the treatment of women in India by identifying a scriptural tradition. The nationalist response was to construct a reformed national tradition and defend it on grounds of modernity. The recovery of a 'national' tradition grounded in an ancient and unsullied past, was, points out Partha Chatterjee, the most powerful and creative effects of the assertion of sovereignty in the nationalist imaginary based on the delineation of its 'difference' with the models of modernity produced in the West. The repository of the reformed national tradition, the 'new woman', was a 'refined' woman distinct from the 'western woman' and the 'street woman' in her dress, demeanour, and education.[15] While she was different from the latter in her cultural refinement and morals, she differed from the Western woman in that her education was not aimed at achieving a competitive equality with men in the sphere of 'outside', and the loss of feminine virtues thereby. An ideal companion to the Indian (Westernised) male, the new woman, owing to the 'discipline' of her refinement, remained untainted by the corrupting influences of the material domain, upholding thereby

---

[15]Throughout the late nineteenth and early twentieth centuries, the recovery of tradition and the reclamation of national pride and identity was linked to the recovery of the 'new woman'. The concept and ideology of the 'new woman' in vogue in Europe in the nineteenth century was eagerly adopted by both men and women of the bourgeoisie. Kassim Amin's book on women's emancipation in 1901 was called *The New Woman*. In 1919, some Egyptian women formed the 'Societe de la Femme Nouvelle'. In the same year an 'Association of New Women' appeared in Japan, while in China (also in 1919), a feminist magazine was titled *The New Woman* (Jayawardena 1982, 142).

the sanctity of the nation. The new patriarchy advocated by nationalism conferred upon women the honour of a new social responsibility, and by associating the task of female emancipation with the historical goal of sovereign nationhood, bound them to a new subordination which drew its legitimacy from the idiom of the nation (Chatterjee 1989a; 1989b; 1994a).

It may be reiterated here that the women's question articulated in this historical period and its resolution in the form of the new woman was primarily a class-based formulation indicating a 'differential' construction of the public sphere. For the middle-class women, the 'new woman' marked their 'partial emergence' into a new kind of economic sphere into which they carried the constraints of conduct dictated and inculcated by the 'discipline' of the private sphere. For the large numbers of poor women, capitalist expansion and the specific forms of extraction in colonial conditions meant a shift from the traditional 'public' sphere of agricultural labour into the modern, industrialised sector. It also meant, however, that women, who more than men were lacking in skills required by the industrial sector and were constrained by social and familial conditions, were to an extent marginalised from the emerging workforce of industrial labour (Banerjee 1989). On the other hand, despite the ideological constraints on women's mobility, because of the growth of industries, especially those associated with textiles, the demand for cheap women's labour grew in all colonies: China (silk and allied manufactures), Japan (textiles), Iran (carpets), Egypt (cotton), India (textiles), and Turkey (rugs and textiles). Similarly, women's labour was crucial in the plantation sector (tea, rubber, coconut, sugar, etc.) and in farm and domestic agriculture in these countries. It is significant that the women's question, which became an important concern for the nationalists, did not focus on questions of work and wage conditions of women in the industry (Jayawardena 1982, 9).

Thus, the recovery of the nation became contingent on the image of the ideal Hindu woman. The construction of a national identity around the idealised Indian (Hindu) woman was based on a series of exclusions around class, caste, and race, the 'homogenisation' of differences, and the 'hegemonisation' of a universal identity.[16] As with all hegemonic forms of dominance, the new patriarchy that accompanied the constitution of the 'new women' combined coercive authority with the subtle force of persuasion. This was expressed most generally in the inverted ideological form of the relation of power between the sexes, in the adulation of women as goddess or as mother (Chatterjee 1994, 130). The dominant characterisation of femininity in the new construct of women as a sign for nation, drew from all the force of mythological inspiration characteristics of femininity, namely, the spiritual qualities of self-sacrifice, benevolence, devotion, religiosity, and so on. The various shapes of the new woman continuously readapted the 'eternal' past to the needs of the contingent present, the woman's body signifying the ultimate and even the last resort of resistance to imperialism in the nationalist discourse. As in the reveiling of the Algerian women and the insistence of the Kenyan women to exercise agency over their bodies, Sarkar sees in the early nationalist discourse an obsessive preoccupation with sati—the freedom of the Hindu widow to bring about her own self-destruction. Through this agency over her body, she preserved her independence and national independence. Very often an implicit continuum was postulated between the hidden innermost private space— chastity—to political independence at the level of the state, as if through a steady process of regression, this independent selfhood had been folded back from the public domain to the interior space of the household and then further pushed back into the hidden depths of an inviolate, chaste, pure female body.

[16]Basing her analysis on the representation of women in calendar art, Patricia Uberoi explores the construction of a national identity through a series of exclusions, the 'homogenisation' of differences, and the 'hegemonisation' of a 'universal' identity. It was the legacy of the colonial period, points out Uberoi, that the construction of such an identity became contingent on the image of the ideal Hindu woman. The genre of calendar art represents a ground in which the tension between 'unity' and 'variety' or 'hegemony' and 'pluralism' is played out through the use of women signifiers (Uberoi 1990).

Independence, like a hidden jewel, could be detached from external surroundings that spelt defeat and secured/concealed in the very core of the woman's body (Sarkar 1987, 2014).

The homogenising and hegemonising discourse of the ideal-typical formulations of womanhood was, however, traversed by other strands manifesting the contradictory pulls and predicaments that have historically confronted women and the manner in which these dilemmas have been articulated/resolved. Thus, while much of the nineteenth-century Bengali literature shows the use of women signifiers in nationalist imagination in forms consonant with the expectation of the times with no discernable changes in the figuration of women as the embodiment, the ultimate site, and even the last refuge of freedom, there were also some shifts and departures. In particular, the moral initiative that the woman came to wield within the nationalist ideology marked a rupture in the structuring of gender relations. The role ascribed to women of helping men retain or regain their moral status in the face of the humiliation of subjugation they suffered in the public domain represented a subtle reordering of power relations within the family. Even as the patriotic, self-sacrificing woman continued to animate much of the nationalist literary imagination, the ubiquitous trope of motherhood, in particular, was given a 'national' character so much so that the mother's mantle was seen as embracing an entire 'race of mothers', *mayer jati,* invoking in women the duty of participation in *national regeneration* (Sarkar 1987). The dilemmas of passive domesticity also unfolded, however. Jasodhara Bagchi's examination of the figure of Shanti in Bankim's *Anandmath* evokes the dilemmas that women faced in the historical conditions that called for action and drew attention to the forces that constrained them into passive domesticity. The unharnessing of Shanti's 'unusual energy'—'her affective self—towards the *liberation of the Motherland* necessitated that Shanti should sever her links from the 'enclosed space of domesticity' (Bagchi 1985). The image of the *virangana* or the 'warrior heroine' distinct from the earlier tropes of the *exemplary wife-heroines* (Sita and Savitri) or the *powerful mother goddess figures* (Durga and Kali) was a largely overlooked 'alternative paradigm'. The attributes of the virangana model (valour, male attire, leadership of women and men) were at variance with the ideals of the earlier models, viz, passivity and self-abnegation in the case of one, and motherhood in the other. Significantly, all warrior heroines (for example, Rani Lakshmibai, Ahalyabai Holkar, etc.) were nonconformists, who rejected sati and *jauhar*, the expected norms of behaviour, to stand in and rule till the time the male heirs to the throne attained maturity. What is significant, however, is that their nonconforming is seen as compensated by their practising an even greater virtue, that is, patriotism, serving the country. Thus, the *sat* of the virangana is constructed not in terms of her relationship to a man as wife or widow, but in terms of her relationship to the nation. It is not a coincidence, then, that these historical figures, which endure today, took form in the emerging political and social ideologies of the nineteenth century as inspirational figures, as symbols of the nation itself *(Mother India)* and were engaged in a valiant and righteous struggle against the immoral rule of the coloniser (Hansen 1988).

Similar figuration of the 'inspirational' woman is seen in Gandhi. There is a predominant 'homogenising tendency' in the 'construction and reconstruction of women', rooted in the specific historical contexts of the early twentieth century in which Gandhi's *Woman* takes shape. While the figuration draws affinity with the nineteenth-century social reformers' imaginary of the pure, chaste, and virtuous woman-at-home imagery, an element of dynamism seeps into this construct, owing to its specific space in Gandhi's political ideology. The large-scale participation of women in mass movements and their imprisonment alongside men in the 1930s, in particular, necessitated that the woman-at-home image be reconciled with the new 'activist' woman. An alternative model which also coexisted with the earlier models, ostensibly expanding women's choices, was conceived in the image of a Hindu widow, a 'renunciator', whose social behavioural code was laid out in precise terms (service of the nation), yet her membership of society remained ambiguous and even transcendental, in the sense that she 'sacrifices' her 'femininity' and 'reproductive aspects' of married life to become the 'universal mother', a repository of moral good of all mankind. What is significant is that as in the earlier discussed construct of the 'warrior heroine', Gandhi's *Woman* too is abstracted from an urban, middle-class, upper-caste imaginary, despite the fact that Gandhi perhaps more than any other 'national' leader of the time was familiar with rural India and also with the fact that by 1921, of the 33 per cent of women workers 11 per cent were in industry (Patel 1988). The image of woman as goddess or mother served to erase her sexuality in the world outside the home. Samita Sen has shown how motherhood became the major element around which the identity of the Hindu middle-class women was centred. This identity extended into a national identity where the metaphor of the nation as motherland was employed as a symbol of resistance (Sen 1993).

If nationalist ideology of nineteenth-century Bengal legitimised the subjection of women under a new patriarchy, its history also reflected struggle. The unravelling of this history of struggle has shown that the struggles were multifaceted and not confined only to the public space. It has been pointed out that, working with archival resources of political history of this period, women would appear in the history of nationalism only in a 'contributive' role. Such a study 'generally signifies an addition of women into the framework of conventional history…In this sense, with a few exceptions, the women worked within boundaries laid down by men. The history uncovered in this way is a contributive history' (Jayawardena 1986, 260–61). Because of the specific conditions of colonial society, a history of this struggle is to be found, some scholars suggest, in the inner spaces of the middle-class homes. The evidence of women's struggle, therefore, is to be found not in the archives, but in autobiographies, family histories, religious tracts, literature, theatre, songs, paintings, and such other cultural artifacts (Chatterjee 1994, 133–38). Malvika Karlekar develops a concept of *antahpur*, literally translated to mean 'inner house', for the private sphere consisting of a set of rooms, courtyard, terrace, roof, and kitchen, in which women lived and worked and had limited access to the outside world. The antahpur was symbolic of the physical and emotional experiences of its women members. The relationship of the antahpur to the outside realm of men was that of patronage and superiority. A hierarchical relationship between conjugal partners was reinforced and legitimated through the notions of separate spheres. The male world of 'work' and public intervention carried more prestige and status than the female world of domesticity. Karlekar's accounts of the memoirs from the antahpur, 'varied voices from the inner recesses of the home', however, reveal that many women worked out meaningful roles within it for themselves. They wrote, read, thought, and communicated. An example cited by Karlekar is that of Rajalakshmi's mother voicing a sentiment which was at variance with the taboo on education of women:

> so many girls today are being educated: are they becoming widows? To lose one's husband is a matter of fate...brooding on this and not being educated is hardly the solution to such a problem...if one does become a widow but has some education in one's stomach, then why should one be afraid? The girl who knows how to work with her hands and is intelligent will somehow or the other manage to live her life in dignity (Karlekar 1991, 86).

Women's writings seem to be occupied with the theme of change and how best to cope with change. The anthology *Ideals, Images and Real Lives*, especially the section titled 'Real Lives', portrays the complex ways in which women understood the messages the mythical models and fictional heroines lay out for them, and their own responses to them in terms of compliance, adaption, and resistance (Thorner and Krishnaraj 2000). An examination of autobiographies of Bengali women of the period by Srabashi Ghosh shows the diversity of contexts in which these responses made themselves manifest as ranging from the inner quarters of the family and the household to peasant insurrection in Tebhaga

(Ghosh 1986). The most striking feature employed by them is the way in which the very theme of disclosure of self remains suppressed under a narrative of changing times, changing manners and customs, changing values, their struggles to read and write, and also the urge to compensate for their husband's 'adjustments' in the world. Partha Chatterjee suggests that this strategy, worked out within the space of the emergent nationalist middle-class home, anticipated the form of a more general strategy, which political nationalism would later use to make the solidarity of cultural communities compatible with the requirements of the modern state (Chatterjee 1994, 147).

Up to the Gandhian mass movements, where women came out in large numbers, the sanctity of the privacy of the female space and its representations were not eroded. Even the ritual of nationalism—the spinning of the *charkha* could be performed at home. Some nationalists, such as Saratchandra in *Pather Debi*, sought to resolve this contradiction by casting it in the shape of an extraordinary sacrifice demanded of a select few at a rare moment (Sarkar 1987, 1015). But, the agency of women at this juncture witnessed a break from their constructions in the nationalist project. Meena Alexander discusses this contradiction and the dilemma as reflected in the writings of Sarojini Naidu, who was elected the first Indian woman president of the Indian National Congress in 1925. It is significant that Naidu went to the extent of advocating violent measures to combat the British. Her venturing into the political realm is seen by Alexander as the breaking free of the 'agonised self' from the immobilisation portrayed in the female images in her own writings. Alexander sees this passage of her resistance as a process of empowerment generated by the confrontation with the 'tragic bonds of her own culture', which gave her the power to attack the public bonds laid down by a colonising power (Alexander 1985).

A similar trauma is witnessed in the memoirs of Shudha Mazumdar compiled by Geraldine Forbes. Mazumdar was born into a high-caste, rich, landowning family, and she is remembered for her translation of the *Ramayana* published by Orient Longman in 1958. Living in the times when the nationalist movement had acquired the proportions of a mass movement, she has been described by Forbes as interested and aware of the events around her, secretly reading proscribed literature by the revolutionaries, preparing bandages for volunteers who went to fight in the First World War, attending Congress meetings to hear Gandhi speak, and going to watch the parade when young Congress volunteers first wore military uniforms. Although from her vantage point the political events were peripheral and never central to her existence, the trauma is evident in her writings:

> I had read much but apparently digested little, for as far as I look back I find I was obsessed with a good deal of self pity…My discovery of the ephemeral quality of the things of the world tinged my thought, making me less interested in my home and surroundings. I prayed long, fasted occasionally…I remember having strange dreams at this time about flying through space, and would awake unfreshed and weary (Forbes 1989, 134).

The Diverse Manifestation of The 'New Women'

The ideological constructions of the 'new woman' did not account for the various ways in which women were in fact struggling against oppressive structures—ways which did not necessarily conform to the prescriptive codes of behaviour laid down by the bourgeois nationalists. While in several situations women 'transgressed' behavioural codes to assert their individuality beyond the boundaries laid down by religion and tradition, in some situations women confronted oppressive structures, and in still other situations they defied traditional prejudices in organisations and joined political movements, trade unions, and guerrilla organisations.

In some Islamic countries, for instance, women asserted freedom by 'throwing-off the veil', the symbol of women's confinement and seclusion. Making a statement of defiance to the feudal order, several prominent women appeared unveiled in public. Queen Surayya of Afghanistan and the Queen of Iran appeared without the veil in 1920 and 1936 respectively

(Jayawardena 1982, 143). For Palestinian women, the national movement against Zionism provided the context in which the struggle for women's emancipation also struck roots. Flouting conventional and religious norms, Palestinian women first demonstrated against Zionism in 1921 though they were heavily robed and rode in closed cars. Eight years later, in 1929, two hundred delegates attended the first Arab Women's Conference of Palestine. The very act of attending the conference was, asserts Matiel Mogannam, '...a bold step to take in view of the traditional restrictions, which until then prevented the Arab women in Palestine from taking part in any movement which might expose her to the public eye' (Antonius 1982, 63).

Often women directly confronted structures of oppression in their immediate environment. In southeast Nigeria, for instance, Igbo women carried on a unique protest, which they called the Women's War (1929–1930), against taxes imposed on them by British colonisers at a time when profit from land was declining. This protest, emulating the traditional women's protest termed by the Igbo as 'sitting on a man', involved public persuasion and/humiliation of a man by women. It involved the women's converging in the man's hut and singing songs ridiculing him until he was embarrassed and expressed repentance. In November 1929, thousands of Igbo women animated by the rumour that women's possessions were about to be taxed, 'ridiculed' and 'demanded the caps' of the warrant chiefs of sixteen native courts in Calabar and Owerri provinces. The women activated their strong grassroots network and vented their fury on the chiefs who were perceived as corrupt. British authorities perceived these traditional forms of protests as riotous and fired on the women on two occasions in mid-December, killing fifty and wounding several others (Leonard 1998, 452).

The national movement in Algeria against French rule gained momentum after 1956. The National Liberation Front waged an armed movement against the colonisers in which women assumed important roles by smuggling ammunition and terrorist bombs under their robes, serving as nurses and spies, hiding rebels and feeding them, and also engaging in combat as members of the Front (Leonard 1998, 453). Armed revolt broke out against the British in Kenya to recover their land and independence. The imprisonment in 1953 of Jomo Kenyatta the leader of the Kenya African Union, the political face of the secret society of Mau, led to widespread agitation and a spurt in underground revolutionary activities in which both rural and urban women participated as scouts, nurses, and spies. Women were consciously involved in the independence movements in sub-Saharan Africa. The African Party for the Independence of Guinea and Cape Verde succeeded in ending 90 years of Portuguese rule in 1974, after fighting a guerrilla war for nearly twelve years. Struggles against Portuguese rule were waged in Angola and Mozambique as well. The Party mobilised women in large numbers and assigned them specific roles in the guerrilla war. Women mobilised others to participate in the movement, fed guerrillas, cooked food, gathered supplies and water, and marched long hours to the hidden base camps to replenish them. Some women also trained as guerrillas. The struggle of the Eritrean people for independence from Ethiopia entered a new phase with the beginning of the armed struggle in 1961. Peasant women provided the basic needs for a movement that was functioning underground, that is, food and shelter, and urban working women organised themselves to give financial help to the movement (Davies 1982, 111).

Women revolutionaries have recounted the political implications of such participation, the risk of torture, death, and rape, and, in many instances, at the expense of their families and children. Talking about their double exploitation as colonised and as women, which gave them no political rights and legal personhood to own property or to have rights of ownership over what they produced, women in armed struggles in El Salvador, Eritrea, Namibia, and Zimbabwe, among others, felt that the struggle for national liberation gave them a standing as individuals and as women. Ellen Musialela, who became involved in the armed struggle for Namibia's liberation in 1964, found that women's struggle alongside men 'on all three fronts of the struggle—diplomatic, military and political'—earned them 'great respect by men'. Not only did men not look on women as weak, women were not assigned separate work, which was shared by all irrespective of a person's sex. As a result, she felt that the central leadership of South West African People's Organisation (SWAPO) consisted of both men and women. More importantly, it provided the opportunity to build the groundwork for seeking women's rights, especially those pertaining to education and economic independence, alongside the struggle for national liberation. Thus, the SWAPO Women's Council (SWC), founded in 1970, described its primary aim as striving 'to achieve equality for women as well as their full participation in the struggle for national and social liberation' (Musialela, 1982, 84–5). Similarly, the National Union of Eritrean Women (NUEW), founded in 1979, with its headquarters in Rome, saw in itself a manifestation of the development of women's struggles and the raising of political consciousness and organisational ability of women. The formation of the NUEW would, they hoped, accelerate the development of women's movement and their participation in the ongoing national struggle under the vanguard of the Eritrean People's Liberation Front (EPLF) against 'colonial oppression' and 'feudal exploitation' for 'social transformation' (Davies 1982, 108).

The aspiration for 'social transformation' was being expressed by women's organisations, which pressed for political rights for women alongside their struggles for national liberation. Perhaps the most prominent demand for political equality in the early twentieth century, around which women were mobilised and organised, was the demand for suffrage. In several colonised countries, the demand for voting rights for women was posed and gained momentum during heightened anticolonial struggles. Given that under colonial conditions only a small minority of men could vote, it is significant that the demand for women's suffrage was made, as in India, within the framework of 'universal suffrage'. Thus, women demanded not only voting rights for women on an equal basis with men, but also voting rights for all the adult population. Various organisations in India including the All India Women's Conference, Women's India Association, and National Council for Women in India, agitated for reforms to broaden the eligibility criteria to include more women voters. At first, the women's conferences dealt with women's education, but gradually they adopted political issues of sexual equality, votes for women, and reform of personal laws. The women's organisations succeeded also in getting women's political equality included in the political programme of the Indian National Congress that was at the forefront of the national liberation movement in India.[17]

Apart from women's organisations, feminist literature and journals of the period throw interesting light on the 'women's question' as it was articulated in the context of anticolonial struggles. The magazines, novels, didactic tracts, articles, and books that proliferated during the period concerned themselves, among other issues, with women's subordination. They contributed significantly to the dissemination of information on women's movements, especially the suffragette struggles in Europe and rights issues in other countries. Egyptian women, for example, read about innovations and legislative reforms in Turkey. Among the earliest journals was the Egyptian journal *Al Fatah* (1892), the Turkish weekly *Newspaper for Ladies* (1895), the *Chinese Women's Journal* (1907), *Knowledge*, an Iranian Women's Journal (1906), and *Seito* in Japan (1911). Novels with explicit feminist concerns were also published. Li Ruzhen wrote the first Chinese feminist novel, *Flowers in the Mirror*, in which

---

[17]See Forbes (1998). In Costa Rica, however, the women's movement for political rights took place after the country gained independence from Spain in 1821. The first proposal for women's suffrage was made in the legislature in 1890, long after the country became free. The fight for women's right to vote and contest elections was taken up by Liga Feminista (Feminist League), which supported women's rights to suffrage, education, and social welfare. The league became active during the following three decades when popular demands for social reform also increased. Women finally got the right to vote and contest elections in 1941 more than a century after the country gained political independence (Leonard 1998, 449).

sex roles were reversed in a society where women ruled and men had bound feet (Jayawardena 1982, 144–45).

Conclusion

Anticolonial movements were a significant part of the experience of a large number of countries of Asia, Africa, and the Americas. The movements coalesced a wide range of struggles, waged against various forms and structures of oppression. The strand of struggle that assumed primacy was the struggle for national liberation where liberation came to mean the restoration of popular sovereignty and dignity to *a people* sharing a common past and destiny as a nation. The specificity of this national identity derived from resources gleaned from history, from a tradition unsullied by colonial domination. The figure of the woman constituted the core ingredient in the construction of national identity. The 'new woman', reformed, educated, and steeped in 'traditional' values, became the repository of national identity and essence. The construction of the 'new woman', however, exhibited the class concerns of the nationalist elite. A large number of women were a part of the industrial workforce, who struggled against wage and work conditions under a capitalist economy that prospered under colonialism. Issues of women's equality and emancipation within the context of colonial modernity were fraught with contradictory pulls and the lives of women reveal the ensuing strains. The 'private pain' and anguish seen in the poems of Sarojini Naidu, for example, sought the redemption of the 'agonised self' in vigorous political/public activity. Women participated in significant ways in national liberation struggles in roles ranging from passive resisters to armed revolutionaries. In order to understand the content of women's participation, one must look at the questions such participation raised or sought to resolve about women's social roles. It is important to note that even when the nationalist elite proposed that the 'women's question' had been resolved, women themselves interpreted their struggles as directed not merely against colonial domination. They have rather seen themselves as struggling on multiple fronts as women—against dowry, against rape, against genital mutilation, against discrimination in the workplace—seeking in other words not only national liberation but social transformation as well to end their social, economic, legal, and political subordination as women. In the chapter which follows we shall open up for critical interrogation the domain of the 'home'—the 'domestic'—which was an enduring arena of contestation between the coloniser and the colonised. The domestic was not only the realm where the nationalists sought to 'resolve' the women's question and resist colonial intervention, it was also the realm where the limits of women's behaviour were sought to be drawn and her unequal position within the hierarchised structure of the family, nation, and state, affirmed.

3

The Domestic, Domesticity, and Women Citizens in Late Colonial India

This chapter explores the specificities of the notion of 'domestic' as it emerged in the context of colonial India and examines some aspects of the complex ways in which it unfolded in late nineteenth- and early twentieth-century India. It builds on studies which show that the contours of the 'domestic' took shape in the course of the contest between the colonial state and the nationalist elite, as a contested space for the assertion of 'legitimate' authority. While retaining the argument that the construction of the domestic in the colonial context was accompanied by a reconstitution of national tradition, the chapter proposes that there existed a dialogical and interactive relationship between the domestic and public. While the basis of this relationship is indeed embedded in the contests between the colonisers and the nationalist elite, the meanings which accrued to the domestic in the course of this contest were not fixed nor reducible to a framework of oppositional relationship. They, rather, manifest a complexity and mobility, reflecting the diverse terrain of conflict, resistance, dialogue, and negotiation between the coloniser and the colonised and demonstrate the ways in which the boundaries of the domestic were made permeable.

The chapter looks in particular at didactic tracts/prescriptive conduct books and pamphlets in Hindi—to show how within a specific sociohistorical context, the domestic was being articulated within a complex network of relationships, the ideological, spatial, and temporal connotations of such articulations, and the implications they had for envisaging the terms of women's membership as citizens within the emergent polity. The recourse to didactic/prescriptive writings is to add another dimension to the existing research in this area. While a substantial bulk of this research focusses on nationalist writings in journals and in fiction by men and women, the texts relied on in the present chapter are different insofar as the messages they carry are overtly instructive and not shrouded in fiction or essays. Significantly, some of these texts were part of the study curricula of *kanya vidyalayas* (schools for girls) and had, therefore, an authoritative character. The proliferation of such texts in the late colonial period may be seen also as reflecting the anxieties of a period of change where gender roles, far from being settled, manifested domains of contest and struggle.

The Domestic in Western Modernity: Implications for Women's Citizenship

Modern notions of citizenship evolved from the ideological, material, and social formations of modernity set in motion by Enlightenment thought, the bourgeois revolutions of the seventeenth and eighteenth centuries, and the models of modernisations put forth in the course of development and expansion of capitalism. These ideological, social, and material formations affected women of different classes in dissimilar and even antithetical ways. The idiom of 'domesticity' was a significant axis on which this difference made itself manifest. Domesticity may be seen as broadly referring to an ideology pertaining to the specificity of the nature and scope of activities in the realm of the domestic. The notion of domestic may then be seen as having certain 'spatial', 'temporal', and 'ideological' connotations. It follows from this that the meanings which 'domestic' and 'domesticity' signify are not fixed and reflect their temporal, spatial, and ideological contexts.

The idea of the domestic, signifying a sphere of female activities distinct from the public (male) sphere of activities, relatively inferior yet complementary to the latter, emerged in the context of the historical transitions from feudal, agricultural, artistocratic, to industrial, bourgeois-capitalist societies. The development of capitalism changed the manner in which production process and labour were organised in feudal and household economies, bringing about a segregation of production for the market and private housework and generating a split between the public and domestic spheres. This split was primarily determined by the fact that the economic activities of the household were distinct from that of the public/civil society where production took place for profit, and the relationships of production were nonfamilial and impersonal. Moreover, the distinction between the two spheres became gendered as each sphere came to be seen as separate in terms of male and female sphere of activities. The idea of separate spheres of male and female activities, and the devaluation of household work was justified by strands in Enlightenment thought that espoused biological determinism or a linkage between biological constitution of male and female bodies and their 'natural' suitability for specific social roles. Nature, asserted Rousseau, made women inherently different from men, suiting them physically, morally, and intellectually to their primary task of reproduction. Their education and place in society, therefore, should reflect this difference and their natural feminine instincts channelled advantageously into 'civilised domesticity'. In his manual of education, *Emile*, Rousseau articulated the Enlightenment view of the female body as *a new scientific view* of sexual difference, as the moral and social imperative for organising social life. Declaring that 'men and women were made for each other', Rousseau cautions that 'their mutual dependence was not equal':

> ...We could survive without them better than they could without us...Thus women's entire education should be planned in relation to men. To please men, to be useful to them, to win their love and respect, to raise them as children, care for them as adults, correct and console them, make their lives sweet and pleasant; these are women's duties in all ages and these are what they should be taught from childhood (Rubinstein 1986, 202).

The emergent bourgeois culture thus redefined sexual roles, bringing forth the idea of the domestic woman, to whom the care of the family could be entrusted. In this new definition of social roles, the domestic came to symbolise the sphere in which women preserved the values of selflessness, love, and care that had been driven out of the hard materialist and powerful world of the market. The propagation and universalisation of the image of the 'housewife' as the ideal image of the 'modern woman', was accompanied by a process of 'housewifization of women' (Mies 1998, 40). The process of housewifization, as Maria Mies terms it, was part of a continuing history of violence against women and the rise of the 'White Man', the coloniser of women, of nature, and of foreign people.[1] Mies points out that the

---

[1]Maria Mies has shown that capital accumulation presupposes the exploitation of ever more 'non-capitalist' milieu and areas—the colonies—for the appropriation of more labour, more raw materials, and more markets necessary for initiating the process of capital accumulation. The main colonies of capitalism in the process are countries of the third world, women, and nature. These colonies constitute the hidden underground of the economic system, which can be compared to an iceberg. The visible part above the water constitutes capital and wage labour, the invisible part under the water represents nonwage labour, particularly of women, nature, and the third world. Capitalism, avers Mies, creates a worldview in which man appears as totally independent of nature (or God). The new power by which man is able to set himself over and above nature—and women—is, together with modern science and technology, the power of 'money', or capital. Capital here means money that is able to give birth to more money, 'money breeding (*contd.*)

domestication of women was by no means a peaceful history, but was immediately preceded by at least three centuries of brutal violence against millions of women in what has been put down in history as the witch hunt. The largest mass killing of women in modern history, significantly, did not occur, as is commonly believed, in the Dark or the Middle Ages or as a result of superstition, but later, at the time of the inception of the modern economy and of the modern state.[2] Feminist research has not only shown the interconnection between this brutal attack on women, particularly on healers and midwives, and the rise of modern medicine, which subsequently became a monopoly of men, it has demonstrated in particular that not only modern medicine, but also modern physics and mechanics and the new 'scientific' relation to nature rose up from the fires of the witches.[3] In these fires, the old organic relation of women to their bodies, their knowledge about health, disease, and about the healing powers of nature, were all burnt to ashes. One aspect often overlooked in the analyses of the witch pogroms is the accumulation of wealth through such witch trials. The wealth accrued from such 'hunts' and the property confiscated from the 'witches' and their families were used to finance wars and modern projects.[4] The brutalisation and subordination of 'bad women' were followed in the eighteenth century by the idealisation of the domesticated, tame, weak, and dependent

---

(*contd.*) money'—the real god of capitalism, the creator and preserver of all life. This new life-giving power of money replaced the life-giving capacity of women and of the earth. Maria Mies, 'World Economy, Patriarchy, and Accumulation', in *Women in the Third World*, ed. Nelly P. Stromquist (1998, 37–45).

[2]Ibid. This witch hunt, which raged through Europe from the fourteenth to the seventeenth century, is the largest mass killing of women in modern history; estimates place the numbers at 500,000 to several million.

[3]Some of these writings are, B. Ehrenreich and D. English, *For Her Own Good: 150 Years of Experts' Advice to Women* (1979); Carolyn Merchant, *The Death of Nature: Women, Ecology and the Scientific Revolution* (1983).

[4]See Maria Mies, *Patriarchy and Accumulation on a World Scale: Women in the International Division of Labour*, (1986).

'good woman', the housewife in the households of the rising bourgeois class. This ideal woman soon came to symbolise progress and became a model to be emulated by the lower classes,[5] and a standard by which other civilisations could be measured.[6]

A number of feminist writings take recourse to the 'domestic thesis' to explain the disparate chronological sequence of the acquisition of citizenship by men and women. This thesis claims that the gendered organisation of spaces, the uses made of them, and meanings attached to them have been responsible for the exclusion of women from public roles, institutions, and citizenship. Proponents of the thesis point out that the construction of separate and contrasting spheres, public and private, having gendered attributes, masculine and feminine, has been a feature of Western political and social thought and practice.[7] The gendered organisation of social relations around 'separate and

---

[5]The European working class, which even as it fought against capitalism, adopted this image of woman and the bourgeois family as models of progress. It was an important aim of trade-union struggles that the proletarian man should also earn a 'family-wage' so that he could keep a 'nonworking' housewife at home (Mies 1986, 107–8).

[6]The image of the ideal housewife was transmitted by missionaries and colonialists all over the world as a model of 'civilisation and enlightenment'. The rise of the 'White Man' became in some ways contingent on the apotheosis of the domestic woman, 'the angel of the household'. The process of housewifization thus was accompanied by the process of colonisation of far-away lands in Asia, Africa, and South America. These two processes were directly and causally linked. Colonialism provided the material source for the increase of productivity of human labour, which then gave a boost to industrial expansion. In this process of colonisation, the 'White Man' could count on the loyalties of local patriarchal values and institutions as a base for modernisation and capital accumulation (Mies 1986, 40).

[7]See Carole Pateman, 'Feminist Critiques of the Public/Private Dichotomy', in *The Disorder of Women: Democracy, Feminist and Political Theory* (1989, 118–40); Jean Bethke Elshtain, *Public Man, Private Woman: Women in Social and Political Thought* (1981); Nancy C.M. Hartsock, *Money, Sex and Power: Towards a Feminist Historical Materialism* (1983); Susan Moller Okin, *Women in Western Political Thought* (1979); Carole Pateman, *The Sexual Contract* (1988).

contrasting space' takes the specific form of the construction of the 'domestic woman', which becomes instrumental in confining women to the private space, and far from generating equality, which formed the framework of universal citizenship, prepared the grounds for a separate timeline of citizenship for women. While citizenship for men may be seen to have started from the eighteenth century with the acquisition of civil rights, for women, the same century saw the beginning of a corresponding history of greater dependence.[8]

While the significance of the domestic ideology in influencing social roles and spaces in modern times cannot be denied, there is a degree of scepticism among social scientists about the evidence and analytic procedures underlying the thesis. A number of them feel that historical evidence supporting the dominance and acceptance (by women) of the ideology of domesticity is uneven. As *a set of ideals* surrounding the role of women, the domestic ideology, they argue, did not necessarily correspond to nor was inspired by the lived experienced of *all women*. Instead, these ideals were generated with respect to a rather small category of women—the married upper, and upper-middle class women.[9] The thesis, moreover, suffers from

---

[8]It is little wonder then that the French Convention declared in 1792 that women were not citizens. Lieteke van Vucht Trjssen sees in these roles the underlying tendency to restrain the participation of women in the labour market. See Lieteke van Vucht Trjssen, 'Women Between Modernity and Postmodernity', in *Theories of Modernity and Postmodernity*, ed. Bryan S. Turner (1990).

[9]Anthony Giddens would understand women's roles neither in terms of a gap between theory and practice nor in terms of self-imposed transgression by women. He would rather see it in terms of the absence of any rigid difference between the formalised and fully articulated discursive consciousness and the pragmatic and often tacit practical consciousness. The difference in other words is between what is only *said* and what is *simply done*. Anthony Giddens, *The Constitution of Society: Outline of the Theory of Structuration* (1984, xxiii–xxvii, 3–7, 15–16, 21–25). Looking at 'what was simply done', recent feminist epistemology and sociology identifies women's standpoints as sites that, although infiltrated by formalised and textually mediated forms (*contd.*)

analytic weakness that lies in its dependence on a series of straight dichotomies.[10] These dichotomies, they feel, tend to simplify rather than explain the intricate and complex manner in which human experiences actually unfold. A number of feminists, especially Joan Wallach Scott and Denise Riley, while conceding that ideological climate did inhibit women's publicness, argue that women had complex and multiple roles which were not necessarily circumscribed by binary opposition of sociopolitical relations.[11]

In the exploration of the 'domestic' and 'domesticity' within the colonial context and its implications for articulating the citizenship of women, this chapter sees the domestic as denoting a terrain of conflict, of resistance, and dialogue among multifarious socioeconomic and political forces placed in a conflictual relationship. Steering clear from approaches that conceive it in opposition to some other category, it sees the domestic as emerging at the interface of a diversity of distinctions, not necessarily dichotomous or binary in character, exhibiting a mobility of meanings, and as a rallying point for a multiplicity of identities. The notion suggests a plurality of meanings, defying any rigidity, thereby giving the term a degree of dynamism. These diverse and shifting meanings of domestic and

---

(*contd.*) of discursive consciousness, are also sufficiently autonomous to become sites of difference in which hegemonic paradigms and theories can be contested. Dorothy Smith, *The Everyday World as Problematic: A Feminist Sociology* (1987, 105–11); Patricia Hill Collins, *Black Feminist Thought* (1991, 21–33); Joan Wallach Scott, 'The Evidence of Experience', *Critical Inquiry* (1991, 773–97). Klein argues that the discussions of 'public' and 'private' have often assumed a common knowledge of the meaning of these words without investigation. The point is that even when 'theory' was against them, women did have public life and engaged in public practices. Lawrence E. Klein, 'Gender and the Public/Private Distinction in the 18th Century: Some Questions About Evidence and Analytic Procedure', *Eighteenth Century Studies*, (1995, 102).

[10]See Lawrence E.Klein.

[11]Joan Wallach Scott, 'Women's History' and 'Gender: A Useful Category of Historical Analysis', in *Gender and the Politics of History*, (1988, 15–50); Denise Riley, '*Am I That Name?' Feminism and the Category of 'Women' in History* (1988).

domesticity can be seen as deriving significance from the broader contexts of the anticolonial struggle and assuming form both as a *space* defined by the frameworks of the contests and as an *activity* not necessarily bound by notions of space.

In the light of the above propositions, we shall examine the meaning(s) of domestic as a site of social (re)structuring and its implications for the lived experiences of women. This examination shall serve as a background for an exploration of the ways in which the idea of domesticity emerged in late colonial India, at the interface of the contest between the colonisers and the nationalists over the demarcation and delimitation of the 'domestic' as a space for the assertion of legitimate authority. It can then be proposed that the meaning of the domestic and its contours were not only shaped by the terms of the contest, but were also the sites where old meanings were reinforced and new ones generated. To substantiate this, the colonial and nationalist formulations of the 'domestic' will be explored to see how in a specific historical context the domestic was being articulated within a complex network of meanings. Such explorations will serve as a framework for understanding the nature of women's membership as citizens in the emergent body politic.

The Domestic Ideal and the Colonial Context

The notion of 'domestic' and the idiom of 'domesticity' within the colonial context assumed significant spatial, temporal, and ideological connotations. At the intersection of a colonial policy of domination and exploitation and the various struggles for national self-determination, the 'domestic' came to assume several meanings, which were sometimes inconsistent and irreconcilable with one another. It emerged, (i) as a *terrain of contest* (domination and resistance) between the colonisers and the nationalist elite, (ii) as *an exclusive sovereign domain* where the nation was acting on its own, resisting colonial penetration, (iii) as *an inclusive repository of tradition*, history, and culture of a 'people', where the nation was seen as having survived unsullied by colonial domination, and, (iv) as *a gendered category* having important implications for the manner in which women's social roles were being defined. These meanings may be seen as emerging in the process of (i) the unfolding of practices of colonial rule, and, (ii) nationalist resistance to colonial rule and the assertion of an Indian modernity. In the sections which follow, an attempt will be made to explore how these diverse meanings of the 'domestic' are thrown up in the course of these two broad processes.

In order to explore and interrogate the above meanings, it would be worthwhile to reflect on some of the following questions: (i) If the domestic was grounded in the claims to sovereignty and self-determination, what were its 'special' characteristics? (ii) How were its boundaries defined—was it simply the home, or the cultural community, or the nation, or a political community constituted within a wider political imaginary? (iii) How did it come into existence? Was it contingent, contextual, or had concrete/discrete boundaries signifying the area where the domestic ended and the political/public began? (iv) Was the domestic nonpolitical as it is made out to be? (v) What tussles and contests characterised the internal dynamics of the domestic—seen in the order— home, community, nation? (vi) How were these struggles accommodated in the homogenous/homogenised 'domestic', and how were these played out in the public/political. In other words, how do these fissures and their negotiations make themselves manifest in the language of citizenship? (vii) How has the domestic been seen in literature on colonial history, gender studies, and how does the literature of the period portray it, and, (viii) How did women define what constituted the domestic?

The domestic in the colonial discourse and practices of rule

The domestic can be seen as encompassing a set of meanings emerging from the imperatives of colonial rule which dictated that the colonised population be made intelligible to the coloniser. Underlying such imperatives was the assumption that the colonised cultures could not be properly understood until the domestic or the 'native culture' had been opened up to scholarly [orientalist] study and governmental scrutiny. This assumption permeated much of European writing and thinking on India in the eighteenth and early nineteenth centuries. In the process of understanding the colonised, the domestic came to assume specific cultural connotation and was imbued with meanings which denied coevalness to the colonised. The figure of the colonised emerged within this framework as a 'domesticated', apolitical subject-citizen, marked by cultural attributes that were inadequate for citizenship. The idea of the 'domestic' became part of the civilisational critique of the colonised culture and the rationalisation of a differential colonial rule. The edifice of the critique was based on the so-called 'women's question' which condemned Indian civilisation as inferior. The idea of 'civilisation' itself emerged from the coloniser's world view which saw the world as hierarchical and at the same time united in a scale of hierarchies binding it into a universal within which different civilisations could be slotted (Chakrabarty 1993, 1–7).

The contours of the domestic were also shaped in the attempts by the British to institute a system of governance, which reflected and reinforced their understanding of the colony (India) in cultural terms and which denied the colonised the status of a citizen. The understanding of the colony in cultural terms, slotted in a universal civilisational hierarchy, denied coevalness to the colonised. Citizenship was seen as rooted in modern Western contexts and, therefore, not applicable to societies where 'premodern' forms of social relations persisted. The nonapplicability of this manifestation of Western rationality was justified in terms of an inadequacy and incapacity on the part of the colonised to transcend the medieval to the modern. Thus, Alexander Dow in the *History of Hindostan*, first published in three volumes between 1770 and 1772, lamented: '...to make the natives of the fertile soil of Bengal free, *is beyond the power of political arrangement*...their religion, their institutions, their manners, *the very disposition of their minds form them for passive obedience*.' This passivity that Dow finds ingrained in the mentality of the 'native' population would, states Dow, reap results quite the opposite of those which ensued in Western societies, when certain basic conditions of 'self-determination were achieved: 'to give them property would only bind them with stronger ties to our interests, and make them subjects; or if the British nation prefers the name—more our slaves'.[12] Thus, as Dipesh Chakrabarty phrases it, subjecthood but not citizenship remained the cornerstone of imperial ideology and the colonial practices of rule as the native was never considered adequate to the latter (Chakrabarty 1992, 6).

The techniques of governance, which the colonial state deployed, reflected and reinforced the manner in which the colonisers made sense of and in the process described and defined the colonial subject in relation to itself. 'Modern' governmental practices of measurement, enumeration, and classification of the subject population were developed to facilitate administration (Chakrabarty 1995). This in turn made precise the definition of what was within the competence of the state.[13] On the other hand, this delineation of the colonial state's sphere of competence was contested by the nationalists who sought to contain and constrict this widening sphere of state influence.

---

[12]Alexander Dow, cited in Dipesh Chakrabarty, 'Postcoloniality and the Artifice of History: Who Speaks for the Indian Past' (1992, 1–26), (emphasis added).

[13]The colonial state attempted to govern its subjects by adopting techniques of measurement. Bernard Cohn and Nicholas B.Dirks remark that the modern (European) state, unlike the premodern state, made its power visible not only through dramatic, theatrical displays, but also through 'the gradual extension of officialising procedures and routines through the capacity to bound and mark space, to record transactions such as the sale of property, to count and classify their populations, to gradually replace religious institutions as the registrar of the life-cycle facts of birth, marriage, and death...'. Bernard S. Cohn and Nicholas B. Dirks, 'Beyond the Fringe: The Nation State, Colonialism and Technologies of Power', *Journal of Historical Sociology*, 1, no. 2, (June 1988). In his study of the history of communities in pre-British and British India, Sudipta Kaviraj says, that 'communities' in pre-British India had 'fuzzy' boundaries, implying boundaries which did not have concrete divisions. In British India, these 'fuzzy' identities become 'enumerated' and in the process standardised and frozen so as to ensure governability. Sudipta Kaviraj, 'On the Construction of Colonial Power: Structure, Discourse, Hegemony', in *Contesting Colonial Hegemony*, eds. Dagmar Engels and Shula Marks (1994).

The domestic as the site of nationalist resistance

In the course of the struggle for their respective spheres of competence, the realm of the domestic emerged not simply as the field of domination and practices of (colonial) rule; it emerged also as an arena of contest, as the site of resistance to colonial rule where the colonised recovered their freedom. If the colonial discourse domesticated, depoliticised, and subjugated the colonised, the nationalist discourse reclaimed the domestic as the site where a resisting, liberatory, self-identity took form.

The delineation of the domestic in the colonial context reflected nationalist aspirations to a modernity, which would qualify them to 'sameness' with the colonisers, and, at the same time, reflected their 'difference' or distinctiveness. It was, effectively, the latter, that is, the assertion of difference, the claims to being a 'unique people'—a 'nation'—which logically formed the ground for the assertion of a sameness and equality with the colonisers and was expressed as a right to political sovereignty and national self-determination. It was this claim to both sameness and difference that was reflected in the constitution of an impregnable realm of home, where the nation acted on its own without the interference of the colonial state.

The domestic as the site where a resisting self-identity took form can be seen as unfolding at two layers in the process of the narration and constitution of the nation. It involved the invocation of an overwhelming, homogenous national identity deriving from a shared historical past and destiny. The invocation of this national identity was also hegemonising in the sense that it involved the containment of (heterodox) possibilities into a single national essence. This nation was the domain of national sovereignty within colonial society. If the outside, the domain of economy, statecraft, science and technology, was the alienating and emasculating domain where the East had succumbed to the West, it was the domestic, the realm reclaimed in thought and practice from the outer world of foreign (colonial) rule, where the superiority and distinctiveness of the nation was asserted. The inner domain of culture became coterminous with the nation—sovereign, impregnable, and 'non-negotiable' with the colonial state. It was in this sovereign space of the domestic where Partha Chatterjee identifies the 'most powerful, creative and historically significant project' launched by nationalism, that is, the construction of the reformed, national tradition with the 'woman' as its repository (Chatterjee 1994, 129).

On the other hand the enunciation of the nation involved, also, the articulation of the domestic in the form of a democratised civil society where modern notions of rights and citizenship could assume form and substance. The earlier section discussed the 'bureaucratic-rational' impulses of the state, which involved the definition and enumeration of the colonised people not as individuals but as constituents of 'supra-communities' as in castes, sects, 'martial races', all of which were deemed by the state to be apolitical.[14] This enumeration reflected the public-political organising by the colonial state of its sphere of

---

[14]The replacement of fuzzy communities with enumerated ones (numerical description of communities as Bernard Cohn calls it) depicted not only the way in which the colonial state attempted to 'know' and subsequently govern the colonised, but it also affected in important ways the understanding of the people about themselves. Bernard S. Cohn and Nicholas B. Dirks, 'Beyond the Fringe', *Journal of Historical Sociology*, (June 1988). As Kaviraj has pointed out again, the fuzziness of the communities (though precise for all purposes of social interaction) did not require its members to ask how many of them there were in the world. Cohn points out that this numerical description of the colonised—their classification into specific religious or caste communities or even criminal ones—did not reside exclusively in the colonial imagination but it shaped in turn the subsequent forms of mobilising the people seeking representation in the state domain as belonging to a particular caste or religion. This enumeration of the colonial population as specific communities was the reaffirmation, however, of the colonial attempts to define the colonised in terms different from them—as an ensemble of communities. Apart from the standardisation, the construction and definition of identities itself affirmed the rule of difference which legitimised colonisation and produced the colonised as a non-rational other of coloniser. Sudipta Kaviraj, 'On the Construction of Colonial Power', in *Contesting Colonial Hegemony*, eds. Engels and Marks (1994).

competence and influence. On the other hand, corresponding to such enumeration, a realm of civil society emerged, where a process of democratisation of the civic life of the nation was unleashed. Whereas colonial practices of rule involved the enumeration of communities as indicative of religious and cultural activities, numerous struggles rallied around these cultural-community identities and questioned their marginalisation within socioeconomic and religious hierarchies and hegemonies which marked Indian society. While the domestic as the sovereign, inner, homogenous, cultural realm of the nation was articulated as the boundary restricting colonial interference, the domestic as a melange/ensemble of communities, depoliticised and domesticated within the colonial discourse, became a realm marked by struggles for socioeconomic reconfiguration and rearticulation of power relations. In other words, the struggles of democratisation of the hitherto existing power relations were to set the grounds for the institution of modern structures of self-governance, replete with the language of rights and citizenship—the initiation, in short, of the formation of a political community marked by relationships of horizontal camaraderie.

The domestic and gendered citizenship

As pointed in an earlier section, the production of knowledge about the colonised denied them coevalness. The denial of coevalness, based on the treatment of women as indicators or signs of a degenerate civilisation, and the feminisation and depoliticisation of Indians in the colonial discourse has been discussed earlier. If difference constituted the basis for the colonial state's legitimation of deferral of citizenship to the colonised, the nationalists lay claims to citizenship by disrupting the colonialist notion of modernity as something that had already taken place somewhere. The domestic became the arena where the nationalist (male) ventured to mark and define an Indian modernity. This modernity, conceived as the enduring spirit and essence of Indianness, was culled and sifted from a past unstained and unsullied by alien presence and domination.

Throughout the late nineteenth and early twentieth centuries, the nationalists sought to confirm this spirit by recovering, resurrecting, and reaffirming a 'national' culture from the folds of history. The domestic was the space where the retrieval of the national culture took place. Women, in their specific roles as biological reproducers, became the 'natural' symbols of the continuity of a national culture and identity. The apotheosis of the idealised Hindu woman was an integral part of this process of recovery and rejuvenation of a national tradition. Produced and reproduced through extensive writings laying down behavioural norms for women, the body of the idealised Hindu woman came to symbolise the ultimate and even the last resort of resistance to imperialism in the nationalist discourse. Tanika Sarkar expresses this significant yet paradoxical relationship: 'Independence like a hidden jewel, could be detached from external surroundings that spelt defeat and yet be concealed in the very core of the woman's body' (Sarkar 1987, 2014). Yet, because freedom in the public/world was dependent upon the liberation that was asserted within the domestic, there appears also to be 'an implicit continuum' between the woman's body, signifying chastity, to political independence at the level of the state. Significantly then, seen from the other end of this spectrum, political freedom, sovereignty, and citizenship become dependent upon 'a steady process of regression', a reversal in the case of women. The process of individuation and citizenship for women reverts as her 'independent selfhood' folds back from the public domain to the interior space of the household and then is further pushed back into 'the hidden depths of an inviolate, chaste, pure female body' (Sarkar 1987).

The writing of the history of the nation thus implicated women as the integral principle of the national essence. In this context, the figure of woman unfolded in various shapes. Iconic forms were garnered from history and rendered meaningful and relevant to the present struggle. A range of modular forms from heroic womanhood in the virangana model (Lakshmibai, Ahalyabai Holkar, Durga, and Kali) to the exemplary wife model typified by Sita and Savitri, were deified and projected as authentic social roles for women. All these forms, whether exemplifying resistance and obduracy or sacrifice and 'self-abnegation, had a common thread of meanings running through them. This thread pertained to the idea of woman as the sustainer and reproducer of the nation, as the indispensable ingredient which gave life to the nation and at the same time partook of the moral responsibility of fortifying the nation, making it impregnable to foreign domination. These deified and thereby authenticated roles for women constituted a national identity based on a series of exclusions,[15] the homogenisation of differences, and the hegemonisation of a universal national identity. In this context, domestic behaviour and relations came to be assigned new meanings and ascriptions, meanings that connected the imaginary of the family and community with that of the nation. These meanings gave a new significance to family, and the manner in which the family came to be implicated in the notion of the community and the nation.

Domesticity: A Public Discourse Surrounding the Private

The ideal of the housewife/family and the discussion around domesticity, that is, the manner in which the domestic or private was to be ideally organised, reflects the contests that accompanied the struggles of Indian nationalists to present themselves as a sovereign and autonomous people. In this section we shall examine journals, books, and pamphlets to see how the ideal of domesticity, located within the normative frameworks of familial, community, and national relationships and bonds, was transmitted through didactic writings. While most of the writings discussed are in Hindi, wherever possible the

---

[15]For the manner in which such exclusions are brought about see Sumanta Banerjee, 'Marginalisation of Women's Popular Culture in Nineteenth Century Bengal'; Nirmala Banerjee, 'Working Women in Colonial Bengal: Modernisation and Marginalisation'; and Uma Chakravarti, 'Whatever Happened to the Vedic Dasi? Orientalism, Nationalism and a Script for the Past', in *Recasting Women: Essays in Colonial History*, eds. Kumkum Sangari and Sudesh Vaid (1989).

examinations will be substantiated by analysis of such writings in other Indian languages. We shall explore, in particular, how these writings were imbued with multiple meanings of the domestic; how the personal/domestic was distinguished from the community and public; how, interrupting the colonial discourse about the subject/citizen and colonial modernity/civil society, the domestic formed part of the discourse on nationalism; and how the Indian model purported to be different (original) from the received models (Western) for relating the personal/ private to the public world of civil/political life.

It may be pointed out at the outset that as in other kinds of writings including fiction, articulation of domesticity was textual and of a public nature, constituent, therefore, of the modern print culture and the public sphere. What distinguished the didactic writings from other texts, however, was their overtly normative/prescriptive character. The publicness of these texts was, therefore, circumscribed by the fact that their instructive nature was intended as a closure of debate and dialogue. Their claims to authority through recourse to religion and mythology as well as by the fact that a number of them were written by figures of authority in 'girls' schools' and were prescribed texts, effected further closure. It may be reiterated that these texts were intended for only a small group of people, the Hindu middle-class women. They reflect, however, the manner in which the national project sought to construct a homogenous Hindu identity and in the process ironed out and effaced other existing traditions. Moreover, the public discourse on domesticity, imbued with symbolic associations with the nation, as pointed out earlier, played a significant ideological role, pleading for a truncation of women's individuation by 'fixing' her within the 'natural' units of family, caste, community, and nation and for a different and dependent role for women in the emergent nation-state. The extraordinary proliferation of such writings in the period may indeed be symptomatic of an intrinsic anxiety and impending social chaos as nationalism gained momentum as a political movement unleashing energies that sought to tear down traditional structures of authority in all its manifestations.

An examination of the public narratives of the domestic in the course of the national movement shows two parallel and mutually disparate descriptions of its association with the nation. A different conception of the domestic and women's figuration in relation to the nation, therefore, appears in each relationship. While the conception of the domestic in both is in terms of a gendered space of feminine activity and attributes, in one, the domestic is conceived of as a sphere of activity subordinate to the public sphere where the masculine civil-political project of national liberation unfolds and the struggle for national liberation is waged. The domestic, in this formulation, bears the stigma of inadequacy and incompetence for its incommensurability with modern times. It represents what Dipesh Chakrabarty calls the 'unhappy consciousness' of the early nineteenth-century imaginations in Bengali domestic writings. Whereas the domestic represents the unhappy present, worldly activities are perceived as pursuits for happiness (freedom) to be achieved in a historical future. This perception was based on the imagination of the *griha* or the home/domestic as lacking in the discipline and beauty that marked the 'English home'. The domestic in this relationship bore the burden of being an 'embarrassment', needing reform and improvement. It bore also the burden of 'guilt' for being the cause of embarrassment and emasculation of Indian men in the public sphere of male activities.[16] Implicit in such a formulation was the acceptance of the 'universalist' (colonial/Western) paradigm involving the acceptance of a hierarchical imagination of the world.[17] Embedded in this

---

[16]Alongside the narrative of liberation/freedom/happiness also existed an antithetical narrative of degeneration or *kaliyug*. The use of 'woman as signifier' of the quality of times is reflected in the portrayal of Bengali women. The emphasis on their ignorance features alongside the figuration of men under the pressures of the coercive public sphere. See Sumit Sarkar, 'The Kalki Avtaar of Bikrampur: A Village Scandal in Early Twentieth Century Bengal', in *Subaltern Studies Vol. VI*, ed. Ranajit Guha (1989).

[17]See Ranajit Guha, 'Dominance Without Hegemony and its historiography' in *Subaltern Studies Vol. VI*, ed. Ranajit Guha (1989).

imaginary of the present was the need for a rigorous prescription for improvement. This civilisational-cum-nationalist body of thought proliferated in the second half of the nineteenth century and tied the domestic intimately with the idea of nation and the belief that the nation would improve with the improvement of the latter.

In the second formulation of the relationship between the domestic and the nation, the domestic became a site where continuity with 'mytho-religious' (Indian) society was asserted. Unlike the previous association in which the domestic was an 'embarrassment' requiring corrections in order to be 'modern', in the second form of association, the civil society becomes a problem, a constraint whose coercive nature was to be tolerated but never enjoyed. The domestic, in this formulation, was the site of self-recovery and self-respect. The civil-political society, unlike the earlier formulation, is not conceived in terms of a space holding the promise of future happiness, but a space of dehumanisation, dissociation, and even the amputation of the human body from its real self—its soul. The domestic is the space which kept alive the self and nourished it. Whereas the domestic is eulogised as the space of redemption and preservation of the self, the world is the space where the human body is regimented and controlled by the coercive properties of colonial society, of capitalism, work, and bourgeois regimes of discipline. Alongside a mourning for the compulsion to bend to the coercive regime of the public sphere, there may be seen a recurrent cautioning and exhortation against letting this coercive regime find its way into the self and colonise it. The griha or the domestic was, thus, not only imbricated in the mytho-religious (backward looking) time of the nation, it is seen as thereby providing redemption against the dehumanising effects of the colonised public space. The need to buttress the space of the domestic in a manner that did not rupture continuity with the past was asserted. Simultaneously, the need to reorganise it in a manner commensurate with its role in the changed times was also emphasised. While the discourse on change and improvement made its way in this formulation as well, the domestic was not conceived as a space marked by 'degeneration', but redemption and rejuvenation. The public-political was the place of humiliation, but also the space of struggle, drawing moral strength and vigour from the domestic. Thus, in this formulation as well, albeit in a different manner, the narrative of freedom and liberation in the public was tied with and depended upon the domestic.[18]

While the two formulations have sometimes been seen as signifying two phases of the nationalist movement, the former marking the period of reform and the latter the phase of nationalist revival (Chatterjee 1994, 116), they appear to coexist in domestic writings in Hindi of late nineteenth and early twentieth century. What is significant, moreover, is that in both formulations, there does not appear to have been any real break in the manner in which women were seen as signifying the domestic. Thus, whether as signifiers of degeneration needing correction or as reproducers of the pristine past, women were conceived as objects to be reformed and educated. 'Educating women' was, moreover, grounded in a presupposition of their ignorance, which in turn implicated them in the 'emasculation' of men in the body politic. Further, the deviation of men from their *karma* (action)[19] in submitting to the coercion and indignities of life in the public sphere was projected on the women in their neglect of their *dharma* (duty). Thus, personhood or selfhood, although unhappy and in bondage, was conceived as masculine, while women embedded within the folds of the (joint) family, the (Hindu) community, and the (Hindu) nation, unlike men, could not dislodge themselves from the 'mytho-religious' time of the *kula* (family/community/nation) to

---

[18]For a discussion of the nature of the domestic in both these formulations within Bengali literature, see Dipesh Chakrabarty, 'Postcoloniality and the Artifice of History', *Representations* (1992).

[19]The concept of karma lays down that the quality of actions, including both merit and demerit, determine the future of all beings; the theory of inevitable consequences.

insert themselves into the historical narrative of secular time looking towards a future of liberation and freedom.

Thus, *Vanita Vinod* (1906; 1912),[20] a conduct book with sixteen articles written for 'married women', emphasises the symbiosis between the *parivar/kutumba* (family/extended family), the *jati* (community), and *desh* (nation). That the symbiosis between the family and community extends also to the nation may be seen from the fact that women are enjoined to develop traits of *atma-vismriti* (self-forgetfulness or selflessness) and *atma-tyag* (self-renunciation) as the primary precepts for organising the family. The lack of or deviation from these precepts is seen as having led to *paradheenta* (subjection of the self to another, in other words, subjection to colonial rule). While atma-vismriti and atma-tyag are the desired behavioural norms for women, described as both 'essential' and 'useful', the realisation of the male self is seen in *atma-nirbharta* (self-dependence or self confidence in the autonomous self) and *atma-gaurav* (pride in the self). The restoration and recovery of (male) self-pride and independence depended in particular on the renunciation of their self by women. This renunciation could be achieved by adhering to the rules (*niyam*) designed especially for them by the *shastras* (religious-scriptural texts).

It is significant how the discourse on the degeneration of the domestic and its improvement could appear to give agency to women, while actually excising it. While submitting women to what the author of *Vanita Vinod* admits as extremely demanding and exacting rules, he turns them into evidence of the greater accountability (*jawabdehi*) that women have on account of bearing the exhausting yet honourable burden of improving the *manava-jati* (humanity). The task of *making* these rules is entrusted to men. The masculine activity of framing rules is, however, projected as being in effect a limited function. The author stresses emphatically that making rules is the *only* thing men have in their hands, for the more important and significant

---

[20]Shyamsundar Das, ed., *Vanita Vinod*, (Kashi: Nagari Pracharini Sabha, 1906; 1912).

task of following them, *manana, bartana*, is the share of women. Atma-vismriti, atma-tyag, and *pati-bhakti* (devotion to husband) are some of the conditions that are seen as enabling women in accomplishing the tasks for which they are accountable to all of humanity. It is in this framework that the book talks of some 'womanly virtues', which women of the past possessed and put to good effect in the exercise of their duties as women. Important among these virtues were *krodh shanti* (control of anger), *dhairya* (patience), and *saahas* (courage). These virtues, it may be noted, took a specifically gendered form when exercised within the domestic by women, seen as they were as instruments for the effective accomplishment of their pati bhakti, which was the *mool mantra* (essential principle) of organisation of human life. These virtues were manifested, for example, by the mythological figure of Damyanti who, when left in the jungle by her husband, did not lose dhairya and saahas, which enabled her to reunite with her husband and also preserve, even in the face of several temptations, her chastity (*satitva*) described as a jewel (*ratna*)—*satitva-ratna*—a jewel, more precious than a woman's life. The author subsequently laments that such virtues seemed to be absent in the modern women (described significantly as *abala* denoting woman in a state of helplessness and incapacity). The modern woman or abala is seen as lacking in both dhairya and saahas and put in Damyanti's situation was more likely to perish in the jungle or succumb to wild animals. A similar illustration is sought from history to bring out the weakness of modern women as compared to her more admirable female ancestors. The example, this time, is that of a mother who sends her young son to the battlefield to replenish the army of the Rajput king Jaimal fighting against the Moghul emperor Akbar. In this case, the mother not only knows that her young son is going to die, she sends him into the battlefield with the instruction to meet the death of a true *kshatriya* (warrior class). Not satisfied with sending her son to his death, the mother along with her daughter-in-law follows the son into the battlefield where all die fighting the enemy. With this illustration, the author seeks to establish continuity with the nation's past, drawing from the imaginary of a land that had been consecrated and sustained by the blood of courageous women (*veer baalaa*). The lament of degeneration, however, closely follows this apotheosis of the past, and modern women are again indicted for not displaying, even in their dreams, a thousandth iota of the courage shown by the valiant women of the past.

Significantly, it needs to be reiterated here that both the 'guilt' of degeneration and the onus for improvement was placed on women. The majority of writings in journals, books, and pamphlets for women exhibit simultaneously the lament of degeneration with an exhortation for improvement. Most of these writings, thus, took the form of instructions/preachings (*upadesh*) to women to educate themselves. *Nariratnamala,* for example, carries forty-six stories of heroic women (viranganayein), meant to serve as emulatory models for modern women, encouraging them to inculcate virtues which women of the past possessed, virtues which were needed to sustain the nation.[21] It needs to be pointed out that quite a number of such writings drew attention towards certain decadent traditions (*ku-ritiyan*) such as *bal vivaha* (child marriage), *bahu vivaha* (multiple marriages), illiteracy among women, and the social oppression of women. These enumerations of social decadence and oppression addressed to women, while providing a framework of remedies, did not fail to put the blame on women for such practices. Thus *Vanita Vinod* declared that the majority of 'ridiculous' rituals (*moorkhata ki rasmein*) prevalent in India owed their existence and perpetuation to the stupidity of women (Das 1912, 100). Once again the indictment of women is stretched to include a lament for the unhappy present. The practice of bal vivaha, responsible for the generation of a debilitated and feeble (*durbal*) race, is identified as one among the many decadent traditions being sustained by ignorant women. In a different vein, Shrimati Hardevi, the author of *Striyon Pe Samajik Atyachaar* (Social

---

[21]Pandit Baldevprasad Mishra, *Nariratnamala*, (Bombay: Shri Venkateshwara Steam Yantralaya sam.1965).

Oppression of Women 1892), points out that the numerous forms of oppression against women, including discrimination against the female child, discouragement of female education, etc., continue only because of women's stupidity (*moorkhata*, *avidha*), which, asserts Hardevi, in so many ways stands in the way of the progress of the nation (*deshonnati*). Women, deprived of education, confined lifelong as slave women (*dasi*) within the prisonlike caverns of the house (*aajanma kathin kaaraagar ki kandara*), dispossessed of God-given liberty and freedom, are debilitated mentally and physically. How could such a woman who never in her life inhaled a single breath of freedom, asks the author, bear courageous (*shoorveer*), clever (*tejvaan*), and independent (*swaadheen*) children (Hardevi 1892, 3). *Vanita Vinod*, too, steers clear of casting any aspersions on Indian men. In a different context, viz., the problem of men's love for music and consequently for the dancing girls and prostitutes (*veshya*), the author attributes the misdirected affections of men on the curious turn of times when men seem to have lost the capacity of thinking and working independently, so much so that they were not self-reliant even for their leisure and entertainment. The author then instructs women to restore the self-reliance of men by becoming proficient in music themselves and provide men entertainment at home (Das 1912, 107).

We mentioned earlier that the domestic ideal restricted woman's individuation by 'fixing' her within the 'natural' units of family, caste, community, and nation. Women were seen as providing the foundational mainstay of such social/cultural groupings. Endowed with the important duty of marking and sustaining these significant boundaries, women's subjectivities were constituted differently from the individuality which accrued to men in the political public sphere. Thus, a recurrent theme which emerges in these public narratives about the social life of the family was that 'the highest form of personhood' was that constituted by the idea of denial and abnegation of the self. The subjectivity of women was constituted, unlike men, not in the secular spirit of civic virtue but in a spirit of subordination to the principles of dharma founded not on a principle of camaraderie and equality, but on a hierarchical unity symbolic of power and domination, often translating into cruelty and violence. While political freedom (swadheenta) held the promise of citizenship for men as equal and self-governed participants in the public-political, for women, freedom lay in their continued embedment within the domestic—the family and community (parivar, kula, kutumba). The latter embodied a space where her identity was constituted in the various aspects of her relationship with the (public) men, as mother, wife, daughter, each relationship based on her biological specificity, 'natural' predispositions, and emotional incapacities. Thus *Vanita Vinod*, in its fifteenth chapter, *Grihacharya* (norms/routines of the household), stresses not only the special traits of women's character which made her suitable (only) for domestic work, it goes on to turn it into a normative ideal. Suggesting the natural inferiority of women and their work and their subjection to men (*purushadheen*), it urges men to be benign and sympathetic to women and to not treat them with contempt. Women in turn are advised not to despair, but seek redemption by devoting themselves to serving men:

> Compassion, affection, love, empathy and dedication may not have been witnessed in this world, had God not created women—who as mothers, wives and daughters fill the world with such pleasant emotions...*All (other) visible objects in the world today have been made by men and women can only comply with it.* God has made the female species delicate and fragile both physically and emotionally, pitiably incapable of self defence. They are destined thus by God to remain in male protection—of father, husband and son—all their lives. Women should, therefore, not despair, but feel obliged that they can dedicate themselves to the service of men (Das 1912, 166).

The kutumba/parivar (family/extended family) was bound by the normative codes of *grihaacharan* and *grihacharya* founded on the natural suitability of women and men for the social/cultural and political aspects of life, respectively. Compliance with the codes of the griha was shown by the persuasive rhetoric of the nation. Very often, consent and endorsement of grihaacharan came from women themselves, showing what may be called the 'ideology of patriarchy of the kula'.[22] Women writing in *Bamabodhini Patrika* concede that knowledge became graceful in women only when they retained, at the same time, all the good qualities to be found in the Hindu woman such as modesty, humility, softness, patience, [and] self-sacrifice (Borthwick 1984, 55–6). A number of writings by both men and women stressed these qualities as essential elements of grihaacharan. Shyamsundar Das, the author of *Vanita Vinod*, stresses, for example, that *lajja* (modesty) and *namrata* (politeness) were the jewels (*aabhooshan*) of women without which women were not fit for the status of womanhood (*stripad*). Women were instructed to talk less, and not to laugh loudly or indulge in arguments (Das 1912, 170). Only by following the norms of grihacharya could women accomplish their true womanhood (*satitvadharma*). Yashoda Devi, an exponent of ayurvedic medicine and the author of several books pertaining to women's health, expresses similar sentiments in her book *Nari Dharma Shiksha* (Educating Women in their Dharma), one among the several books of the series *Pativratadharma Mala* (Devotion to Husband series). The book lays down that *nari dharma* lies in the observance of *pativrata dharma*. The characteristics of a woman who observes the norms of devotion to her husband (pativrata) are described alongside a pictoral illustration of Sita, the quintessential mytho-religious, exemplary wife. The pativrata is described as one who never looks at her husband with anger, is chaste and pure in mind, speech and body, and obeys her husband. The exhortation to denial of the self is completed by asking women to be like a shadow (*chhaayaa*) of their husband, ready to be his friend and companion and when required his maid (dasi) and helper (*anuchari*).[23] It is

---

[22]The expression is borrowed from Dipesh Chakrabarty, 'Difference-Deferral of (A) Colonial Modernity', *History Workshop Journal* (1993, 27).

[23]See Yashoda Devi, *Pativratadharma Mala—Nari Dharma Shiksha*, 3rd edition, (Colonelganj, Allahabad: Vanita Hitaishini Press, 1934), 8.

noteworthy that the book declares at the outset, as a subtitle to the book, its nature and purpose—*stri jati ke upkar ke liye*—for the upliftment of the female species. Repeated reminders that the principles were derived from the *dharmashastras* authenticated the frameworks of this upliftment. The claim to authenticity was further and recurrently emphasised by the illustration of principles of pativratadharma through religious-mythological exemplary wives, for example, Sita, Savitri, Anusuya, Kaushalya, etc. The majority of the principles of pativratadharma were conveyed through influential female religious-mythological figures thereby reinforcing the pressure to comply and sustain the continuity with tradition. One is informed that Sita, when dissuaded by Rama from accompanying him to the forest when exiled for fourteen years, explained to him her pativratadharma and admonished him for standing in the way of her compliance with it. We are told that Sita had received education in pativratadharma from her own mother and, after marriage, from none other than Ram's mother, Kaushalya, herself an epitome of the ideal wife. During her stay in the jungle, Sita is given further lessons (upadesh) in pativratadharma by Sati Anusuya, wife of Sage Vashishtha, who advises her that the husband is for a woman the sole male on earth, that his feet are sacred and should be worshipped.

The motif of pativrata nari, thus, while endorsing womanly virtues, circumscribed women's self and sexuality by norms directed towards the stability of the family. Thus *Nari Dharma Shiksha* advises that a pativrata woman should worship her husband as god, even when he was ugly, given to philandering, unreliable, sickly, choleric as the devil, alcoholic, old, stupid, dumb, deaf, blind, broke, or a coward. Without vanity, anger, or desire for reward, the book advises that the wife should please her husband and abstain from amusing other men or even liking the company of other men (*Nari Dharma Shiksha* 69–70). She should eat her husband's leftovers as god's blessings (*prasad*); when the husband enters the house, the wife should get up, listen with devotion to what he says, her eyes fixed on his feet, serve him, sleep only after he has fallen asleep, and get up before he wakes up in the morning. Even if the husband continues to sleep till the afternoon, the wife should awaken him with humility and with the following entreaties:

> O Master, your bath is ready, so is the food, preparations for your daily rituals are also complete, your clothes suitable for the time of the day are ready as well, visitors are awaiting you.
> (*Nari Dharma Shiksha*, 87)

The wife then finishes by saying, 'there is no *other* hurry' (emphasis added). It is significant that the woman does not appear in any writing to be making a demand on the time of the husband for her own self. For her part, she is instructed to submerge herself within the demands and needs of the husband and, thereafter, the family. The boundary of her world is marked by her bedroom; she speaks only as loud as her friend can hear; her happiness is determined by her husband's happiness, her laughter by his approval. She is instructed to bathe daily, keep herself fragrant, speak with love, and eat and talk frugally. If she feels the desire to go on a pilgrimage, she should wash her husband's feet and drink the water. If her husband goes abroad, a dutiful wife abstains from beautifying herself and wears old clothes. Addressed by several denotations, *sadhvi* (one who is an ascetic), *sheelvati* (one who is chaste), *vasumati* (one who has patience), *lajjavati* (one who is shy/diffident), *tanvi* (one who is slim), *smitvati* (one who smiles), the *kuleen stri* (respectable woman) of the past was described as possessing these traits (*Nari Dharma Shiksha*, 79–87).

The noble qualities of the pativrata nari are contrasted with her opposite the 'fallen woman' (*neech nari*). While the pativrata exhibits endearing qualities of equanimity of temperament and agility, the neech nari is lazy and neglects her children. She is also immoral in that she looks at all men with fascination. This neech nari is not to be trusted, as her judgments are influenced by passion; she covets other men and looks at strangers through the screens in the window (*Nari Dharma Shiksha*, 43–44). The descriptions of the fallen women are often accompanied by their dehumanisation and premonitions condemning them to rigorous punishment after death. *Nari Dharma Shiksha* notes that a woman who answered back or argued with her husband was like the village dog. If a woman disobeyed her husband, howsoever stupid and impoverished, she became a snake after her death and suffered widowhood in successive births. On the other hand, a woman who adhered to the norms of pativrata lived in heaven for three and a half crore years. In another work, *Nitigyan* (sam.1982), Yashoda Devi cautions women who defy their husbands. The evil woman (*dushta stri*) is warned that her acts of defiance reduce the life of her husband, and women like her are condemned to live in hell after their deaths. Mentioning that there are more than a thousand kinds of hell (*narak*), the book goes on to describe twenty-nine categories in which women can expect to be lodged after death, depending on the degree of their defiance. From the *Namistra Narak*, where women who covet other men and money may find themselves suffering thirst, pain in the eye, and blindness, to the *Asipatravan Narak*, where headstrong women who have defied the *vedas* and the *shastras* by defying their husbands suffer whiplashes from *yamdoots* and painful injuries from trees which constantly shed their razor-sharp leaves, the narak is presented as a condition from which their can be no relief.[24]

In another formulation, the regulation of women by the principles of pativratadharma and her unsuitability for public work are seen as deriving not from her finer womanly traits and sensibilities (love, emotion, compassion, etc.), nor from her natural physical and emotional inferiority, but from the innate disruptive attributes of her character. Thus, in a chapter titled *Swatantrata ke liye Striyon ki Ayogyata* (the unsuitability of women for independence), Jayadayal Goyandeka, the author of *Nari Dharma*,[25] argues that it was essential and expedient for the well-being of human society, the nation, and the human species

---

[24]See Yashoda Devi, *Neetigyan*, (Prayag: Vanita Hitaishini Press, sam.1892), 39–45.

[25]Jayadayal Goyandeka, *Nari Dharma*, 8th edition (Gorakhpur: Geeta Press, sam.1994), 5.

in general that women should not be independent. Women, points out Goyandeka, have certain 'special natural vices', which make them especially unsuitable for independence, viz., bodily passions (*kaam*), anger (*krodh*), impertinence (*duhsaahas*), obduracy (*hath*), stupidity (*buddhiheenata*), falsehood (*jhooth*), craftiness (*kapat*), harshness (*kathorta*), defiance (*droha*), pettiness (*chhotapan*), and impurity (*ashauch*), all of which, if not curbed, would lead to grave consequences for the nation and society. Women, therefore, ought never be left independent but, as Sage Manu prescribed, always in the custody of and subject to the father in their childhood, husband in their youth, and son in their old age (Goyandeka, 6).

It may be pointed out that womanly virtues and duties, as manifested and circumscribed by pativratadharma, were distinguished in these books from the masculine karma or action. The notion of karma is brought out as a form of action that has the deterministic quality of changing the future conditions of living things. Thus, men are portrayed as the creators of the visible/material world, including the rules and norms which should ideally govern its functioning. Both Shyamsundar Das in *Vanita Vinod* and Yashoda Devi in *Nari Dharma Shiksha* endorse these special aspects of men's actions that determine the constitution of the 'world' held in common by all mankind. While women's activities are directed by the natural and emotional relationships under the overarching pativratadharma, men's actions are directed by more material, worldly, and contractual obligations. The story of Raja Harishchandra is rendered in *Nari Dharma Shiksha* to show how *satya dharma* (duty towards truth) is the primary guiding force behind the actions of King Harishchandra. Working as a *dome* (one who removes carcasses, an untouchable) in the cremation ground while in exile, Harishchandra, true to the terms of his employment, does not let the emotional appeals of his wife to allow the cremation of their son without a levy come in the way of his *swami bhakti* (duty towards his master/employer) (Devi 1934, 59–64). Women, however, are not only seen as incapable of karma, they are not expected, therefore, to show any disregard for emotions and duties that tie them to the kutumba and kul. In fact, the pativratadharma, for which women are found naturally suited, requires that women be trained in it from their childhood, binding them to a grihacharya (home+routine), a diurnal routine specific to the 'home', and a different set of behavioural norms of the home (grihaacharan).

There appears, then, in almost all books, a recurring concern for the education of women in grihacharya and grihaacharan. More often than not, justification for women's education itself was derived from their 'visible', 'natural' domestic skills and guided by the aspiration of education to achieve better domestic labour. Shrimati Manavrata Devi, writing *Nari Dharma Shiksha* in 1928 for the benefit of 'all the mothers and sisters' in India, claimed that there was no important subject useful for women which had not been covered by her in the book. These useful subjects, it follows from her list, were: education of children (*bal shiksha*), housework (*grihakarya*), attitude towards members of the house (*gharwalon ke saath bartava*), raising children (*santan-paalan*), treatment of ailments (*rog chikitsa*), and recipes (*vyanjan banane ki vidhiyan*).[26] The book seems to have sold in large numbers in all its editions: the first in 1928 (2000 copies), second in 1931 (2000 copies), third in 1932 (2000 copies), fourth in 1933 (2000 copies), fifth in 1934 (2000 copies), sixth in 1938 (2000 copies). One thousand books were published in its seventh edition. Endorsements and recommendations from teachers, headmistresses, newspapers, and magazines figure in the last few pages. One Parvati Devi recommended that the book should be part of the curriculum of kanya vidyalayas in the higher classes, and Lakshmi Devi, the head administrator of the Kanya Gurukul at Hathras, agreed with her. *Aryamitra*, the newspaper of the Arya Pratinidhisabha of Samyukta Pranta, felt that all 'girls' needed education on the lines laid down by the book before they got married. The popular women's magazine *Manorama* recommended that every household have a copy of

---

[26]See Manavrata Devi, *Nari Dharma Shiksha*, 7th edition (Kashi Pustak Bhandar 1942), 18–19.

the book (Manavrata Devi 1942, 113). In the book, Manavrata Devi proposes that education is equally essential for women and men. For women, however, education had to be of a different and special kind, since the primary responsibility of looking after the household (*grihasthi*) lay with women (*stri samaj*). Again, transmitting her message through the consenting voices of religious-mythological women, she reminds women that marriage was a *mahayagya* (an exalted ritual) for the sustenance of society (*samaj*) and not for the satisfaction of physical needs and passion of the senses. This is in line with Pandit Baldev Prasad Mishra's prescription to women in *Nariratnamala* about marriage being the means for the procreation of healthy species. Marriage, women are told, did not mark the end of *brahmacharya* (celibacy), but continued to be governed by its norms (Mishra sam.1965). While facilitating and improving the management of domestic work, education was not to interfere with nari dharma of pativrata (woman's duty of devotion to husband) with its underlying principle of '*swami sewa*'. Draupadi is thus called into force by Manavrata Devi, who educates Satyabhama on how Draupadi kept her five husbands happy: 'I abjure passion, anger, arrogance and self-respect and look after my five husbands and their wives with complete sincerity'.[27] This sincerity was manifested in a rigorous daily routine that included cleaning the house, the utensils, cooking, feeding the family, etc. Education itself was not to interfere with the '*ghar ke kaaj kaam*' (household chores) and was ideally imparted in leisure time, as seen in *Strishikshavidhayak* (1823), an anonymous Calcutta School Book Society textbook in khari boli.[28] In his book *Stri Shiksha* (1912), Mahendralal Garg writes about schools which had been set up for 'women' and 'girls'. Among them, *Vanita Ashram* near Surat was opened for girls in 1909 (they had only nine 'girls' at first) in order to give them an education in

---

[27]Manavrata Devi, *Nari Dharma Shiksha*, 7th edition (Kashi Pustak Bhandar 1942), 18-21.

[28]See Kumkum Sangari, 'Amenities of Domestic Life: Questions on Labour', *Social Scientist* 21, nos. 9–11 (1993): 20.

housework *in their free time* (that is, from housework). Garg, points out, 'the women studying in *Vanita Ashram* find ample time to do their housework. They come to the Ashram after finishing the morning work and reach home after school, in time for the evening work'.[29] Garg expresses hope that in the next few years, women's education would make enough progress to produce wives who were true companions of their husbands (*sachchee sahadharmini*) (Garg 1912, 152).

The education that was proposed for women was to serve very different objectives. The issue at hand was not education for women as individuals, but for the sake of the (Hindu) nation. As a Bengali newspaper of 1889 declared in the midst of a raging debate over women's education:

> The best system of education for Hindu females will be that which will take note of their character, capabilities and lifework, and implant in their minds those priceless domestic virtues which it is necessary for Hindu wives to possess. Considered from this point of view it is not desirable that the Hindu girls should be given the denationalising education which is given to the Hindu boy (Borthwick 1984, 92–93).[30]

While domestic education purported to achieve proficiency in household work, as discussed earlier in the chapter, national redemption was a major concern underlying the reform of the

---

[29]See Mahendralal Garg, *Stri Shiksha* (1912, 106).

[30]Meredith Borthwick, *The Changing Role of Women in Bengal 1849-1905* (1984, 92–93). Sucheta Mazumdar points out that after much impassioned debate from the 1830s and with the influence of the reformist Brahmo Samaj on the wane by the 1880s, the curriculum of nationalist education for most women's schools had been firmly established with the study of Sanskrit, Bengali, arithmetic, moral textbooks, and culinary skills, and the learning of various puja (worship) rituals. The best puja performer received a prize. The Hindu bourgeoisie at Mahakali Pathshala accepted this curriculum and was the signal for the general acceptance of education for women in Bengal, with minor variations in the rest of India. Education for women was to become a new class-caste demarcator, as long as the women were not 'denationalised' by this education. See Sucheta Mazumdar, 'Women, Culture and Politics: Engendering the Hindu Nation', *South Asia Bulletin* (1992): 7.

domestic. The theme of the freedom of the nation was tied with the idea of domesticity in the sense that the domestic was the space where the different meaning of 'freedom' in the Indian tradition made itself manifest. While the Western notion of freedom was seen as based on the idea of possession and selfishness and the idea of an assertive ego, the Indian notion was presented as based on the idea of freedom from ego and the voluntary abnegation and denial of the self. The reformed household and the educating of women in domestic virtues was a manifestation of this freedom. The liberating nature of women's education in domestic virtues was stressed in domestic writings, which took pains in asserting its nonmaterial and spiritual nature. In the chapter *Vidya ke Laabh* (Benefits of Education), *Vanita Vinod* brings out the selflessness of women's education and the manner in which it made itself manifest in women's roles as mothers and wives. A father talks to his daughter (*dhatri shiksha*) of how education was of supreme value because it was incremental, it increased when shared and could not be stolen. The optimum manifestation of these qualities of education, the father points out, could be witnessed within the family and household (Das 1912, 47–50). In a similar demonstration of the selfless aspects of women's education, Mahendralal Garg talks of systems of education in *Seva Sadan* in Poona and Bombay where women were trained in the virtues of compassion. Women, who are naturally more compassionate than men, says Garg, take the *seva vrat*, that is, the pledge to serve (with compassion). These *seva vrat dharini*(s) (those who have taken the pledge of service) visit the sick in hospitals, empathise with them, and ease their pain and sufferings (Garg 1912, 155–57). In most cases, as we saw in the discussion of pativratadharma earlier, prescriptive norms sought to assure the exercise of such womanly virtues within the domestic space.

The reformed household, particularly through the agency of women, received a prominent place in the nationalist vision of the redemption of the sense of deficiency in the nation's present. The reform of the household worked within the nationalist framework that sought to rejuvenate the enfeebled (national) body to render it healthy and Hindu-national.[31] A nationalist medical discourse around the notion of the (ailing) body focussed on women, setting them up as symbols of Vedic virtues and the Hindu nation and established a regulatory ideal of conduct for them.[32] Yashoda Devi, whose work was discussed earlier in a different context, ran an ayurvedic clinic in Allahabad. She started a journal for women in 1908, followed it up with two more in 1910, and started yet another in 1930.[33] Yashoda Devi's book *Grihini Kartavyashastra, Arogyashastra arthat Pakshastra* (1924) gives ample sense of the nature of 'improvement' and the disciplinary regimen addressed to women.[34] The book concerned itself with food and offered directions on cooking based on rules

[31]A body culture developed that was aimed at sculpting strong, vigorous physiques and brought within its ambit traditional arenas of wrestling, gymnastics, and other sports. It was to transform this weak, disease-prone body that Gandhi had secretly experimented with by eating meat during his youth. Attention also turned to sexuality as several Indian intellectuals argued that India had fallen to foreign rulers because Indians had been rendered weak and passive by self-indulgence. Sharing these views, prominent late nineteenth-century religious reformers such as Swami Vivekanand and Swami Dayanand advocated the practice of sexual discipline as a means of national regeneration. Attempts to sculpt Indians into a muscular nation produced prescriptions for self-discipline that were authorised by the invocation of traditions and were widely circulated in the middle-class culture. The discussion on the body and liberatory ideology based on nationalist medical discourse through the agency of women is based on Gyan Prakash, *Another Reason: Science and the Imagination of Modern India*, (2000, 143–44).

[32]In addition to promoting female education, the Arya Samaj published journals addressed to women and directed at applying medicalised disciplines. One such important journal was *Panchal Pandita* which started in 1897 as a bilingual English and Hindi periodical, but became an exclusively Hindi publication in 1901. It focussed on diffusing modern knowledge authorised by the invocation of the *Vedas*, and it regularly published articles on healthy diet, cleanliness and hygiene, the care of children, the follies of astrology and other such topics (Gyan Prakash 2000, 143–44).

[33]These are noted in Shaligram Srivastava, *Prayag Pradeep* (Allahabad: Hindustani Academy, 1937), 161.

[34]See Yashoda Devi, *Grihini Kartavyashastra, Arogyashastra arthat Pakshastra*, 3rd edition (Allahabad: Hitaishi Yantralaya, 1924).

of health and hygiene, catering towards revitalising the body rather than pleasing the senses. The directions pertaining to health and hygiene unfold in the narrative of a fictional tale of a man whose improper eating habits make him seriously ill. The man's near death becomes the basis for a dialogue between two women, who, drawing lessons from this incident, discuss the nutritional qualities of different kinds of food and the rules to follow in cooking and managing the household. This dialogue on ill-health caused by ignorance also paves the way for the author to outline the elements of proper Indian womanhood. The boundaries between health, hygiene, morals, and social institutions blur as instructions on preparing healthy food lead to the injunction that women must take full responsibility for maintaining the health of the household. A responsible Indian woman, the text suggests, rises early, takes charge of the household, and prepares food according to the laws of nature and the season. She must, directs the book, dispense with the servant, who has no knowledge of the rules to be followed. In fact, women are instructed to dispense with the servant whose presence encourages indolence and detracts women from their responsibilities. No sleeping late, no lazing about, no gossiping with neighbours after the husband leaves for work and the children have gone to school; make the beds, bathe, cook food appropriate for the season, look over the household accounts, and perform other household chores. The evening routine is more of the same—cook, manage, and facilitate the running of the household (Yashoda Devi 1924, 47–66, cited in Prakash 2000). Yashoda Devi's extraordinary prescription for women is triggered of by the fictional yet symbolic near death of a Hindu male caused by the neglect of the rules of nutrition by his wife. Curing the body, however, served as the justification for the formulation of rules and routines calculated to render the body useful, healthy, and productive.[35]

---

[35]What shaped the language and provided an arena for the reconstitution of gender relations was the attention to governance, the concern with the health of the population that developed during the second half of the nineteenth century. The middle class debated the status and relevance (*contd.*)

Thus, the domestic discourse incorporating the nationalist idea of improvement, displayed an overriding concern with 'order', 'routine', 'discipline', 'obedience', 'punctuality', 'time' manifested in the discipline/order/cleanliness of the house. The cover page of *Nari Dharma Shiksha* invites one to look for a picture of the *aadarsha grihani* inside the book. The picture shows three women, one of them working on the charkha in a meticulously neat kitchen, the other sitting at a table in the sitting room reading a book, and the third sitting on a mat in the same room, playing with a plump and happy child. It may be noted that this tranquil picture of the idealised home conveying a message of meticulous order, discipline, smoothness, and leisure shrouded the daily drudgery which these conduct manuals lay down for women (*Nari Dharma Shiksha* 1942). Consider, for example, a list of eighteen rules laid down by Jayadayal Goyandeka, in *Nari Dharma*. The notation *shri ram* at the top of the page enforces the prescriptive character of the rules deriving from religious authority. Titled *Striyon ke Palane Yogya Sadharan Niyam* (simple rules suitable for the guidance of women), the rules read as follows: (i) remember God when you get up in the morning and then again while going to bed; (ii) get up in the morning before sunrise, otherwise observe fast; (iii) pay ritual homage to the Sun after your bath; (iv) chant the *hare ram mantra* one thousand five hundred and twelve times;

(*contd.*) of Western medicine, homeopathy, ayurved, and yunani in its search to define what was appropriate to India. In this search, a range of therapeutics—some new, some old, and some of different provenance—found eager enthusiasts concerned about having disciplined bodies. These included chromopathy (a system of therapeutics based on colours), mesmerism, hypnotism, and mechano therapy and were circulated widely among the middle class through the nineteenth-century print culture. Books, pamphlets, and newspapers frequently advertised and discussed these systems, and the efficacy of different patent medicines were items of urban middle-class conversations. Such discussions were not always systematic or learned, and they did not seriously threaten the dominance of Western medicine. But, they were important for an elite obsessed with defining appropriate therapeutics for India. See Gyan Prakash, *Another Reason* (2000, 150).

(v) remember God at least once every hour; (vi) touch the feet of all elders; (vii) never get angry; (viii) pray to God; (ix) never grumble; (x) if you look at any man other than your husband, remember God; (xi) never criticise; (xii) be impartial while feeding; (xiii) never be rude; (xiv) never be sarcastic; (xv) never hurt the feelings of others; (xvi) speak the truth; (xvii) never hide anything; (xviii) if you break any rule chant the *hare ram mantra* a hundred and eight times (Goyandeka samvat.2002, backpage). While such rules were to take care of women's mental and spiritual disciplining and strength, physical strength was to accrue not from exercising or playing games, which were expressly denied, but from household labours such as washing utensils, cleaning the house, grinding wheat, removing the husk from rice, filling and storing water, etc. (Goyandeka Samvat. 2002, 29). It is significant how the dull, monotonous, and repetitive labour epitomised by both the *chakki* (the grinding stone/wheel) and charkha (spinning wheel) were presented not only as prescriptions for women's health and leisure, but as the means for the restoration of the strength and vigour of the nation. The decreasing use of the two wheels (by women) had, suggests Manavrata Devi in *Nari Dharma Shiksha*, made the nation weak and dependent for food and clothes on outsiders (1942, 53, 82).

This framework of women's labour seems to have been closely associated with the control of female sexuality. Domestic labour was seen as having restraining abilities, the purifying effects of ablution. It emerges also as a form of surveillance as wives could not be wholly restrained through violent measures. Domestic routine was blended with clock time with the wife's getting up before her husband, cleaning utensils, sweeping the home, respecting elders, cooking, etc. Pandarinath Prabhu approves of keeping women engaged in housework so that 'they may not get idle moments for thinking of or doing any undesirable or shameful act'.[36] Consider, for example, the Hindi pamphlet,

---

[36]Pandarinath Prabhu, *Hindu Social Organisation*, 4th edition, (Bombay: Popular Prakashan, 1940), 238, cited in Kumkum Sangari, 'The Amenities of Domestic Life', *Social Scientist* (1993): 24.

Arogya Vidhan: Vidyarthi Jivan (1929) a book of advice focussing on sexual discipline authored by Yashoda Devi.[37] The purpose of these texts was to promote a nationalist discipline of the body that aimed to restore its health. The text on sexual discipline was addressed to students and offered advice on how to maintain healthy bodies and dispositions tied with what she sees as the culture and health of the nation. Conceding to sensual pleasures was viewed as a sign of cultural/national weakness. Yashoda Devi's prescription of conduct for young men and women was offered within a framework of cultural self-discipline. Thus, a denunciation of sensuality was followed by the recommendation of *brahmacharya*.[38] The notion of marriage as a means of procreation and sustenance of a race for a healthy Indian nation recurs in most such writings. Shrimati Manavrata Devi in *Nari Dharma Shiksha* writes about the norms of *stri brahmacharya* (abstinence by women). A *brahmacharini*, she points out, is one who does not marry till the age of sixteen and remains ignorant about the sexual aspects of life until her marriage. The notion of *brahmacharya*, however, is seen as perfectly compatible with married life. For a married woman, brahmacharya consists of living a routined, disciplined life (of pativratadharma) and engaging in sexual intercourse with the husband as a duty of married life, never for pleasure (1942, 155–56).

While facts about female sexuality and women's knowledge of their bodies were to be filtered out till they attained the age of sixteen years, women's textbooks concerned themselves with education in feminine/domestic virtues. From the age of seven till and through marriage, girls were to be first learners and then practitioners of these virtues associated with the management of housework. Most tracts were detailed in the nature and division of domestic labour and daily routines and methods of time management. This was often accompanied by tirades against

---

[37]Yashoda Devi's ayurvedic practice, which included a small hospital in Allahabad and clinics in Benaras, Patna, Muzaffarpur, and Gaya, specialised in the treatment of infertility. See Gyan Prakash (2000, 152–53).

[38]See Gyan Prakash (2000, 152–53).

alasi (lazy) women and against 'fallen women' who neglected their children and housework. Significantly, the association of scientific and disciplined domestic labour with the 'educated' (middle class) women makes it almost imperative for the authors to constitute the 'illiterate' woman as the aberrant woman producing a factual anomaly in the narration of household labour by women. The disciplinary texts efface the domestic labour of illiterate women and block their ideological incorporation into new familial models and from constructions of 'womanhood'. Prescribing adherence to a hierarchy within the household, the texts also uphold a hierarchy of labour among women within the household.[39] The good daughter-in-law must do all the work while the mother-in-law is urged to be gentler in her teaching and supervision. As we saw in the discussion of stri brahmacharya, it is significant that in none of these texts is there a vision of the withdrawal of women's labour from the household at any age or stage. While the prospect or the reality of women working outside the household is never entertained, marriage and domestic labour seem to be the only activity available to women. Even in the case of widows, the option of renunciation is witheld and marriage is eternalised. The widow is advised to lead a peaceful life, never waste a moment, start the day by remembering her husband, desist from the company of men, eat pure food, and suppress all desires.[40]

Conclusion

The extraordinary plethora of domestic texts and the ideals surrounding domesticity in late colonial India have to be understood within the context of the complex framework of ideological and sociocultural forces of the period. Understanding the ideological and sociopolitical forces constituting the realm of the domestic is particularly important for locating the terms of

---

[39]See for a detailed discussion Kumkum Sangari, 'The Amenities of Domestic Life' (1993).

[40]Ibid, 160–61.

women's citizenship. While Dipesh Chakrabarty would see the invocation of household duties in manuals as 'a cryptic cultural code'—'a culturally shared code of conduct referring to the qualities of grace/modesty and obedience',[41] we have seen in the preceding discussion that the disciplinary regime representing 'cultural code' does not present a picture of emotional bliss. It rather gives a picture of daily drudgery, of domestic toil, of violence and oppression involved in the life of the upper-caste woman. For Kumkum Sangari, the idiom of domesticity would seem to show the explicit class concerns of the nationalists, fraught with the tensions of 're-entering' (and thereby sustaining and perpetuating) existing practices into 'new evaluative systems' and 'pulling back' women's widening social agencies into 'normative modes'. The idiom of domesticity seemed to provide a 'resolution' of this tension by forging a 'non-contradictory', 'symbiotic' relationship between the education of women and their duties (labour) within the family (and by implication to the nation).[42] The fact that domestic manuals felt the need to repeatedly point out the special historical role and status that women were assigned, their moral superiority over women who neglected domestic duties, the fact that household labour did not reduce them to the status of slaves or servants but made them suitable for a higher life (after death), and the repeated warnings about the dreadful outcomes which followed noncompliance,

---

[41]See Dipesh Chakrabarty, 'Radical Histories and Question of Enlightenment Rationality', *Economic and Political Weekly*, 30, no. 14 (1995): 751-68.

[42]The ideologies concerning women's roles within the domestic space, have been attributed by Kumkum Sangari to the process of class formation in the nineteenth century. The reform agendas were themselves part of this process of class formation, encoding and effacing this other history of domestic labour and inequality. Unwilling to contest the gender-based division of labour and marriage as an institution regulating it and faced with the difficulty of making domestic labour congruent with emerging class formations, reform agendas foreclosed many possibilities for substantial social equality. Kumkum Sangari, 'Amenities of Domestic Life' (1993, 22–23), and Kumkum Sangari and Sudesh Vaid, 'Introduction', in *Recasting Women*, eds. Sangari and Vaid (1989, 9–10).

indicates a field of tension around the personhood of the educated woman rather than a realm of consent and harmony. These tensions unfolded in the writings by women nationalists, some of which have been discussed in the course of this work. The dilemma is reflected, for instance, in the writings of Sarojini Naidu who saw her entry into the political realm as the 'breaking free' of an 'agonised self' from the immobilisation of the female images embedded in her own writings. A similar trauma was seen in the memoirs of Shudha Mazumdar whose awareness of the political events around her left her with 'strange dreams about flying through space' leaving her 'unfreshed and weary'. Within the domestic texts these dilemmas appear in stray cases of writing by women taking the form of ridiculing men who attempted to clean the *rajmarg* (public road/road to the government) while their own homes were filthy. Shrimati Hardevi, for example, advises men to first take notice of the condition of women closeted within the caverns of their homes and then ask themselves if at all they deserve to be called civilised and capable. In the next chapter we shall see how organised struggles by women for voting rights opened up issues concerning the 'home' and 'Indian womanhood' for public scrutiny. We shall see, in particular, how, like the 'domestic', the issue of voting rights for women was braided within the questions of the status of India/Indians within the British Empire and the character and extent of rights to which the subject population was entitled.

4

The 'Womanly Vote' and Women Citizens: Debates on Women's Franchise in Late Colonial India

This chapter explores the formation and gendering of Indian nationalist ideologies of citizenship through an examination of suffrage debates in India from 1917 to the 1940s. Starting from the premise that the defining parameters of citizenship in India emerged in the historical context of the anticolonial movement and the assertion of a national self-identity, it shows how in this context the 'vote' assumed significance as a claim to equality and to the political rights of citizenship that were denied to colonised subjects. The debates surrounding the vote as a measure of equality disclose, however, complex intersecting layers of sociopolitical forces—nationalist, colonialist, feminist, masculinist, and conservative. This chapter focusses on the debates over women's franchise and the manner in which gendered meanings came to be attributed to the 'vote'. An attempt will be made to unravel the meanings surrounding 'vote' and 'women' at the intersection of the ideologies of colonialism and nationalism, the social and political forces and practices which informed these meanings, the manner in which these meanings changed in association with each other, and their implications for articulating 'women' as citizens. The chapter sees women's struggle for suffrage both as part of other struggles sharing common ground with them and as having some specific characteristics of its own. The struggle for political rights and equality by women, it is proposed, occurred in dialogue with other struggles, and its forms and expressions were determined by the contours of the dialogue.

Anticolonial nationalist ideologies were couched in the language of national self-determination, popular sovereignty, equality, and freedom. In this context, the ideal of citizenship, premised on equality and national sovereignty, evolved as a powerful ideology of resistance against the colonisers. National liberation movements emerged increasingly as struggles for constitutional status as citizens, while the nation as a historico-cultural unity came to play a significant role in defining the political identity of citizens as members in a political community. It is not surprising, then, that the right to vote became meaningful in the national movement as a measure of belonging to the nation and of claims to equality with the colonisers.

One is perplexed, however, at the difficulty of weaving together a single thread of events or debates that can be labelled *the* suffrage debate or *the* suffrage movement.[1] The purpose of

---

[1]Several works on the organisational aspects of the struggle for the vote for women in India, the biographies of women at the helm of these struggles and its peculiar relationship of collusion and conflict with the 'national movement' have, however, appeared over the years. Aparna Basu and Bharati Ray, *Women's Struggles: A History of the All India Women's Conference 1927-1990* (1990); Hanna Papneck and Gail Minault, *Separate Worlds: A Study of Purdah in South Asia* (1982); Gail Pearson, 'Reserved Seats: Women and the Vote in Bombay' (1983, 47–65); Barbara Southard, *Women's Movement and Colonial Politics in Bengal* (1995); Geraldine Forbes, first Indian edition, *Women in Modern India* (1996); Vijay Agnew, *Elite Women in Indian Politics* (1979).

this chapter, however, is not to refute or substantiate the often-repeated contention that there was no suffrage movement in India. We would rather show that amongst the 'myriad' 'events' and 'conversations' in the early part of this century, one conversation concerned itself with the right of women to vote. The struggle for freedom and equality by women, like all events and conversations, occurred in 'dialogue with so many others' and its forms and expressions were necessarily 'in connection with all the other lyrics being sung' at the time.[2]

Voting rights for 'Indian women' was an issue braided within the questions of the status of India/Indians within the British Empire and the character and extent of rights to which the subject population was entitled. The imperial ideology of *difference*—racial, civilisational, and gender—prepared the ground for the *distancing*—spatial and temporal—of the colonised and the *deferral* or *denial* of conditions that were considered legitimate rights of people in the metropole. The nature and course of the debate were thus determined largely by the colonial relationship between India and Britain, especially at a time of a growing crisis of legitimacy for the colonial government in the face of *a* popular movement for national self-determination. The various strands in the debate reflected in turn the multifarious relations of domination and subordination, the nature of colonial authority, and the complex sociopolitical forces and ideological formulations that structured the narratives of 'womanhood'. Thus, the 'vote' at this historical juncture not only signified a claim to the exercise of political rights of

---

[2]History according to Elsa Barklay-Brown is like everybody talking at once, multiple rhythms being played simultaneously. The events and people written about do not occur in isolation but in dialogue with myriad other people and events. In fact, at any given moment millions of people are all talking at once. As a historian, one tries to isolate one conversation and to explore it. But the trick is then how to put that conversation in a context which makes evident its dialogue with so many others—how to make this one lyric stand alone and at the same time be in connection with all the other lyrics being sung. Elsa Barkley-Brown, 'Polyrhythms and Improvisations: Lessons for Women's History' (1991).

citizenship which were being denied to the colonised subjects, it symbolised also a terrain where numerous social and political forces existed in a curious blend of conflict and camaraderie.

The Right to Vote and Women 'Citizens'

Organised activism by women for voting and representation emerged in the context of the reforms in 1917 promising the gradual evolution of self-governing institutions. It gained pace with subsequent reform declarations and all but withered away in the 1940s. The decline in the 1940s was symptomatic of the unyielding primacy that the issue of political independence had assumed. It is important to point out at the outset that while a small minority of men could vote on the basis of a property qualification, women in India had no voting rights.[3] While the removal of sex disqualification formed the basis of women's demand for voting rights, it is significant that women's organisations that took up the issue with the colonial government placed it within the larger agenda of universal franchise. 'Fair field and no favours' was the preferred slogan. The women's delegation that met Montagu asked that when the franchise was drawn up, women as 'people' in a self-governing nation within the Empire should be 'allowed' the same opportunities of representation as men.[4] This prioritisation of universal franchise, rather than an emphasis on women's

---

[3]Citizenship's relationship with property goes back to the Aristotelian tradition whereby ownership of property was considered essential to be a 'solid citizen'. This view was expressed in modern times by the restriction of suffrage and membership to men of certain defined economic standing. Giving the vote to propertied men was thus tantamount to elevating some over others in the hierarchy of citizens.

[4]'A Ladies Deputation to Mr. Montagu', *New India* (25 October 1917, 5); 'Women's Deputation to Mr. Montagu', *New India* (13 December 1917, 5); J.H. and Mrs. Cousins, n.d., *We Two Together* (Madras: Ganesh and Co, 310); 'A Copy of the Address Presented by the All-India Women's Deputation to Lord Chelmsford (Viceroy) and Rt. Hon'ble E.S.Montagu (Secretary of State)', pamphlet, suffrage-India, Fawcett Collection. See also Frank Moraes, 'In Political Life', in *Women in India*, ed., Tara Ali Baig (1958).

franchise, placed women's demands in consonance with the nationalist demand for 'national' citizenship and sovereignty. A careful avoidance of a critical stance towards 'their' men, while appealing to the coloniser, was a consistent characteristic of the women's campaign. While grievances could be addressed to the nationalist men, the coloniser could not form the medium through which or the forum where complaints against their men could be addressed for rectification.[5]

The provision of 'universal adult franchise' in the charter of rights adopted by the Indian National Congress, in its Karachi Convention in 1931, was, in effect, the ultimate public manifestation of this 'harmony', apparently achieved without the acrimonious 'sex war' suffrage had provoked in the West. This consensus, however, was a veneer which served to blanket the fundamental and contentious issues which the issue of voting rights for women raised. The contours of the debate, submerged in the consensus, reveal a complex interlocking of ideological formulations—colonialist, nationalist, masculinist, and feminist—over the issue of women's proper place and the extent/nature of rights which suited it. The debate discloses the critical social tensions pertaining to gender, class, and community and the multifarious ways in which these tensions manifested themselves in the context of colonialism.

We shall first outline the sociopolitical forces which formed the context in which the demand for women's political rights was formulated and which influenced the content, form, and outcome of the demands. Most of the activism concerning suffrage was directed at influencing the legislators, colonial officials, and nationalist opinion. It involved only a section of women of the middle class, the demographic section, which, in Partha Chatterjee's words, 'effectively constituted the 'nation' in late colonial India' (Chatterjee 1994, 119). While issues of

---

[5]An influential group, however, including some English women such as Eleanor Rathbone, a section of Indian women, and the official opinion was in favour of *restricted* enfranchisement of women in a specific *proportion* to the enfranchised male population.

representativeness and 'real women' recur intermittently in the course of the debate, the universalisation of the abstract woman emblematic of true Indian womanhood and Indian tradition persists in all arguments, both for and against suffrage.

The nationalist and colonial constructions of tradition and womanhood, thus, formed one set of paradigms in relation to which the formulation of women's demands for voting rights took place. The women in the suffrage movement took up, therefore, 'Indian womanhood' as a concept already constituted for them, that is, as emblematic of Indian tradition.[6] The internalisation of this formulation of Indian womanhood by women in the suffrage debate points to their apparent *complicity* with the (male) nationalists in a 'shared' struggle for 'equality' with/against the coloniser. The articulation of Indian womanhood, however, frequently came to be used as a rallying point by women for criticising conservative nationalist opinion on political rights for women and for nationalist policies and practices on the family and family law. The silence on the women's question that Partha Chatterjee sees as having followed the nationalist resolution of the women's question was interrupted by women's organised struggles and the franchise debates in public/elected bodies. The resolution, as we shall see in later sections, was opened up by women for scrutiny, renegotiation and, contestation.[7]

---

[6]See Forbes ' Caged Tigers' (1979). The manner in which tradition was constructed selectively and patriarchies reconstituted through discursive and political processes and the implications of this for the definition of women both as a category and lived experiences have also been explored in the essays in Sangari and Vaid (1989).

[7]In her Ph.D dissertation (1990, 32), Kamla Visweswaran points out that it is no coincidence that this so-called resolution followed the split within the nationalist discourse between social and political reform. The Indian Social Conference was founded in 1887 two years after the Indian National Congress, and the two organisations held joint meetings every year until 1895 when Tilak forced the Indian Social Conference out. Thus, on a rather elementary level, she says, the nationalist discourse no longer 'speaks' the women's question because it has produced a minor, though necessary, (*contd.*)

Women's activism in this phase around the issue of suffrage also took shape in relation to suffragist feminisms in other countries and was influenced by Irish and British suffragists active in India.[8] The Irish feminists found India a preferred site to propel their criticism of British colonial policies in India and Ireland by bringing together nationalist and suffragist demands for citizenship, while British suffragists strove to broaden the scope of their activities for political rights in a 'universal sisterhood'.[9] Indian feminists collaborated with the British and Irish feminists in their goal for the creation of women citizens. If the contest between Indian nationalists and Indian feminists on issues of the family and family laws demonstrates this universal sisterhood, there were moments when this sisterhood was fractured by the nationalist anxieties of Indian feminists. Frequently, therefore, the latter resisted their Western sisters' condemnation of Indian social structures as oppressive and the

(*contd.*) oppositional discourse as a subset of itself. This is the language of social reform, which, while it dogs nationalist 'political' discourse, no longer forms a basic part of its precepts. Yet, it is no accident that this 'resolution' is contested precisely at the moment when social reform planks are included in the platform of the Indian National Congress in 1917. For this year also marks the founding of the Women's Indian Association (henceforth WIA) and the regendering of social reforms discourse.

[8]The upsurge of nationalism during the war had created pressure to extend voting rights in many nations. The surge of movements for female suffrage across the world and the trend towards enfranchisement of women and the successes enjoyed by the suffragists in Britain, the United States, and many European Countries towards the end of the First World War had undoubtedly encouraged Indian women. A Bill introduced in the British Parliament in 1917 and enacted into law in 1918 broadened the male electorate and gave a limited franchise to women in Britain. Many European countries such as Russia, Germany, and Poland also adopted women's suffrage between 1917 and 1919; Scotland, Wales and other states affiliated with Britain such as Canada, Ireland, British East Africa, and Rhodesia approved women's suffrage. See Barbara Southard (1995, 71).

[9]Mrinalini Sinha (1990) provides an excellent account of the relationship between British and Indian suffragism within the framework of imperial social and political structures.

figuration of Indian women as 'gendered subjects of an irrational patriarchal system'.[10]

The colonial relationship of dominance and subordination with its strong racial/civilisational connotations was extremely influential in determining the nature and terms of the debate over women's suffrage in India. Indeed, notwithstanding the Chartist movement for political manhood and the suffrage movement for women's enfranchisement, masculinity (as opposed to an inherent human right based on reason) formed the fundamental basis for citizenship in Britain. Masculinity was affirmed in relation to paternal/political/proprietory authority over women/family, colonial subjects, and the working class. Through much of the nineteenth century, the debate over franchise for women and the working class in Britain saw the vote being defined increasingly in national imperialist class and gender terms. Opponents of universal franchise compared the working class to colonial 'natives', both of them requiring firm, unflinching, and unsentimental control (Hall 1992, 285). The constant reiteration of this authority was important for the continued subjection of these sections of the population by the white, propertied male. Those opposed to women's suffrage in Britain drew sustenance from the philosophy of the jurist, James Fitzjames Stephens, who, from his experiences of imposing a 'consolidated code of law on India', linked force in government to a rigid patriarchy in the home. Stephens compared women to 'natives', both of whom were unable to enforce their will. Manhood, he claimed, rested on physical virility (Stephens 1874, 284).[11] The

---

[10]Kamla Visweswaran calls these moments of agreement and conflict the *thematic* and *problematic* of Indian and Western feminisms. In her work, she explores the writings of Dr. Muthulakshmi Reddy (the first woman legislator in the Madras Presidency) and the journals put out by the WIA to study the negotiations which first-wave feminism had to make between nationalism on the one hand and Western feminism on the other (1990, 32).

[11]As British imperialism faced growing challenges from the Boers and competition from Germany, opponents of women's suffrage asserted that the defence of the Empire required virile men and submissive, fertile (*contd.*)

assertion of this intractable and unbridgeable racial and civilisational difference between the coloniser and colonised was reflected in an influential strand of opinion that was subscribed to, among others, by General Smuts and that rejected the rationale of 'equal citizenship' behind the demand for franchise. Justifying his dismissal of the claim for equal franchise rights, General Smuts opined that such a claim arose

> ...from a misconception of the nature of British citizenship... not from the fact, but from the assumption that all subjects of the king are equal, that in an Empire where there is a common king, there should be a common and equal citizenship and that all differences and distinctions in citizen's rights are wrong in principle...On the contrary there is every imaginable difference. The common kingship is the binding link—it is not a source from which private citizens derive their rights....[12]

A Chronology of Events

The focal point of the debate on women's franchise was the announcement on 20 August 1917 by Edwin Montagu, secretary of state for India, to gradually develop 'self-governing institutions in India with a view to the progressive realisation of responsible government' and his subsequent visit in November 1917 to ascertain Indian opinion on specific reform proposals.[13] The demands by Indian women for voting rights emerged in this context of promise for political reforms. Montagu's announcement in the House of Commons was followed by a visit to India in November 1917 with the object of learning

---

(*contd.*) women. Whereas working men had been criticised in 1867 for having very large families, early twentieth-century anti-reformers lambasted suffragettes for concentrating on politics instead of childbearing for the Empire. For more details on James Fitzjames Stephens' views, see Anna Clark, (1996, 249).

[12]General Smuts quoted in Srinivas Shastri, *The Indian Citizen* (1948, 50).

[13]Montagu's 20 August announcement of the British government's policy in the House of Commons was followed by his visit to India in November 1917. Montagu toured the subcontinent for five months with the governor general of India, Lord Chelmsford.

more about Indian opinion on various aspects of political reforms. A number of 'prominent' Indian women 'organised' by the Irish feminist Margaret Cousins and Saraladevi Chaudhurani requested an audience with Montagu for members of the WIA and the Bharat Stri Mahamandal, respectively, to discuss education and social reform. The women's delegation that sought a meeting with Montagu was told that only deputations with political subjects would be received. The issue of political rights for women, thus, gained precedence in women's activism in this phase. Margaret Cousins writes about how the first demand for women's franchise was born soon after: 'I then circulated a couple of extra sentences about political rights or rather "opportunities" in the draft of the memorandum. I know the women interested in the deputation believed in being citizens of their country and they wrote agreeing to the addition, *so the vote was born*' (Cousins 1941, 33).[14] On 15 December 1917, a 14-member women's delegation led by Sarojini Naidu met

---

[14]Emphasis added. The Theosophical Society and the WIA which was started by Dorothy Jinarajadasa on 8 May 1917 at Adyar, the headquarters of the Theosophical Society, were closely involved in the organisation of this deputation and in subsequent lobbying in later years. The composition of the deputation reflected a convergence of the two streams of Cousin's influence—the Indian Women's University, of which she was a member of the Senate, and the WIA of which she was the joint secretary. The support of other women's association was also canvassed. The Gujarati Stree Mandal of Bombay, which was patronised by some men (such as Purushottamdas Thakurdas) who supported the WIA, held a meeting for Annie Besant (who extended her influence both through the Theosophical Society and her Home Rule League) in October 1917. The deputation which finally met Montagu consisted of members of several women's organisations such as *Seva Sadan*, the *Mahila Seva Samaj*, the Indian Women's University at Poona, and the Women's Branch of the Home Rule League. See Gail Pearson, 'Reserved Seats', (1983), 49–50; Frank Moraes 'In Political Life', in *Women of India*, ed. Tara Ali Baig (1958, 91–92); Geraldine Forbes, *Women in Modern India*, (1998, 92); Barbara Southard, *The Women's Political Movement and Colonial Politics in Bengal*, (1995, 70); 'Ladies Deputation', *Indian Social Reformer* (1917, 121); Vijay Agnew, *Elite Women in Indian Politics*, (1979, 108); Muthulakshmi Reddy ed., *One Who Knows, Mrs. Margaret Cousins and Her Work in India*, (1956, 4).

Montagu and Chelmsford to present their demands for political rights. Montagu's entry for the day in his diary noted that '[the women's deputation] assured [him] that the Congress would willingly pass a unanimous request for women's suffrage'. It is worth mentioning, however, that Montagu thought of the deputation as nothing more than *interesting* and the Montagu-Chelmsford Reforms made no mention of it. His notes focussed on 'one very nice-looking woman from Bombay, Dr. Joshi', Sarojini Naidu, 'the poetess, a very attractive and clever woman, but [he believed] a revolutionary at heart', and Mrs.Cousins, 'a well-known suffragette from Bombay' and 'one of Mrs. Besant's crowd' (Moraes 1958, 91). A WIA publication records that many years later, Sarojini Naidu was to recall that the idea of meeting important people such as the viceroy of India seemed a 'bold and daring' adventure to the deputation. The delegates subconsciously spent a lot of time 'worrying over their appearances', wishing somehow to reinforce their arguments 'by a colourful and picturesque appearance' (Reddy 1956, 8).[15]

It is significant that since women's organisations were not political at that point in time, the blessings of the Indian National Congress (henceforth INC) had become almost a necessity for the validation of their demands. The women worked to garner support for their cause through women's meetings and appealed for help from the INC and other political organisations. It was crucial for women to put their demands in such a manner as to convince the male nationalist opinion that voting rights for women were consonant with the language of equality in the political domain and yet in harmony with 'tradition', or was rational *precisely* because it was in congruence with tradition. Thus, in August 1918, Sarojini Naidu exhorted a large special session of INC in Bombay attended by 5,000 delegates, assuring her audience that extending the franchise to women was rational, scientifically and politically sound, compatible with tradition, and consistent with human rights

---

[15]Muthulakshmi Reddy cited in Agnew (1979, 108).

(Forbes 1998, 94). The resolution was passed by a 75 per cent majority.[16] Saraladevi Chaudhurani presented the resolution supporting the vote for women in the thirty-third session of the INC in December 1918 in Delhi.[17] Meetings of provincial and district Congress conferences and of women's organisations to express support for women's franchise followed in the rest of India, and similar resolutions were passed.[18] The India Home Rule League and the Muslim League also approved resolutions supporting women's franchise in the same year (Agnew 1979, 109).

Women's groups in India and Britain as well as Indian political parties submitted petitions favouring women's franchise to the various committees established to formulate the details of the Montagu-Chelmsford reforms. When the Southborough Committee, which dealt specifically with the franchise issue, toured India, a women's delegation led by Annie Besant, with Sarojini Naidu as one of its members, met it to press further for women's franchise.[19] In their final report, published in April 1919, however, the Southborough Committee, while acknowledging the support for women's franchise from educated Indians and political parties, including the INC and the Muslim League, decided against enfranchising women. The committee concluded that the demand for women's franchise in India was a 'limited' one, confined to a small group of educated women, and that Indian women in 'general' did not want the vote. Even if they

---

[16]*Report of the Special Session of the Indian National Congress*, Bombay, August 19–31 and 1 September 1918, 109–10.

[17]*Report of the Thirty-Third Session of the INC*, Delhi, December 26–31, 1918, 118–21.

[18]In 1918, the provincial conferences of Bombay, Madras, and Andhra Pradesh passed resolutions to remove sex disqualification from the reform bill.

[19]Prominent among the organisations which met the committee were the WIA, including representatives from its 40 branches, the Women's Graduate Union of Bombay and the Women's Branch of the Home Rule League. In addition, the women of Bombay organised a petition signed by 800 'ladies' reiterating their demand for the vote. Muthulakshmi Reddy, (1958, 14), cited in Vijay Agnew, (1979, 109).

did, the committee claimed that the social disabilities of women under Indian customs would hamper a general implementation of female enfranchisement.[20] It was argued that the low rates of female literacy in India and the prevalence of *purdah* would give rise to practical administrative problems in giving women the vote.[21] The Joint Select Committee of the House of Lords and the House of Commons set up to consider the Government of India Bill also rejected franchise for women despite persuasive evidence presented before them by Besant and Naidu.[22] While the drift towards women's suffrage in Britain and the precedent established elsewhere in the world made it hard for the British to ignore these petitions, political worries about offending the conservative sensibilities of influential (propertied) groups in

[20]Mrs. Herabai Tata, 'A Short Sketch of Indian Women's Franchise work', pamphlet (n.d.), Suffrage-India, *Fawcett Collection* (henceforth FC).

[21]It may be pointed out that 'practical administrative problems' were indeed experienced in the implementation of franchise, with the increase in numbers after the Government of India Act of 1935. These problems were compounded by the restrictions imposed by the Act on the process of registering women voters. While propertied women entered the electoral rolls automatically, women who qualified under the literacy clause had to register their names, with the provinces differing in their methods of registration. In Bengal, the government sent forms to the leading men requesting them to prepare the list; in Bombay, application forms were to be circulated by village officers; in the United Provinces women could register by mail or through their husbands; Madras required the women voters to present their applications personally to the registration officer which caused some discomfort for women in purdah and to other women for various reasons. Citations from the editorial, *Stri Dharma*, May and June 1936, and Aruna Asaf Ali, 'Women's Suffrage in India', in Shyam Kumari Nehru, (n.d., 358), and Vijay Agnew, (1979, 125).

[22]Local branches of the WIA held meetings, passed resolutions, and forwarded their comments to London. Letter from M. Cousins to 'My Dear Sisters', 28 May 1919, *AIWC Files*. In Bombay, women held a protest meeting and sent letters and telegrams to members of parliament. Mrs.Jaiji Jehangir Petit, chair of the Bombay Women's Committee for Women's Suffrage, sent this cable to London: 'women ask no favour but claim right and justice. If the vote is denied it will mean serious check to women's advancement in India'. See Forbes (1996, 95).

India, traditionally British allies and vehemently opposed to any change in women's roles, evidently took precedence. Montagu observed that conservative opposition to female franchise was almost a 'religious feeling', and 'dangerous' to provoke. He urged the House to pass the India Bill as it existed with a proviso allowing provincial legislative councils to add women to the list of registered voters.[23] In 1919, a British parliamentary committee recommended that female franchise should be considered a 'domestic' subject, leaving it to the provincial legislatures to decide the matter. Thus, the Government of India Act, 1919, while not enfranchising women, left the question of votes for women to the Indians to decide.[24] In the 1920s, therefore, the focus of women's struggle for the vote shifted to a new emphasis on organisation and agitation at the provincial level.

By 1929–30, the nine provinces that elected members to their provincial legislatures had given franchise to women based on the criteria of age and property. The Bombay and the Madras legislative councils granted women voting rights in 1921, the United Provinces in 1923, Punjab, Bengal, and Assam in 1926, Central Provinces and Bihar and Orissa in 1929.[25] The removal of disqualification for women at the provincial level meant that enfranchised women could also vote for the central legislative assembly. The admission to the right to vote was, however, largely symbolic as only a small minority of women was enfranchised, of which only a few exercised their voting rights.[26]

---

[23]H. Tata to J.J. Petit, 7 December 1919, *AIWC Files*, Joint Select Committee on Government of India Bill, vol. I, *Report and Proceedings of the Committee, Parliamentary Papers 1919*, vol. IV, part I of the Preamble.

[24]See Barbara Southard (1995, 71–72).

[25]Vijay Agnew suggests that the Central Provinces passed the resolution in 1926. For Forbes, the year Assam, the Central Provinces, and Bihar and Orissa conceded was 1930.

[26]In the 1923 elections, only 18.3 per cent of these women eligible to vote in Bombay exercised their right. In the 1926 elections, the proportion of female voters to the adult female population of the province was only 0.8 per cent and only 20.1 per cent of those eligible actually voted. (*contd.*)

The following table illustrates the relative proportions of women and men voters.[27]

Province	Electors to population	Adult men voters to adult men population	Women voters to adult women population
Madras	3.2	11.6	1.0
Bombay	3.9	13.4	0.8
Bengal	2.5	9.7	0.3
United Provinces	3.5	12.4	0.4
Punjab	3.4	11.9	0.5
Bihar and Orissa	1.1	4.6	—
Assam	3.7	14.2	0.2
Central Provinces & Berar	1.3	5.2	—

While 'propertied women' now had the right to vote, they did not as yet have the right to sit in the legislatures. Women's organisations, the WIA in particular, sent letters to the secretary of state and the secretary of the Reforms Enquiry (Muddiman) Committee, and met the Muddiman Committee at Simla, seeking the removal of sex disqualification from election to the legislatures. The Muddiman Committee recommended that the bar against women's election or nomination to either chamber

(contd.) Report Showing the Result of Elections in India (1923), 8; Report Showing the Results of Elections in India (1925 and 1926, cmd., 2923), in Gail Pearson (1983, 51).

[27] Indian Statutory Commission, A Survey Report, Government of India, (1930, 191). The high percentage of voters in Madras and Bombay, according to Agnew, indicates the level of literacy among its female population, the money allocated by the government to women's education in these provinces, and their attitude towards social reform. Bengal's attitude towards social reform was liberal but its elite (largely landed aristocracy) and nationalists resisted political reforms. See Vijay Agnew, (1979, 113).

of the Indian legislature or to the provincial councils should be removed after resolutions were passed in the chambers and councils.[28] A year later, in April 1926, the governor-general-in-council directed that such an amendment could be made to the electoral rules, provided the requisite resolutions were passed. No woman stood for the 1926 election in Bombay, though two contested unsuccessfully in Madras. The women turned their attention to seeking the *nomination* of women to provincial and central legislative bodies. The All India Women's Conference on Education and Social Reform (henceforth AIWC), formed in 1926, joined hands with the WIA to press the issue.[29]

The struggle for women's franchise was again spurred with the appointment of the Simon Commission in 1927 to enquire into 'constitutional matters leading to the formulation of a new India Act'. The WIA expressed its willingness to cooperate with the commission and asked for the inclusion of a woman

---

[28]*Report of the Muddiman Reforms Committee* (1924–25, 119).

[29]The All India Women's Conference (AIWC) was set up by women to organise themselves to pursue reforms in the system of education through linkages with various women's organisations. Margaret Cousins issued an appeal in the newspaper and wrote to over 500 women who were renowned educationists and social reformers or were associated with relevant organisations. It was suggested that women organise committees in their provinces with representatives from various local organisations and different strata of society. While the primary concern of AIWC was educational reform, they campaigned for social reforms such as the Rai Hari Bilas Sharda Bill for prevention of child marriage, the removal of legal disabilities of women in matters of marriage and inheritance, and the right of women to vote. It entered into the struggle for political rights without aligning itself to any particular political party. Its members included women from various parties. It espoused a strong nationalist stand and demanded equal rights for women in all spheres. See All India Women's Conference, Souvenir, (1927–70, 12). The AIWC membership comprising wealthy, educated women from large urban centres as acknowledged by its secretary, president, and chairperson in a letter to Nehru: 'Our members are drawn from all classes of the intelligentsia or Western educated women, the ignorant and the illiterate while attending our meetings are non-vocal'. *Jawaharlal Nehru Papers*, vol. I, 47, in Vijay Agnew (1979, 118).

member. WIA was joined by the AIWC, which, by 1928, emerged as a powerful campaigner for women's political rights.[30] By the time, however, the 'white seven' (men) comprising the commission arrived in India in February 1929, the WIA and the AIWC had joined the nationalist boycott against them. But other women, acting outside the ambit of the major organisations, met the commission and suggested giving the vote to literate women or reserving seats.[31]

Prior to the publication of the *Simon Commission Report*, the then governor general, Lord Irwin, announced in November 1929 that a Round Table Conference would be held in London to discuss the next step towards dominion status for India. The WIA asked for the names of three women, Sarojini Naidu, Muthulakshmi Reddy, and Rameshwari Nehru to be included.[32] The INC, however, decided to boycott the conference because Irwins's declaration read 'discuss' and not 'implement'. Despite having laboured hard on the franchise issue, the WIA, too, decided to withdraw.[33] In the meantime, the Statutory (Simon) Commission rejected 'immediate' adult franchise as 'impossible'. It advocated designing a scheme that would enfranchise about 20 per cent of the adult population. In an attempt to strengthen the position of women, it proposed an increase in the proportion of women voters to 33.5 per cent of the entire electorate. This was a substantial increase since women constituted only 5.59 per cent of the total electorate.[34] Neither the proposed Round Table Conference in London nor the Statutory Commission's proposals

---

[30]AIWC proposed that political emancipation was the first step towards releasing women from their 'shackles'. *Annual Report*, AIWC, Seventh session, (1933, 30).

[31]'Indian Statutory Commission', *Indian Annual Register*, vol. 1, nos. 1 and 2 (January–June 1929, 54–56). A women's deputation met the commission members, pointing out the low number of enfranchised women, and they argued that participation should be assured through reserved seats.

[32]Muthulakshmi Reddy (1956, 79).

[33]*WIA Report*, (1931–33, 3–4).

[34]Gail Pearson (1983, 52).

were, however, well received by women associated with the nationalist cause.

At the London conference, which began its meetings in November 1930, Indian women were represented by government nominees Begum Shah Nawaz and Radhabai Subbarayan, who emphasised the 'awakening' of Indian women and the significant role they could play in promoting social change. Most customary disabilities faced by women including purdah, they claimed, would decline if women gained the vote.[35] In a departure from the position of women's organisations, they expressed their willingness for special reservations for women. Margaret Cousins and Muthulakshmi Reddy from the WIA, Mrs. Hamid Ali and Rani Rajwade from the AIWC, and Tarabai Premchand from the National Council for Women in India (henceforth NCWI)[36] together with Sarojini Naidu, issued a joint memorandum in disagreement with Radhabai Subbarayan and Begum Shah Nawaz. Other women who had previously supported nomination and reserved seats came out in support of universal adult franchise with 'equality and no privileges' and a 'fair field and no favour'.[37] It is quite apparent that without giving up their commitment to women's franchise, the women's organisations attempted to place the nationalist position—no cooperation without a firm commitment to ending British rule—above their desire for wider female enfranchisement.[38] The Karachi Session

---

[35]Begum Jahan Ara Shah Nawaz was already attending this conference as her father's (Sir Muhammad Shafi's) private secretary. Mrs. Radhabai Subbarayan had attended Somerville College, Oxford and was familiar to British suffragists. While both these delegates were longstanding members of women's organisations, the British had appointed them without consulting these organisations.

[36]The NCWI was founded in 1925 to provide a link among various organisations within and outside India, working for the welfare of women in India.

[37]'Reservation of Seats for Women', *The Hindu* (17 November 1931, 5).

[38]Letters from Mrs. P.N. Sirur to R. Subbarayan (22 April 1931), R. Subbarayan to E. Rathbone (1 May 1931), folder no. 5, *Rathbone Papers*, Fawcett Library; Letter from E. Rathbone to M. Reddi (12 March 1931), (*contd.*)

of Congress in 1931 passed the fundamental rights resolution, affirming its espousal of universal adult franchise.[39] With this resolution, the women's demand for equal franchise with men was further strengthened and they reiterated their faith in universal adult suffrage and mixed general electorates, and they opposed reservation, nomination, or co-option for women. With the Gandhi-Irwin Pact of March 1931, INC agreed to participate in the Second Round Table Conference to draw up a plan for federation and responsible government with the reservation of certain powers. The women's organisations following the Congress lead agreed to participate and sent Sarojini Naidu as their representative. Gandhi was the sole representative of the INC, and the British again nominated Begum Shah Nawaz and Mrs Subbarayan. Begum Shah Nawaz had, by this time, changed her position on reservation and firmly supported the Congress demand for universal adult franchise. But, Radhabai Subbarayan withstood pressure from her friends in the WIA and continued her support for reserved seats.[40]

At the close of the Second Round Table Conference, a White Paper recommending an increase in enfranchised women was presented to both houses of parliament. The complexity of the franchise question compelled the Franchise Sub-Committee of

---

(*contd.*) M. Reddi to E. Rathbone (9 March 1931), M. Reddi to E. Rathbone (1 May 1931), M. Reddi to E. Rathbone (6 May 1931), folder no. 1, *Rathbone Papers*, Fawcett Library.

[39]In its Karachi session in March 1931, the INC passed the resolution on fundamental rights and the national economic programme. Gandhi, while moving the resolution, said that it was 'meant for those who are not legislators, who are not interested in intricate questions of the constitution, who will not take an active part in the administration of the country'. Its purpose was 'to indicate to the poor inarticulate Indian the broad features of Swaraj'. The promise of 'franchise on the basis of universal adult franchise' was among the seventeen items on the charter of freedom. See Mihir Kumar Sen, *Elements of Civics* (Hindustan Publications, 1946).

[40]Radhabai Subbarayan, *The Political Status of Women Under the New Constitution*, (Madras: n.p., n.d., 16); Letter from M. Reddy to 'Dear Madam' (16 November 1936), *AIWC Files*, no. 135.

the Round Table Conference to recommend setting up a committee to investigate the demands of various groups and the opinion of provincial governments in India itself. Thus, the Indian Franchise Committee, chaired by the Marquess of Lothian, was constituted in December 1931 and started its work in February 1932. This committee planned to tour India in 1932, collect evidence and opinions, and submit concrete proposals for the next India Act. Radhabai Subbarayan and Mary Ada Pickford were the two women appointed to the Lothian Committee.[41]

In March 1932, when the Lothian Committee visited Bombay, there was an anti-Lothian hartal. The Civil Disobedience Movement had recommenced, and the Congress refused to cooperate with the Franchise Committee in its investigations. A number of non-Congress women, however, involved themselves in the work of the Committee.[42] It is significant that recommendations of the committee for increased enfranchisement of women agreed on the inevitability of enfranchising women in the distant future. The increase of women voters at this stage emerged from the need to prevent any drastic steps the government might have to take in future to rectify the discrepancy between the numbers of enfranchised men to enfranchised women. The committee voted, therefore, to 'substantially increase' the number of women voters. Apart from the existing qualifications of age and property, three more qualifications were introduced to increase the numbers of

---

[41]Eleanor Rathbone, a member of the House of Commons for the Combined English Universities since 1929, had long been interested in women's causes and 'discovered' India when she read Katherine Mayo's *Mother India*. Her own book, *Child Marriage: The Indian Minotaur*, described the Sharda Act as an 'ornamental legislation' and won the praise of some Indian women. Despite her exclusion from the committee, she decided to tour India and meet Indian women. Her object was not to elicit their opinions but rather to advise them how to fight for the vote. Barbara N.Ramusack, 'Cultural Missionaries, Maternal Imperialists, Feminists Allies: British Women Activists in India, 1865-1945', in Nupur Chaudhuri and Margaret Strobel, (1992, 126–28) and Gail Pearson, (1983, 53–54).

[42]Gail Pearson (1983, 56).

women voters: A wife over the age of 25 of a propertied man could vote; a widow of over 25 years of age was qualified to vote if her husband was franchised at the time of his death; women graduates over 21 years of age could vote.[43] By this addition, the committee aimed at securing a ratio of one woman to four men, and estimated that in Bombay their proposals would result in the enfranchisement of about 14.3 per cent of the total female population and about 33.5 per cent of the total adult population.[44] The Lothian Committee also suggested that 2 to 5 per cent of the seats in the provincial councils be reserved for a period of 10 years. The recommendations of the Lothian Committee were rejected by women's organisations as violative of their inherent fundamental human rights as citizens and as a 'vitally integral part of the body politic'.[45]

The question cropped up once again with the communal award that confirmed reserved seats for Muslims and also extended reservation to the depressed classes. Gandhi maintained that the lower castes, the 'untouchables' or *harijans*, were Hindus and should not be treated as a separate group. He began a fast in opposition to the award. The Poona Pact of September 1932, a compromise measure, granted reserved seats to the depressed classes within the total Hindu constituency. The women, who denounced the Poona Pact and the communal awards as divisive for women, considered the acceptance by the Congress leaders of the award an abandoning of the position on universal franchise.[46] Since the award was favoured by Muslim men, Begum Shah Nawaz and a number of other Muslim women advised women's organisations to accept the decision to promote religious harmony.[47]

---

[43]*Report of the Franchise Sub-Committee of the Round Table Conference* (1931, 80–81).

[44]Gail Pearson (1983, 57).

[45]*Annual Report of the All India Women's Conference*, (1933–34, 252).

[46]WIA, 1932, *AIWC Files*, no. 20.

[47]'Women and the Communal Decision', *Indian Ladies' Magazine*, vol. 5, (September–October 1932, 510).

In the meantime, the Civil Disobedience Movement had commenced, and as long as the movement continued, no Congress representative could be expected to participate in the Joint Parliamentary Select Committee to discuss the White Paper Proposals for the Constitution. The proposed members named for the Indian delegation to the Joint Parliamentary Select Committee did not include a single woman, despite agitation by British women. The three major women's associations, the AIWC, the WIA and the NCWI (supported by the Bhagini Samaj and Gujarati Hindu Stree Mandal), prepared a joint memorandum to be submitted to the Joint Select Committee and elected three women to give evidence, on the basis of the memorandum.[48] Begum Hamid Ali, Muthulakshmi Reddy, and Rajkumari Amrit Kaur, who had earlier given evidence before the Lothian Committee at Lahore, were invited to London. The White Paper of 1933 that subsequently came out recommended a marginal increase in the numbers of voting women, but fell short of the expectations of women's organisations which demanded that as many women as possible should be brought on the electoral rolls on the basis of as few differential qualifications between men and women as possible. After much debate the three women's organisations produced a joint memorandum reiterating their demand for adult franchise and objecting to the various schemes for separate electorates and

---

[48]Memorandum II submitted by the AIWC, NCWI, and WIA suggested that the literacy qualification should be modified to include women who could read and write in any one language. They accepted the property qualification, but suggested that it should be made equally applicable to both provincial and federal legislatures. Men and women, 20 years of age and living in large urban centres should be allowed to vote. They reiterated their opposition to communal electorates as an attempt to break the unity of women. *Report of the All India Women's Conference* (1933–34, 19). See also *Stri Dharma* (16 September 1933, 549); 'Memorandum II on the Status of Women in the Proposed New Constitution of India' addressed to the members of the Joint Select Committee (June 1933), pamphlet, *Suffrage*, FC; Minutes of the evidence given before the Joint Select Committee on Indian Constitutional Reform (1934), *Parliamentary Papers*, vol. VIII (IIC) (1932–3, 1617–22).

reservation of seats. The memorandum rejected, in particular, the wifehood qualification. While accepting the property qualification for men and women laid down in the White Paper, women's organisations rejected the educational qualification and recommended in its place a literacy qualification. As a temporary and short-term measure, they agreed to accept the enfranchisement of literate and urban women and decided to work for a franchise ratio of one to five (1:5).[49]

When they were in the last stages of preparing the India Act, the Linlithgow Joint Select Committee decided to examine witnesses from Indian women's organisations. Rajkumari Amrit Kaur, Muthulakshmi Reddy, and Begum Hamid Ali spoke for the NCWI, WIA, and AIWC, respectively. Mrs. Sushma Sen and Mrs. L. Mukherjee spoke on behalf of the Calcutta Mahila Samiti and presented a memorandum, prepared by Radhabai Subbarayan, from 450 women members of municipalities, district boards and taluk boards in Madras and another memorandum from 100 prominent women of Mangalore, prepared by Mrs. N.L. Subba Rao, Mrs. Subbarayan's sister.[50] Lady Layton, Sir Phillip Hartog, and Mrs. O. Strachey presented the position of the British committee for Indian women's franchise. They all insisted on the importance of increasing the number of enfranchised women. A memorandum was presented before the committee, containing suggestions for the period of transition,

---

[49]Not all women, however, agreed with the memorandum. Eleanor Rathbone, in particular, cautioned the women's organisations that insisting on adult franchise and rejecting the wifehood qualification might stifle all schemes to increase the ranks of the enfranchised. Such advice was based on the assumption that universal adult franchise was only a few years away, and she advised Indian women to drop the demand for universal franchise and accept reservations and other special schemes, as any increase in the numbers of women in the legislature would assist in social reform, *Rathbone Papers* (henceforth *RP*), file no. 311. Press Agency (22 April 1933), Rathbone to Reddy (9 February 1933), *RP*, file no. 11.

[50]E. Rathbone to R. Subbarayan, 27 May 1933 and 23 June 1933, *RP*, file no. 5; Mrs. P.K. Sen, FC 'Supplementary Memorandum on the Franchise of women', pamphlet, *Suffrage*.

and it protested against reserved seats for women and indirect representation of women in the federal assembly. The demand was made for the enfranchisement of all 21-year old men and women in urban areas. The secretary of state agreed the evidence was compelling. The Linlithgow Committee commented: 'India cannot reach the position to which it aspires in the world until its women play their due part as educated citizens'. But they declined, ostensibly for administrative reasons, to give women (and India) that opportunity. Provincial administrations complained that too many votes, particularly from women voters as well, would unnecessarily complicate the procedure. Moreover, they labelled the schemes to increase the number of women voters cumbersome and difficult to implement. The final plan approved of a number of different programmes to increase the number of women voters: wives could vote in some provinces, literate women in others, and the wives of military officers in still others.[51]

When the report of the Joint Select Committee was published, the committee appeared to have been little influenced by women's proposals. Some modifications were, however, introduced. In several provinces, excluding Bombay, the application requirement for wifehood qualification was no longer necessary, and in some provinces, including Bombay, the literacy qualification was substituted instead of the educational qualification. Sarojini Naidu vehemently denounced the report and the AIWC rejected it. The Bombay Presidency Women's Council held a special meeting to prepare its detailed criticism for the NCWI. At a meeting in Delhi in January 1935, long after civil disobedience had been withdrawn, the three all-India women organisations met under the presidentship of Sarojini Naidu and jointly condemned the report and rejected the wifehood qualification, reservation of seats, and the system of indirect election from the provincial assemblies to the central assembly, insisting that the literacy qualification should be

---

[51]Joint Committee on Indian Constitutional Reform, Session 1933–34, vol. I, Report 1934; *Parliamentary Papers*, 1933–34, vol. VI.

extended and that the application requirement should be dropped for all provinces.[52]

The Government of India Act, 1935, did not accept universal adult franchise. It introduced special electorates for women, providing for the reservation of 41 seats for women in the provincial legislatures, and it left the task of determining the nature of the constituencies to the Delimitation Committee. Under the Act of 1935, the right to vote was extended to more women. Earlier, the proportion was one woman to twenty men. After the Act of 1935, the proportion was one woman voter to five men voters in an electorate of 35 million voters. Women over 21 years of age could vote, provided they fulfilled one of the following requirements: they were literate, were property owners, or were wives or widows of men having property. Thus, only literate and married women of 21 years of age and above were eligible to vote, provided they had the same property and taxation qualifications as men. In the absence of ownership rights and prevalence of widespread illiteracy, only a minuscule percentage of women constituted the electorate.[53] Women could be elected to the legislature, and 41 seats were reserved for them on a communal basis. They could, however, contest any of the general seats. The constituencies would be small and select and would minimise the difficulty of campaigning in rural areas. They would include both men and women except in the case of Muslim constituencies which would include only women.[54]

The India Act passed in 1935 increased representation but not to the extent expected by organised women. The process of delivering this second franchise decision exposed both the limits of collaboration with the British and the problems inherent in attaching women's rights to the nationalist movement.

The AIWC did not favour the formation of special

---

[52]Gail Pearson (1983, 61).

[53]This Act enfranchised 6 million women and 29 million men, that is, one woman to every five men. Rajkumari Amrit Kaur, 'Women Under the New Constitution' in Shyam Kumari Nehru (n.d., 372).

[54]Ibid., 372.

constituencies for women candidates. They were anxious to be recognised as equal citizens and did not want to be given any special considerations or privileges. They noted that preferential treatment would detract from the status of women as citizens with equal rights and responsibilities. A woman contesting a general seat in a multimember constituency would certainly be more significant than one from a reserved seat and a special constituency. This would also add to their confidence and self-assurance. In the middle of 1935, the AIWC made one last attempt to reject the provisions for female voters. Its standing committee announced that unless the disabilities of the wifehood qualification and reservation of seats under which women were placed were removed, it might not be possible for them to participate in the working of the new constitution. At the tenth session of the AIWC at Trivandrum, however, while continuing their opposition to the wifehood criterion and procedures of application as expressed in a resolution moved by Dr. Sukthankar, they also passed a resolution, put up by Gulbanu Doctor, stating that although the provisions under the new Government of India Act were inadequate, women should take advantage of such powers as they had obtained. The way was cleared for acquiescence to special representation and the challenge, even if not articulated as such, to segregated society receded.[55]

The 'Womanly Vote': The Gendering of the Vote

It would be a mistake to assume from the above account that women's voting rights animated colonial/official or nationalist opinion to the same degree and intensity as social reforms did in the earlier century. The significance of the movement for franchise lay, however, in the manner in which it became the rallying point for women's activism and opened up for public debate and scrutiny women's roles in the family and by implication in the nation and the body politic. As mentioned earlier, organised activism by women for voting and representation

---

[55]Gail Pearson (1983, 61).

emerged in the context of the 1919 reforms that promised 'gradual' evolution of self-governing institutions. It gained pace with subsequent reform declarations and all but withered away in the 1940s. Women's organisations were, in most cases, so closely interlinked with nationalist politics and so averse to follow a collision course with the INC that the franchise issue became a subordinate strand of the national movement and often not easily discernable from the 'national' movement for independence. The growth and intensity of the movement in the period following 1917 show that the channels of constitutional reforms, as long as the nationalist opinion was receptive to it, spurred the movement on. The 'public' harmony between women's demand for the vote and the nationalist position, rooted in the peculiar situation of the debate in the colonial context, would also account for the waning of the movement in the 1940s. The provision of 'universal adult franchise' in the charter of rights adopted by the INC in its Karachi Convention in 1931 was, in effect, the ultimate public manifestation of this harmony, apparently achieved without the acrimonious 'sex war' it provoked in the West.

This consensus over franchise, however, displayed a veneer that served to blanket the fundamental and contentious issues that 'vote for women' raised as well as the complex configuration of the socio-political forces for or against it. If the blanket shrouding the debate were lifted, its contours would reveal a complex interlocking of ideological, colonialist, nationalist, masculinist, and suffragist formulations, over the issue of women's 'proper' place and the extent/nature of rights 'suited' to her proper place. It would disclose the critical tensions within society pertaining to gender, class, and community and the multifarious ways in which these tensions manifested themselves in the context of colonialism. The incorporation of women's political rights in the Congress charter of rights and in the Constitution of independent India do not mark a vanishing point or the resolution of the issues which formed the core of the debate— 'womanhood' and 'citizenship'. They were in effect a 'gloss over', so much so that issues of 'womanhood' and 'citizenship' have returned and rancoured in almost unchanged form in subsequent years in the debates on sati, on rights of Muslim women, on Uniform Civil Code, on women's 'special' rights for representation in parliament, on violence against women, etc.—the list could well be legion.

Keeping the above arguments in mind, we shall now attempt to sift out the meanings structuring the various notions of 'womanhood' and 'citizen's rights' which informed the various perspectives—colonialist, nationalist, suffragist—on the debate on women's franchise. Whereas lines could be drawn dividing those in favour of or against the enfranchisement of women, the divisions could well be seen as transcended by a masculinist camaraderie. Whereas women 'petitioned', 'appealed', and 'struggled' to '(re)present' themselves in committees on franchise reforms and round tables on constitutional reforms, the discussions and debates in 'representative' bodies such as the provincial legislative councils and the various committees concealed/revealed a dialogue among men about 'their' women. Though agitated and emotionally charged arguments were made for and against the issue, the 'us' factor that transcended this apparent conflict of opinion drew from the manner in which womanhood was defined. Notwithstanding the fact that nationalist leaders were themselves ensconced within (colonial) narratives which feminised and infantilised them, a whole series of arguments for or against women's franchise placed women within coordinates of meaning identical to the colonialist narratives of feminisation and infantilisation—wherein women needed to be protected and supported, and wherein they performed essential services for the community/nation such as bearing and raising children. The definition of womanhood and the character of citizenship rights based on it would reveal a remarkable masculinist affinity across various divides (colonised-coloniser, pro-suffrage-anti-suffrage) where a dialogue of men (us) with men (us) about women (them) took place. In this dialogue among men, 'woman' was more often than not defined in terms of a (dependent) relationship to family (husband), and following from it, having respectability, property, education, patriotism, and nationalism. As the terms of the definition of 'woman' would show, the promises of bridges among women across social class and religious community were restricted by a schism within 'respectable' and 'proper' women as well as a schism between them and others who were excluded from the realm of such definitions. All of these contradictions unfolded in extremely complex ways, because, more often than not, groups that otherwise opposed each other ended up adopting the same core narrative—familial ideologies and tropes of motherhood— to bolster arguments both in favour of and against women's suffrage. As mentioned at the beginning of this chapter, these tropes presented womanhood as given, as a problem already constituted for women. Women were, therefore, already entangled within the existing set of assumptions surrounding 'women' and 'womanhood'. Any 'political employment' of 'women' could, therefore, either build upon this 'inherited foundation' or try to undermine it. It could not voice women afresh.[56]

As mentioned earlier, multiple perspectives and discursive practices informed the debate on women's suffrage in India. The colonial relationship of dominance and subordination, as has already been noted in the beginning, with its strong racial/ civilisational connotation, was extremely influential in determining the nature and terms of the debate over women's suffrage in India. The difference of the colonised population and the subsequent denial and deferral of political rights were marked out and effected through a series of exclusionary principles. The feminisation and infantilisation of the colonised and the deployment of racialised and gendered categories by the colonisers omitted the subjects from the category of citizens, because they were inadequate, were not men, or were lesser men. The emasculation of the colonised and the colonial ordering of masculinity emerged alongside racial exclusivity as specific practice(s) of ruling. By this hierarchical construction of masculinity, the coloniser made sense of *himself* in a privileged relationship to the colonised. The depoliticisation of the colonised

---

[56]This premise is borrowed from Denise Riley (1988), Gladys M. Jimenez-Munoz (1993).

subjects, particularly the politically self-conscious, Western-educated Indian, was also effected by placing them in this hierarchy as an unnatural and perverted form of masculinity.[57]

The masculine status of citizenship in Britain was defined throughout the debate on franchise reforms in England in terms that shifted from property holding, to marrying and leading a household, to defending the Empire with violence. Generally, however, electors were supposed to be property holders, since the function of parliament was seen to be the protection of property (Clark 1996, 230–31). The restricting of voting rights in India to property owners was not simply an extension of this principle to the colony; it also assured the continued alliance of this class with colonial rulers. Political worries about offending the conservative sensibilities of influential (propertied) groups in India prevented the extension of franchise to women. The Southborough Committee, appointed to deal specifically with the franchise issue in the course of the formulation of the Montagu-Chelmsford reforms received numerous petitions from educated women, but concluded that female suffrage would be out of harmony with the conservative feeling of the country.[58] Montagu himself hesitated to restrain conservative opposition to women's franchise, urging that this almost 'religious feeling' on the issue would be 'dangerous' to provoke.[59]

It may be noted that the Southborough Committee, constituted to delineate the 'universe' of adult franchise, excluded four

---

[57]Mrinalini Sinha explains the historical processes that constituted the *effiminate babu* in the late nineteenth century. See Mrinalini Sinha (1995, 16–17). Tanika Sarkar considers the emasculation of the colonised to have been achieved by the very fact of colonisation. Manhood being seen in relation to ownership of property, it was this relationship to property that was gradually eroded for the middle classes in the second half of the nineteenth century. See Tanika Sarkar (1992, 213–35).

[58]'Reports of the Franchise Committee and the Committee on Division of Functions', *Indian Constitutional Reforms* (1918–1919, 3).

[59]H. Tata to J.J. Petit (7 December 1919), *AIWC Files*, Joint Select Committee on Government of India Bill, vol. I; 'Report and Proceedings of the Committee', *Parliamentary Papers* (1919), vol. IV, part I of the Preamble.

sections while spelling out the 'qualifications': women; persons under 21 years of age; subjects of a foreign state (but not of a native state in India); and persons of unsound mind. Thus, being a woman reflected an incapacity (as in being underage and of unsound mind) and insensibility (as in being a foreigner) and therefore unsuitability for exercising the vote. This attribute of incapacity was seen again as a civilisational trait, as something emanating from social conditions which were not synchronous with the normative (Western) conditions. It is not surprising, then, that the Southborough Committee considered it premature to extend the vote to women when 'so large a proportion of male electors require(d) *education* in the use of *responsible* vote' (Reports of the Franchise Committee, 1918–19, 4).

While women kept company *en masse* with the irresponsible, immature, unsound, and insensible, ownership of property apparently gave some men the necessary faculty to be responsible electors. The electors were, thus, those (males) in possession of certain property qualification as evidenced by the payment of land revenue, rent or local rates in rural areas, and of municipal rates in urban areas, and of income tax generally (Reports of the Franchise Committee, 1918–19). This limiting of the qualifying criterion solely to possession of property was criticised by others, who pointed out the anomaly of laying down a property qualification while harping at the same time on 'illiteracy' and 'ignorance' as hindrances to adult franchise. N.M. Joshi, a delegate at the Round Table Conference at London in 1930–31 emphasised:

> ...if illiteracy and ignorance is a disqualification, it is a disqualification for all those who are illiterate and ignorant. Unfortunately, that is at present not regarded as a disqualification in our country. People are given vote whether they are literate or illiterate...They are given vote simply because they possess property.[60]

---

[60]N.M. Joshi's deposition before the franchise sub-committee (sub-committee no. VI which was concerned with franchise) of the Indian (*contd.*)

The British legislators took a neutral stance in the debates and, except in Bengal, refrained from voting in the provincial legislatures on the resolution on women's franchise. It is evident that the 'unannounced government policy', as Barbara Southard (1995) calls it, was against giving women the vote.[61] Along with tradition, social conditions and customs became convenient

---

(*contd.*) Round Table Conference, 1930–31. Indian Round Table Conference (12 November 1930–19 January 1931), *Proceedings of Sub-Committees Part II*, 223.

[61]The role of zamindars and title holders, both Hindu and Muslim, and British officials in defeating the suffrage resolution in the Bengal Legislative Council in 1921 was denounced in protest meetings and by the press in Bengal. Mrinalini Sen, vice-president of the Bangiya Nari Sabha (BNS) formed on 13 August 1921 to discuss the resolution on women's suffrage under consideration in the Bengal Council, analysed the defeat as follows: '…most of the Moslem members under the guidance of the Moslem minister and practically all the British official and non-official members and three or four Hindu Landholders who habitually always vote on the official side voted against it in a bulk…'. Southard points out that while the analysis was 'substantially correct', it faltered on two counts: (i) regarding the assessment of the British nonofficial vote, and, (ii) the observation that the Hindu landlords were habitual government supporters. Citing from the proceedings of the Bengal Legislative Council, she shows that of the 15 large landholders or titled aristocrats, 10 were opposed to female suffrage; of the 11 British Legislators 6 voted against and 5 voted in favour, of these 6 out of 7 nominated (official) members voted against, while all the elected (nonofficial) legislators (4) voted in favour. Southard opines that it would be difficult to assume that the private opinions of British official and nonofficial members would differ so radically and prefers to believe that official members' voting against the resolution was more likely to have been an unannounced government policy rather than personal/individual conviction. Again, while the social conservatism of the Hindu landlords is manifested in their voting pattern, their consistent support to government is not brought out equally. Kumar Shib Shekhareshwar Ray vociferous in his opposition to female suffrage was equally vocal in his disagreement to other government policy. On the other hand, P.C. Mitter, elected representative of the landholder constituency and the education minister, voted consistently with the government officials on all bills presented in the Council in 1921, but he voted in favour of women's suffrage. For the details of the voting pattern in the Bengal Council in 1921 see Barbara Southard (1995, 113–24).

parameters for assessing the feasibility of franchise reforms. In the Bengal Legislative Council debates of 1921, the only British official who spoke on the motion highlighted the 'practical difficulties' of giving women the vote (Southard 118). Earlier, the Southborough Committee had cited the 'custom of seclusion followed by many classes and communities', which it felt would prevent female suffrage from becoming a reality.[62]

It may be recalled that the latter half of the nineteenth century had seen both the colonialists and the nationalists rival each other in identifying women as objects to be saved from the effects of a heathen civilisation, or, as in the case of the nationalists, retrieve them as emblems and bearers of the national tradition. In the process, the figure of the colonised woman was inscribed as a monolith. The present period, however, saw the colonialists define their civilising mission differently. As in the construction of the 'bengali babu', the educated product of colonial modernity, as a deviant form of masculinity, the 'new Indian woman', the product of nationalist modernity, was not seen as representing real women. The quintessential Indian woman needing protection was now replaced by the 'poor women' representing millions of ignorant Indians who lived in villages and scorned by the Indian middle class. The Franchise (Lothian) Committee that toured India in 1932 visited the villages to interview 'ordinary people' and see and know for themselves what real women wanted. Ignoring the scare and spectacle the committee created when their ten motorcars roared into the villages, the committee's interpreters ordered people to appear for questioning. Often the women ran away, but on one occasion an elderly widow with inherited property told them that she had always asked her son how to vote. This confirmed the Committee's opinion of villagers as backward and unfit for any form of direct franchise (Forbes 1998, 109).

Although the committee recommended that more women be franchised, to assist social reform, it is significant that the above

---

[62]'Report of the Franchise Committee and the Committee on Division of Functions', *Indian Constitutional Reforms* (1918–19, 4).

experience enlightened the committee not on the absurdity of the existing principle (possession of property) of franchise, but it convinced them of the unsuitability of broadening the bases of franchise. The elderly propertied widow came to signify the backwardness of villagers and became instrumental in excising large numbers of people from the purview of franchise reforms. It may be pointed out that the image of the apathetic, 'progressive women' and their lack of comprehension of the condition of 'masses of women' was also subscribed to by Cornelia Sorabji, whose voice represents a schism within the class of 'respectable' women on the issue of franchise for women. In a confidential memorandum to the government regarding the proposed Montagu-Chelmsfod reforms, Cornelia Sorabji emphasised: '*We* (Indian women) cannot yet make our demands for equal citizenship and equal opportunities—our history forbids this'. Whereas progressive women, Sorabji pointed out, had gone ahead, the majority of women were still illiterate and ignorant. It would be dangerous, she argued, to extend the vote to these 'left behinds' (Forbes, 99).

The spectre of the real women, which continued to haunt women activists in later years, perhaps originated during this period. That real women were poor, rural, and, significantly, traditional was demonstrated also in a nationalist reluctance to effect changes in personal laws. Somehow, the new woman who in the late nineteenth century became the epitome of a reformed, national, tradition now threatened to embarrass the nationalist male before the colonising outsider by asking for changes in their family laws.[63] It was a threat, however, which women activists demanding franchise hoped to ease by persisting with the late nineteenth-century constructions of Indian womanhood and by stressing their own difference from Western women.

On the one hand opposed to the real women, the activist women also ran the danger of being classed as the bazaar women,

---

[63]A similar attempt at defining their citizenship in the emergent polity is seen in roles women envisaged for themselves in planning the economy of the nation. See Chaudhuri (1996).

women in the streets, or of 'manly women'. In the course of the debates on franchise in the Bengal Legislature, the 'gentlemen of the aristocracy' raised the spectre of 'tradition under seige' and warned of the chaos such changes could wreak in the social order. They alleged that only prostitutes/public women, who were free of the constraints of purdah that limited the mobility of respectable women, would benefit by these changes:

> There is a large class of women in almost every bazaar who possess or can possess and I dare say would possess the necessary qualifications by payment of rates and taxes....Our respectable sisters would be nowhere before them, they would be swamped by the formidable numerical strength of these creatures...Their intrusion would be debasing and demoralising.[64]

While other legislatures dismissed such remarks as frivolous and nonissues, the assumption that public women were prostitutes, and prostitutes were not women but creatures, persisted in the definition of true womanhood and delineations of national and cultural identity and citizenship.

In the course of the franchise debates, the monolith Indian women continued to be fractured for convenience into elite women, educated women, real women, poor women, and bazaar women, with the question of who speaks for women's rights assuming focal importance. While the rural, uneducated women gave the coloniser reason to excise large sections of the people from the realm of the political, the compulsion to enlarge the basis of franchise led the Lothian Committee to extend franchise to some women by adding 'wifehood' and 'education' qualifications to the existing qualifications of age and property. Ironically, the basis on which more women were given franchise did not radically change the nature of the electorate in favour of the poor, who had aroused the compassion of the colonisers. If anything, the changes augmented the political power of the

---

[64]Kumar Shib Shekhareshwar Ray, a Hindu aristocrat, made the comments in the Bengal Legislative Council. *Bengal Legislative Council Proceedings* (henceforth BLCP), vol. IV (1 September 1921, 324–25).

propertied classes, further disadvantaging the poor. Women activists were in principle critical of the wifehood and property criteria, which failed to recognise women as individuals. The recommendations of the Lothian Committee were rejected by several women's organisations as violative of their inherent fundamental human rights as citizens and as a 'vitally integral part of the body politic'.[65] The WIA opposed making the citizenship of a woman contingent on her relationship, past or present, to a man, and demanded that in the Declaration in the new constitution, a clause to the effect that 'men and women possess equal citizens rights' and 'no disability should be attached to any citizen on account of sex' should be added. The system of granting votes to women because they were wives or widows of men who possessed the qualification for vote was, they felt, incompatible with the idea of citizenship and equality of women as citizens. (Visweswaran 1990, 39).

Up to this point, two broadly defined premises may be seen as having informed women's demand for franchise: (i) its rootedness within the broader demand for 'universal adult franchise' where the guiding principles were 'fair field and no favours' and a human right to self-determination and dignity; and, (ii) a steadfast refusal to take issue with male nationalists. In other words, an ambivalence in the delineation of citizenship and women's vision of their role in the body politic was rooted in the compulsions of situating 'women's demand' within the wider concern of national sovereignty. Issues of self-determination and sovereignty were frequently expressed by women within a republican framework of basic human rights. Kumudini Bose of the Bangiya Nari Sabha couched her appeal for franchise rights in terms of a basic right women should have as human beings possessing the faculty of reason and judgment. The denial of this basic human right attributed a disability to women as a species from which there appeared to be no redemption.

---

[65]*Annual Report of the All India Women's Conference* (1933–34, 252).

Aliens, lunatics, idiots, children, criminals and women are the persons to whom the franchise has been denied. I leave it to my countrymen to judge with whom the women of their country have been classed and herded together. Minor children will one day become major, lunatics may become sensible and criminals may mend their ways, but a women under the existing arrangement is condemned forever and has absolutely no hope. *Once a woman always a woman.*[66]

It was crucial for women to put their demands in such a manner as to impress male nationalist opinion that giving voting rights to women was both in consonance with the language of equality in the political domain, yet in harmony with tradition; or, inversely, that it was rational because it was in congruence with tradition. While seeking Congress approval for a resolution of woman's suffrage at a special session of the INC in Bombay in August 1918, Sarojini Naidu asserted that extending the franchise to women was rational, scientifically and politically sound, compatible with tradition, and consistent with human rights. While presenting the resolution supporting the vote for women at the thirty-third session of the INC in December 1918, Sarladevi Chaudhurani went beyond Naidu by invoking the principle of equality of all human beings. She stressed that in an age of human rights, justice, freedom, and self-determination, women had as much right as men to chart their own destinies. The world had outgrown certain ideas, she said, particularly the fanciful division of intellect and emotion being the respective spheres of men and women: the 'sphere of women' included 'comradeship with men in the rough and tumble of life and to being the fellow workers of men in politics and other spheres'.[67]

---

[66]The Bangiya Nari Sabha's position on women's suffrage was explained in a series of articles written by Kumudini Bose, published in the journal, *The Servant*. These arguments were later incorporated in a pamphlet which was circulated, used by legislators who favoured suffrage, and also quoted in newspapers. The extract cited above is from the *Statesman* (7 September 1921).

[67]*Report of the Thirty-Third Session of the INC* (Delhi 26–31 December 1918, 118–21).

This articulation of women's political rights within a framework of abstract citizenship was threatened when differences among women surfaced on the issue of reservation of seats for women.

Reserved Seats and Women's Politics

For a long time in the course of the struggle for political rights, women activists had steadfastly refused to endorse the idea of a community of women with special needs and interests distinct from men's, and requiring, therefore, special provisions. A difference among women became apparent, however, on the issue of reservation of seats for women in provincial legislatures. Begum Shah Nawaz and Radhabai Subbarayan, who were appointed by the government as representatives of women at the first Round Table Conference in London, in a departure from the professed position of women's organisations, expressed their support for special reservations, though as a temporary measure.

Unlike the religious minorities or special interest groups like the landed aristocracy and industry, Begum Shah Nawaz and Radhabai Subbarayan did not couch their demands for reservation in terms of a 'wider distribution of power' or a 'declaration of rights' enumerated in a way which made them 'unassailable by a minority community'.[68] On the contrary, they stressed the numerical strength of women ('women constituted one half of the total population') and framed their demands not in terms of a sharing of power, but a sharing of responsibility. Pointing out that 'the political future and welfare of a great section [women]' lay in their 'bear(ing) the full share of *responsibility* in the new India',[69] they drew attention to the inefficacy of the existing franchise qualifications in enabling the

---

[68]See the debate in the Sub-Committee no. III (Minorities) of the Round Table Conference. See Indian Round Table Conference (12 November 1930 to 19 January 1931), *Proceedings of Sub-Committees* (London 1931, 8).

[69]Deposition to the Franchise Sub-Committee by Mrs. Subbarayan. See Indian Round Table Conference (12 November 1930 to 19 January 1931), *Proceedings of Sub-Committees* (London 1931, 231).

women to exercise their responsibility.[70] Significantly both Shah Nawaz and Subbarayan distanced themselves from the *minorities* in the meeting of the Minorities Sub-Committee of the Round Table. Speaking as women they urged the men to be united in a common citizenship. Begum Shah Nawaz persuaded them on behalf of the women of India to come to a settlement: '...as sisters we expect of you, as daughters we beg of you, as mothers we demand of you...'[71] The present, they pointed out, had its difficulties and difference. It was the wonderful future—the development of a common Indian citizenship and Indian nationhood—towards which they asked the men to direct the present.[72]

The Lothian Committee effectively plugged the opposition of nationalist women's organisations by recommending a reservation of 2–10 per cent seats for women in the provincial legislatures for at least ten years.[73] In particular, the communal award, with its provision for communally divided electorates for women, drove a wedge through the public face of unity which the women's organisation had displayed.[74] At least three layers may

---

[70]'Memorandum on the Political Status of Women Under the New Constitution' by Mrs. Subbarayan and Begum Shah Nawaz, Appendix VII, Indian Round Table Conference (12 November 1930 to 19 January 1931), *Proceedings of Sub-Committees* (London 1934, 290).

[71]Deposition by Begum Shah Nawaz at the meeting of the Minorities Sub-Committee. Indian Round Table Conference (12 November 1930 to 19 January 1931), *Proceedings of Sub-Committees* (London 1931, 290, 81).

[72]Radhabai Subbarayan speaking at the meeting of the Minorities Sub-Committee, Indian Round Table Conference (12 November 1930 to 19 January 1931), *Proceedings of Sub-Committees* (London 1931, 290, 80–1).

[73]*Report of the Indian Franchise Committee* (1932, cmd. 4086), vol. I, 86. In its evidence to the committee the AIWC continued its demand of 'adult franchise' and 'fair field and no favours', though as a representative of the WIA, G.J. Bahadurji expressed acceptance for a limited franchise if universal adult franchise was not feasible. A number of other evidences also supported reserved seats for women. They appeared against co-option or nomination of women and favoured the freedom of women to contest their elections in the constituencies. Gail Pearson (1983, 57).

[74]The Lothian Committee met with very few women in India but (*contd.*)

be identified among women on this issue: (i) the nationalist patriots deriving their identity as women from a 'common' and 'equal' citizenship uniting the nation,[75] (ii) women constituting a *we*—identified as a group apart—with special interests requiring special provisions,[76] (iii) minority women, identifying a further specialisation of interest within the category women. It may be pointed out that the emergence of the *we* women and its association with reservation of seats was shortly overshadowed by the nationalist patriotism of women citizens after 1930 under the overriding influence of Gandhi and the national movement. The question of reservation of seats put

---

(*contd.*) accepted a memorandum from the all-India women's organisations. In this document women vented their criticism of all the formulae under consideration: nomination, enfranchising educated women, and the franchise for a percentage of urban women. This was their official stance, though actually there was a great deal of support for special electorates and nominated seats. Amrit Kaur, chairperson of the AIWC in 1932, had to scold Miss Dass, a member from Bihar and Orissa, for organising women's support for a separate electorate: 'Standing Committee members must be loyal', Kaur admonished. Letter from Amrit Kaur to Miss Dass, *AIWC Files*, no. 95 (January 23, 1932).

[75]Sarojini Naidu, for example, argued that the Indian nation ought to have the right to choose every detail of its constitution and that any constitution with safeguards for minorities could not give India freedom. Muthulakshmi Reddy elaborated: '...the only way to bring the Brahmans, the women and the pariahs together on a common platform is by enfranchising the women and the depressed classes on equal terms with others. If the women and the depressed classes are given freedom, power and responsibility, I am sure that they would very soon learn how to rectify the present social evils.' Muthulakshmi Reddy to Eleanor Rathbone, 29 July 1931, RP.

[76]The WIA along with AIWC argued in favour of special representation of women in provincial legislatures in view of the numerous 'social' reform measures which came up in the legislatures for debate. Subbarayan and Shah Nawaz thought that the slogan 'fair field and no favours' was at best illusory, for even with a franchise which produced equal voting power with men, they doubted if 'it would produce any real equality in the political arena'. 'Memorandum on the Political Status of Women Under the New Constitution' by Mrs.Subbarayan and Begum Shah Nawaz, Appendix VII, Indian Round Table Conference (12 November 1930 to 19 January 1931), *Proceedings of Sub-Committees* (London 1931, 290).

women organisations in a situation where the ideal of citizenship, towards which the demand for franchise worked, was fractured by demands for special provisions emanating from among their own ranks. The introduction of minority women as differentiated women problematised both the unitary identity of women and the nationalist patriotism of women citizens.

In significant ways, the issue of reserved seats at this juncture constituted a moment of contest between the nationalist men and an influential section of women within the organisations who were against reservation of seats. The communal award of 1932 introducing separate electorates and including the provision of reserved seats for women was resisted by Gandhi as divisive. While there existed a strong opinion among women that it would be difficult for them to contest elections successfully without such provisions, they supported Gandhi in order not to weaken the nationalist demand. But, when the Poona Pact of September 1932 providing reserved seats for the depressed classes within the Hindu constituency was accepted by Congress leaders, including Gandhi, as a compromise measure, the move was seen by women activists as a betrayal. The Poona Pact and other communal awards were criticised as divisive for women.[77] The AIWC attested to the unity of women at its annual conference at Lucknow in December 1932: 'Our conference has always been united. The Communal Award will divide Indian women. But we so stand for certain ideals and from these we will not budge. No separate electorates and no award is going to separate us.'[78] While some Muslim women, such as Begum Hamid Ali, endorsed the collective stance of the women organisations, a number of Muslim women, including Begum Shah Nawaz, sought to avoid confrontation with Muslim men and dissented, urging that sacrifices [of women's unity] will have to be made for the common good, viz., communal harmony. The favour that separate electorates received from

---

[77]WIA, *AIWC Files*, no. 20, 1932.

[78]Hansa Mehta at the seventh session of the AIWC, Lucknow (December 1932), *Indian Annual Register* (1932, 358).

Muslim women reflected the support the measure had among the Muslim opinion in the country.[79] The unity of women on the issue claimed by the AIWC was a facade that concealed a deliberate obliteration of dissenting voices.[80] The AIWC was, however, vehement in its criticism of what it called a 'humiliating system', which 'ran counter to all real progress'.[81] Women such as Radhabai Subbarayan, who personally favoured reserved seats for women, resented the introduction of the communal principle into the issue. Reiterating that women's seats like seats allocated to those representing labour, landholders, and commerce should be noncommunal, she found it difficult to believe that any woman '...could play her part as an educated and influential citizen if she [was] to enter political life by the communal door and with a communal outlook'.[82]

It is not surprising that the dissenting men saw communally divided electorates for women as the 'extension of a wrong principle into the women's sphere'.[83] The women's sphere in

---

[79]The All Indian Muslim Conference and the All India Muslim League, while supporting the AIWC efforts to enfranchise women on individual merit and not as wives or widows of propertied men, did not agree with the latter's position on communal electorates. In their evidence to the Joint Committee on Indian Constitutional Reforms, the two discussed the question of including women in communal electorates. The general idea that the Muslim community would be at a disadvantage in general elections dominated by Hindus was seen as applicable to Muslim women as well. It was in this context that the communal decision was seen as ensuring representation of Muslim opinion as well as that of Muslim women (Vijay Agnew: 1979, 123).

[80]For example, the dissent of Begum Shah Nawaz was left out from the final report of the AIWC Franchise Committee, because she had not asked for her dissent to be listed. The dissenting note by Muslim women of the Karachi branch of AIWC was ignored on similar grounds. Further, the decision that only majority vote counted meant that the approval to separate electorates given by five Muslim women of Lucknow was seen as numerically irrelevant (Forbes 1979).

[81]*Report of the All India Women's Conference* (1933–34, 182).

[82]*Bombay Chronicle* (22 August 1932, 12).

[83]Minute of Dissent by S.B. Tambe, C.Y. Chintamani, and R.R. Bakhale. *Report of the Indian Franchise Committee*, vol. I, 227.

nationalist imaginings symbolised the sacrosanct unity of the nation, floating pristine amidst the divisions and strife of the political world. In their struggle for political rights, women's organisations, as we shall see shortly, did not contest such constructions, going along with formulations which collapsed womanhood/family with the nation.

Fragmented Women and Gendered Citizens

Two points emerge from our discussion so far. On the one hand, a unified category of women appears unachievable in the face of class and community identities. On the other hand, ideologies of class and community ensure that the category of women, in most cases, signifies the hegemonic propertied and educated women belonging to the majority community. As such the category woman in all its usages is either a fragmented category or an inegalitarian one. Thus, a study of women's rights to vote and political representation at the beginning of this century, while making it a study of a truncated section, nonetheless sheds light on the processes by which this truncated section comes to represent women. Thus, when one says that women got the right to vote between 1921 and 1929, what one actually means is that propertied women got the right. In later years the scope of women was enlarged to include educated women and married, propertied women. Most struggles by women for rights have had to face the pernicious dilemma posed by the impossibility of setting forth a unified category of women. At the same time, as seen in the women's struggle for voting rights, any attempt by women to deny the plurality among them compelled an emphasis on the hegemonic women, and, deriving from this, on the fundamental difference between men and women.

The debate on suffrage in India witnessed women activists' asserting their collective distinctiveness as women seeking, at the same time, to use this distinctiveness to propel them into the anonymous generality of voters and citizens. Kumudini Bose's appeal for the right to political participation for women reiterates the prescription of women's proper place, which is the home, and relieves apprehensions of contest between men and women.

...it is said in the first instance that woman's place is in the home. I do not deny it. No woman ever does. On the other hand every women emphatically claims it as her own world where she is supreme, and all in all the monarch of all she surveys. By getting the suffrage she is not going to be ousted from her home; on the other hand she will, by her vote, influence and control the legislation that is likely to be passed in the Council affecting her home...It is impossible to shut up politics in a compartment and say 'these things are not woman's sphere'. Nothing can be done in the Councils that will affect only one sex. Men and women must work together, the point of view of each being considered for the good and welfare of all.[84]

In a similar vein, Sarojini Naidu dispels (male) fears regarding the enfranchisement of 'Indian womanhood' by assuring that women had no intentions of 'wrench(ing) the power belonging to men': 'Never, never, for we realise that men and women have separate goals and separate destinies and that just as men can never fulfill the responsibility of a woman, a woman cannot fulfill the responsibility of man.' Unless both men and women fulfilled their appointed responsibilities—and here Naidu points at the complementarity of the two sexually differentiated 'horizons'—there could be no fullness or completeness of 'national life'.[85] The emphasis on fulfilment of 'duty' as the basis of claims for rights rather than rights as an enabling condition for the fulfilment of duties is to be noted here.

Notions of sexually defined and differentiated spheres were implicit in the social feminism with which, historically, suffrage movements worldwide have been identified. Indian women, too, claimed political rights on the basis of their usefulness in the life of the nation, but their demands were formulated in an interactive relationship with anticolonial nationalist patriotism,

---

[84]*Amrit Bazar Patrika* (1 September 1921).
[85]Sarojini Naidu, *Speeches and Writings* (1925, 200).

compelling them to stop short of offering a radical critique of the family structure. Women activists in India couched their appeals in a way so as to allay fears of any impending social chaos, the westernisation of Indian women, and the shattering of the premises on which the Indian family (read nation) rested. In their public exhortations, the activists sought to distance themselves from the Western suffragist movement by identifying the differences in their goals and methods. In a speech at a women's college in England, Rameshwari Nehru emphasised that, unlike the suffrage movement in England, the movement in India was a fight against orthodoxy, ignorance, and reaction and not against the other sex. Indian women desired the vote not from a sense of self-aggrandisement but from a desire to fulfil their duties and responsibilities in public life.[86] Similarly, Sarojini Naidu, who had earlier in 1918 assured the INC at its special conference of the compatibility of women's vote with tradition, sketched out at a women's meeting in 1935 the respective fortunes of the suffragette movements in India and the West. The reason why Indian women did not have to 'fight as long and as bitterly' as their Western counterparts lay, according to her, in Indian culture and tradition, which sanctioned equality of women. The cooperation of the male population and the Congress on the matter was, thus, portrayed as symptomatic of this Indian tradition.[87]

The idea that Indian tradition, delineated as belonging to the period chronicled as Hindu, accorded women a high status to which they had to be restored was also evident in a cross-section of male opinion. For example, Professor Hirendranath Dutta, in a speech at a public meeting in Calcutta on 23 August 1921, quoted extensively from the Vedas and Upanishads to argue that modern women in India should be accorded the same status as they had enjoyed in ancient India.[88] Thus, an Indian modernity was selectively sieved from the seams of history and women restored to the status they had purportedly enjoyed in the

---

[86]*Rameshwari Nehru Papers*, Nehru Memorial Museum and Library.

[87]Sarojini Naidu (1925, 194–97).

[88]Letters to Editor, *Amrit Bazar Patrika* (1 September 1921).

'golden age' of India's past. This golden age was frequently contrasted with the 'rigid conservatism' of the medieval period (read Muslim) and the present (in bondage).

The assertion of common bonds of womanhood with Western suffragists was, thus, qualified by a compulsion of complicity with 'their' men. In 1930, both Sarojini Naidu and Begum Shah Nawaz declared that they were not feminists, that there was no such thing as a feminist movement in India, and that there was no need for such a movement because of a high degree of cooperation between men and women in India.[89] Begum Shah Nawaz pointed out the distinctiveness of India to W.A. Jowitt, chairman of the franchise sub-committee of the Round Table Conference: 'There is no such thing as a feminist movement in my country. Both men and women work together and help each other. Our men have been considerate in every way...'.[90] It should be noted that both Begum Shah Nawaz and Radhabai Subbarayan were apologists for reserved seats for women. While the appeal for reserved seats had to be made to the colonial administrator, it was important to emphasise the absence of any antagonism with their men by insisting that the demands for enfranchisement and reserved seats were not feminist demands. Similarly, several years earlier, in her appeal for women's enfranchisement, Kumudini Bose had turned to her countrymen to judge for themselves 'with whom (owing to their disqualification) the women of their country [had] been classed and herded together'.[91] Again, Anusuyabehn Sarabhai seconding the resolution on women's suffrage rights on equal terms as men, which resolution was passed by the INC at its special session in 1918, appealed to the self-respect of her countrymen.

---

[89]Sarojini Naidu, 'Presidential Address', AIWC, *Indian Annual Register* (20 January 1930, 363).

[90]Begum Shah Nawaz, Franchise Sub-Committee Meeting (30 December 1930), Indian Round Table Conference (12 November 1930 to 19 January 1931, 260), *Proceedings of Sub-Committees* Part II.

[91]Kumudini Bose, *The Statesman* (7 September 1921).

You have sympathy for women, will you keep them without rights in subjection—ultimately to turn into rebels? You are all assembled here to preserve your self-respect, to free yourself from the fetters of dependency…I therefore ask you to look upon it as an insult. I therefore ask you my countrymen, whether you will deny to your sisters the rights you demand for yourself.[92]

The idea that the women's struggle for franchise in India was distinctive and did not involve the 'war of sexes' and 'smashing of heads' was also endorsed by sections of male opinion.

It is gratifying to find that in a country where men are accused of treating women as chattels the political progress of women has been more rapid than in England and free from the war of sexes and the smashing of heads and windows which preceded the enfranchisement of women in England.[93]

In subtle ways, Indian suffragists distanced themselves from the guiding hands of British feminists. Carrie Chapman Catt, in her presidential address to the International Women's Suffrage Alliance in 1913, revelled in the 'earnest hope' that her recent tour of Asia would assure that other women, 'comprehending the unity of the women's cause', will be led to carry the inspiration and unity of the movement to the women of Asia, who needed the encouragement and 'practical advice' of Western women. Implicit in the proclaimed 'unity of the movement', however, was a condescending extension of sisterhood and a denial of coevalness to the less privileged Asian sisters. While Western women had emancipated themselves from the most severe mandates of tradition, Asian women, she felt, '*must* continue to struggle under conditions which obtained in [our] Western world *some generations ago*'. This privileged discourse of international sisterhood throve not only on the knowledge that the Asian women lived in societies several generations behind and that they must continue to struggle, but also in the belief

---

[92]*Report of the Special Session of the Indian National Congress*, held on September 1918, 112.

[93]N.M.Dumasia, member of legislative assembly, cited in Forbes 'Votes for Women' in Vina Mazumdar (1979, 6).

that they had long been waiting in a state of inertia with 'rebellion in their hearts' for a liberator—the emancipated Western woman equipped with her knowledge and practical advice.

> ...Behind the purdah in India, in the harems of Mohammedanism, behind walls and barred doors, and closed sedan chairs, there has been rebellion in the hearts of women all down the centuries. There compelled to inactivity, they have been waiting, waiting for a liberator.[94]

Margaret Cousins' memoirs are also interspersed with moments assuming similar privileged knowledge and a distancing which such privilege necessarily involved.

> ...*only I can tell* what led to the vote on women's suffrage in the Provincial Legislative Council of the United Provinces in 1923...to sit there and hear those Indian politicians, and to watch the record being made of a unanimous vote being given in favour of granting women the favour—and that in a province as large as Great Britain. How happy I was amongst my honoured Indian sisters; how glad we had gathered them there (Cousins 1947).

Reactions to Western women's endeavours to save their little brown sisters (recall Katherine Mayo's *Mother India*) centred on the high status of women in Indian homes. Idealisation of the role of women in the home formed the core of such responses. Begum Shah Nawaz remarked: 'In that little kingdom [home] she is not only in charge of finance and of home and foreign affairs, but she is also the custodian of future generations'.[95] Sarojini Naidu preferred to describe a woman as 'the high priestess of home' (Naidu 1925, 199). Both Begum Shah Nawaz and Sarojini Naidu argued that women should be given the right to vote precisely because of their special and predominant role

---

[94]Carrie Chapman Catt cited in Kamla Visweswaran (1990, 42).

[95]Begum Shah Nawaz, Franchise Sub-Committee Meeting (30 December 1930), Indian Round Table Conference (12 November 1930 to 19 January 1931, 260), *Proceedings of Sub-Committees* Part II.

in the household. Begum Shah Nawaz felt that women could deal with the vote and the affairs of the nation because of the administrative skills they had learned in the home: 'Let me point out that a woman is a born administrator, for although the man is the breadwinner, the virtual ruler of the home is the woman.'[96] Naidu believed that the vote was essential for women to imbue their children with the ideals of nationalism (Naidu 1925, 199). The opening lines of Radhabai Subbarayan's convocation address to the Indian Women's University at Poona in August 1933 imply that Indian women's high status in the home is due to the respect given to them by Indian men. the status of women was indeed,. 'one of the most remarkable traits of our national character', which was 'not intelligible' to Western women because of the differences between the two cultures.[97]

The reference here is to 'unpleasant instances' when 'mischievous' visitors from the West after rather 'hurried visits' published their memoirs, presenting them 'to the world as the tale of Indian Civilisation' (Subbarayan 1933, 491). In a speech in London, Sarojini Naidu similarly contested the civilising mission of British feminists: 'Devotion, courage, self-sacrifice, the heroic virtue of quiet daily drudgery, and the more epic ability to face grave and unexpected crises, are not qualities taught by women of one race to another…', even while asserting solidarity with them as women:

> There is no difference between the Eastern woman and Western woman. Beneath all the differences of race, creed, and colour lies the bond that unites all women—a truly international sisterhood which makes all womanhood one. It is a mistake to speak of the debt the womanhood of one nation owe the women of another, for all womanhood is indivisible (Naidu 1931, 86).

Emphasising a shared common oppression as the basis of

---

[96]Begum Shah Nawaz, Franchise Sub-Committee Meeting, 30 December 1930, Indian Round Table Conference, (12 November 1930 to 19 January 1931, 260), *Proceedings of Sub-Committees* Part II.

[97]See Radhabai Subbarayan, *Stri Dharm*, (August 1933), 491.

international sisterhood, Naidu, thus, highlights the relatively dominant position of the Western women and the hierarchy within the sisterhood. Again, even as she unravels the monolith women to point out the racial/colonial inequalities, Naidu retrieves the emblematic woman and emphasises the positive qualities women share in common, namely, 'devotion, courage, self-sacrifice'.

This emphasis accorded to women's pristine, predominant, and indispensable position of responsibility in the home, as also the importance of the judicious exercise of this responsibility to the life of the nation, reinscribed the home as the site where the nation was being built and consolidated. The home was set up as an organic unit of the nation and its constituent (normative) elements (the relationship between a man and woman and their children) reflected the harmony and unity of the nation. The woman's role as mother in the family and the various special functions which emanated from her focal role as mother were taken as a measure of her participation in the nation: 'The family is the unit, the country or nation is composed of many such units, so the mother in the making of good laws and the formation of good governments'.[98] During the course of the debates on women's political rights, we see the usage of family and nation in terms which make the latter a projection of the former and the nation increasingly defined in familial terms.

It is interesting that, more often than not, the core ideas of an array of ideological positions on women's franchise were drawn from the notion of the familial nation. Masculinist narratives, both in favour of and against the vote for women, framed their arguments within the general framework which collapsed family and nation and womanhood and motherhood. They confirmed the broader consensus prevalent in a cross-section of the population active in the debate on women's proper place, despite existing disagreements on the question of women's suffrage. The debates in the various legislative councils and women's

---

[98]Muthulakshmi Reddy, part II, 'Women's Role in Society', cited in Kamala Visweswaran (1990, 46).

campaigns to garner the support of the legislative councilors reaffirmed the collapsing of womanhood with motherhood, the home with the nation, and the distancing of women's specific social activities from the political activities of men. Those in favour of the vote argued that women's maternal role of exercising guidance over their children enabled them to determine the laws guiding an entire population. Those against women's suffrage turned the argument around saying that participation of women in public life would injure family life and distract responsible mothers from domestic duties. The special ethical qualities of women were emphasised by pro-suffrage legislators as qualities that could purify the political arena. The 'spiritual' attributes of Indian womanhood were thus highlighted:

> It has also been urged that politics is a dirty game and that women should not get near it. Is not life itself, as we find it in this happy world of ours, a dirty game too. To whom do we look to purify our everyday existence? To women undoubtedly. So let politics be purified by the association of all that is best and noblest in the womanhood of our country.[99]

Thus, an attempt was made to premise the equality of women with men on their difference from men, a position from which women suffragists did not distance themselves. Women were pictured as a distinctive group that required the vote in order to push social and educational reforms, which would in the long run, benefit the country. Interestingly, those against enfranchisement used the same arguments to plead against the suitability of women for public life. Her 'milder qualities', 'graces of person', 'the constitution of her body and inherent periodical disabilities' provided women the 'aptitude to make her a useful wife and loving mother'. The same qualities, however, made her 'essentially unfit for outdoor work or for the matter of that, for

---

[99]Manmatha Nath Ray Chaudhary, *BLCP*, vol. IV (2 September 1921, 385).

administration and defense of the country...[and for that reason] franchise could not be her birthright'.[100]

It is not surprising, therefore, that women's struggle for the vote and attempts to be part of the electoral process were seen as attempts to combine the social (public/political) with the 'sexual' (private) that interfered, thereby, with the order of sexual roles and class propriety. The perceived threat saw the 'moral issue' being raised in some quarters. Kumar Shib Shekhareshwar Ray's outburst against the corrupting effects of enfranchisement has been noted earlier. Syed Nasim Ali, a legislator in the Bengal Council, likewise exhorted 'every Muhammadan member' of the Council to 'place a hand on his breast' and confess if he actually 'wants that his *zenana* should be dragged out of the purdah'. Following the defeat of the resolution in Bengal, Margaret Cousins described these male fears as an 'exaggeration of facts into fiction'.

> They exaggerated the fact that about one woman to every eight men might (not must) vote in three years into the fiction that every women would compulsorily keep voting all the time and meals would not be cooked. They inflated the fact that purdah polling stations would be provided into which women might enter as unseen as into a ladies carriage, into the terror that 'sexes would mix promiscuously' and that 'Islam did not want Muhammadan women to go hand in hand with men to bazaars, Councils and Courts' (See Reddy 1956, v–vi).

A persistent dilemma for the women activists, therefore, was how to gain admission into the public sphere without generating disruptive identities of manly women or street women and being targeted as instruments of social disorder. The escape from this dilemma was found in the definition of womanhood and women's role in the public-political in terms premised on class distinctions. Under compulsions dictated by a masculinist/nationalist framework, the women suffragists delineated their public-political role in spiritual terms and as comparable to

---

[100]Khan Bahadur Maulavi Wasimuddin Ahmed, *BLCP* (449).

household work. Thus, the contours of a domain of womanly activity—the 'social'—were drawn within the public-political and invested with moral responsibility and respectability. The social was distinguished from the private space of the household as well as from spaces in the public-political, defined as areas of male participation. It also excluded 'public spaces' like the bazaar identified with street women. The social was characterised by a life of charitable abstinence and sacrifice, spiritual participation of respectable women, and higher moral intervention of women for sorting out social problems. By doing so, women were able to collapse the social and political while emphasising their own contribution to this collapsed world in spiritual terms (Jimenez-Munoz 1993). The blurred distinction between women's spiritual participation and such participation within the electoral arena became an important emblem of women's suffrage supporters. Margaret Cousins, for example, insisted that the women's vote, when well-organised by women's associations, for advancing specific interests relating to women such as education, health, morality, prohibition, children's bills, etc., 'may easily be the determining factor in an election result' (Cousins 1921, 328–30). This specific form of participation was seen as enhancing the ethical levels and usefulness of legislative activity, promoting social and public responsibilty.

Conclusion

In this chapter we have analysed the broader social and political meanings and context of the efforts to enfranchise women in the early part of this century. Giving voting rights to Indian women was an issue braided within the questions of the status of India/Indians within the British Empire and of the character and extent of rights to which the subject population was entitled. The imperial ideology of racial, civilisational, and gender differences prepared the ground for the spatial and temporal distancing of the colonised and the deferral and denial of conditions which were considered the legitimate rights of the people in the metropole. The nature and course of the debate was determined largely by the (colonial) relationship between India and Britain, especially at a time of a growing crisis of legitimacy for the colonial government in the face of a popular national movement for self-determination. At this historical juncture, the issue of franchise signified a claim to the exercise of political rights of citizenship that was being denied to the colonised subjects.

The liberatory promise of the suffrage movement lay in the integration of women in the constitutional process and the construction of their political identity as citizens. Women suffragists, however, carried the burden of their ascriptive identity as women into the public sphere. In other words, in the process of asserting their suitability for political participation, they nonetheless bound themselves firmly in their sexualised roles. The liberatory agenda for women, based on the struggle for the vote, unfolded a dilemma, which turns up at every historical moment when women have sought to present themselves as a unified body for the purposes of enlarging their rights. Women seek to assert their separate identity as women, while attempting to submerge themselves in the generality and anonymity of abstract citizenship. At the same time, as seen in the suffrage debates, the definition of womanhood is itself inegalitarian, referring only to the propertied and educated elite. All the same, notwithstanding the fact that it did not contest women's place within the family, the struggle for the vote did emerge in the context of anticolonial movements as a radical demand for equality and for a share for women in the political domain. The silence and subsequent depoliticisation of the women's question, which Partha Chatterjee sees as having followed its nationalist resolution, was interrupted by women's organised struggles and debates in public/political/elected bodies. The resolution was prised open by women for scrutiny, renegotiation, and contestation. This opening up of the women's question reverberated in numerous struggles by women to influence the terms of their incorporation as citizens in the emergent national state. In the chapter that follows we shall investigate how the embedment of women in the national community and cultural-religious community has had important implications for articulating women's citizenship and women's politics. It explores the nature of the language of citizenship that arose at the conjuncture of anticolonial struggles in India and points out the manner in which the nation and the cultural-religious community emerged as the organising principles of a resisting identity and the basis of self-determination, sovereignty, and citizenship.

5

The Nation and its 'Constitution': The Text and Context of Citizenship

The Constitution of India ushered in two sovereigns—a sovereign republic of India, formally constituted with the adoption of the Constitution, and 'we', 'the people', the sovereign citizens of India, who 'gave' themselves the Constitution. The ideas of freedom, justice, and equality, the driving forces in the struggle for self-determination, were included as the foundational principles of a democratic society that the Constitution was expected to usher in. The significance of the nationalist project has been seen to lie in the generation of this 'republican-democratic project' and the balance that it purportedly achieved after 1947 between the upper-caste Congress culture, a republican notion of citizenship with concessions to oppressed castes, and a concept of secularism which sought to recognise and preserve plural identities. The precarious balance that the Constitution sought to build between the national-political community and social-cultural communities, on the one hand, and the abstract individual citizen, on the other, has been tested increasingly in the past years by claims emphasising one over the other. The failure to address people's radical aspirations that were unleashed in the struggles before independence against multifarious structures of oppression has manifested itself in tensions between the concept of citizenship in the Constitution and the hegemonic project of nation-building, which has continually defined membership of the nation in exclusionary terms. The metaphorical pan-Indian wave of anti-imperialism on which the nationalist elite rode has, it appears, descended and splintered into innumerable movements focussing on issues of caste, class, religion, environment, women, etc., belying the nationalist history of inarticulate peasants and spiritual mothers. The present chapter explores the nature of the language of citizenship which arose at the historical juncture of the anticolonial movement in India, the forms in which it got ensconced within the emergent constitution, and the implication of the primacy of collective rights on the rights of women as citizens in the context of ambivalently defined identities of citizenship.

The Nation, Community, and the Citizen

Citizenship, as a legal status and as the organising principle for a sovereign nation and democratic political society, was incorporated in the Indian Constitution in the context of the struggles for self-determination waged against multilayered oppressive structures and discursive constructions of racial and caste superiority. While resistance against oppression spanned all the regions of India and manifested itself in various forms and at diverse sites, it may, even at the risk of simplification, be seen as aspiring to invert oppressive structures at two broad 'layers'[1] of 'collective' bondage: against a hierarchically organised scheme of social relations marked by ascriptive inequalities; and

---

[1]The use of the term 'layer' does not intend to collapse the movements into a hierarchy of types. It rather intends to distinguish between two broad vocabularies of struggle against oppression.

the dominance-subordination relationship between the coloniser and colonised. At both these layers of collectively experienced oppression, attempts were made to articulate the nation/ community as the organising principle of a resisting identity and the basis of self-determination, sovereignty, and citizenship. Within this context, the cultural/religious community, on the one hand, and the national-political community, on the other, acquired equivocal primacy.

Within a hierarchically organised scheme of social relations marked by ascriptive inequality sustained by inequitable power distribution and legitimised by religious beliefs, sanctions, and practices, resistance took the form of struggles against entrenched feudal-Brahmanical-ritual authority and their collusive dominance with (and as) colonial administrators.[2] Innumerable struggles took place against collectively experienced repression and humiliation, rallying around issues of education, respectability of social status, opportunities of occupation and vertical mobility, and improvement of economic status. These anticaste and antifeudal struggles could be seen as aspiring, in their cumulative capacity, to create a civil society in which ascriptive hierarchies of power relations were dismantled and

---

[2]The caste system, a hierarchical system of ascriptively segmented occupational and endogamous castes, manifested differential distribution of power-privileges, and, alternatively, disabilities, sanctified by the dominant (Brahmanic) religious tradition. With regional and intra-regional differences and unevenness, this hierarchical system for more than a millennium manifested remarkably uniform features all over India with the Brahmins at the top, followed by other literary, propertied, and clean castes, and the shudras, the labouring and polluting castes, at the bottom. This religious hierarchy of purity and pollution was mirrored in the production relations and ownership patterns and also found expression in an unequal privilege/disability structure in public life. Colonial intervention did not do away with the old forms and structures of subordination. If anything, it deepened the already existing cleavages. Within the evolving structures of colonial rule, the upper/ruling strata of society, consisting of the Brahmins and other *dwij* castes, were empowered, enlarged and even nationalised. For a discussion of the impact of colonial rule on the 'old order' of Indian society see G.Aloysius, *Nationalism Without a Nation in India* (1997, 21–51).

democratised, through 'an egalitarian spread of power'. These movements signified the emergence of a national-political community—the process of the 'becoming a nation'—as rooted in the idea of sovereign personhood and peoplehood and its formal 'affirmation' within the nation-state through the notions of citizenship and territoriality.[3]

The other instance of collective experience of bondage emanated from the dominance-subordination relationship between the 'Indians' and the 'British'—the coloniser and the colonised. The struggle to invert this 'collective bondage' took the form of *the* national movement for self-determination and sovereignty. The national movement pitted against colonial rule was, however, ambivalently articulated. There appears to have been an aspiration on the one hand for greater share in the governance of the country, reflected in demands of greater opportunities for participation in the central and provincial legislatures and the executive councils, as by the Liberals and Swarajists in the early part of the century. On the other hand, this contest also took the form of noncooperation and civil disobedience in the event of failed expectations as was the case with the Indian National Congress on most offers of constitutional 'reforms'. It is significant that the form and substance of civil disobedience, as articulated by Gandhi, derived from a distrust of the oppressive structures of the modern state, much of which emanated from Gandhi's experiences with the colonial state in South Africa and India[4] and which congealed his commitment to a moral right of the individual to rebel.

---

[3]G. Aloysius describes this process as *homogenisation of power within culture*, in the sense of an even distribution of power and as instrumental in bringing about the nation as a new form of congruence between power and culture. The premodern form of the culture-power fusion was unequal and hierarchical legitimised by Brahmanic tradition and the (present) collusive, colonial power structure (ibid, 52–92).

[4]It is significant that Rabindranath Tagore while defining a 'nation' as an 'aspect of a whole people organised for power', rejects the modern (political/nation-state) form that it takes as 'gigantic organisations for hurting (*contd.*)

At both these layers of collective bondage, attempts were made to articulate the nation as the basis of self-determination, sovereignty, and citizenship. The constitution/formation of a distinctive identity as the basis for the assertion of sameness and an equitable distribution of power became an important condition/ context for liberatory change. The nation as the source of one's *own* distinctive past became at this historical conjuncture an important resource for the constitution of a resisting/liberatory identity. The construction of a distinctive identity as a nation involved not only the 'liberation' of one's 'own' culture from the limiting influences of other cultures, but also a distancing from past forms of unequal and hierarchical distribution of power. Thus, becoming a nation ultimately involved a struggle for equality wherein the 'past' formed the basis and source of self-determination of the national community (or the cultural collectivity) in its totality and also of each of its constituent members, who, breaking themselves free from ascriptive identities and hierarchies, constituted a civil society of citizens.[5]

(*contd.*) others', for 'making money by dragging others back' and for 'seriously impeding *our* freedom'. The *our* in Tagore's formulation, is 'the larger life of a higher civilization', that of the larger humanity. This formulation of freedom as embracing the entire humanity has been compromised because of colonisation. Since India has been ruled and dominated by a nation that is 'strictly political in its attitude', he points out, 'we [too] have tried to develop within ourselves, despite our inheritance from the past, a belief in our eventual political destiny'. See Rabindranath Tagore, *Nationalism* (1917, 97–112).

[5]We must recall here the Marshallian paradigm of development of citizenship, and its promise of full and equal membership of the political community. An important aspect of this membership was minimum social status as the basis for the exercise of civil and political rights or the right to 'live the life of a civilised being according to the standards prevailing in society'. These standards of life and the access to social heritage comprise a broader notion of citizenship (as equality) involving, as Bryan Turner points out, 'the question of social membership and participation in society as a whole' (Turner 1986, 85). Essential to this is a decline in the dominance of hierarchical social structures and the emergence of egalitarian horizontal relationships. The transition to the nation thus signified the continual movement towards the achievement of this (egalitarian) social membership. A.D. Smith points (*contd.*)

The nation, thus, became a vitalising source for large masses of people, whose feeling of unity as a 'people' drew sustenance not only from a shared past but also from a commonality of political purpose and destiny. It became constitutive of their political identity as citizens, as equal members of a political community with not only an equal claim to its past but also to its future. The masses of men and women, who were hitherto excluded from the arena of public power through ascriptive, hierarchical, structures of privileges in society and dynastic rule in polity, emerged politically in this construction and transfer to nation to constitute the new politico-civil society of equal rights and liabilities (Aloysius 1997, 52–92).

It must be borne in mind, however, that while the struggles at both the aforementioned layers unfolded simultaneously, their social bases and aspirations were almost antagonistic. Their construction of the past, which became the source of pride and a resisting identity for equality, was disparate; the forms of resistance were divergent; and visions of the future were dissimilar. In other words, not only was the 'past' of the 'nation' imagined differently at these layers of contestation, the future of the national community was envisaged divergently. The struggle for democratisation of power across a national community, for example, placed the dominant structures of the old (fedual-Brahmanical-patriarchal) order as an adversary to be rolled back. The 'old order' was, however, embedded in the folds of the dominant power structures to such an extent that it opposed these reversive forces not only for the erosions they made into its traditional domain of power, but also on account of the effect of these forces on their bargaining capacity vis-a-vis the coloniser. It is significant that most instances of resistance and struggles mentioned as constituting this layer of struggle would appear to have been outside the scope of the 'pan-Indian' struggle that was being waged by the 'nationalist' against the 'pan-Indian' colonial

---

(*contd.*) out that nationalism as self-determination for the cultural collectivity is inextricably tied to nationalism as self-determination of the individuals within that collectivity. The two are but phases of a single move towards modernity and nationalism. A.D.Smith, *Theories of Nationalism* (1983, 67).

state. The success of this 'pan-Indian' struggle was significantly dependent on the presentation of the struggle as a harmonious aspiration of the people as a whole. The invocation of harmony required a normalisation of these diverse 'micro-levels of struggles' into that for national independence and their simultaneous exclusion/distancing from the national-political by attributing them labels such as 'communal' or 'social/cultural', as opposed to 'national' and 'political'.

Inadequate citizens and the rule of colonial difference

At the interface of these broad frameworks of resistance, the colonial state staked its claims to exclusive sovereignty and to 'legitimately' (re)order the lives of its subjects. This involved not merely the distancing of the 'modern' colonial state from previous (native) regimes of power, but involved also, at a more practical level, the compulsion to 'reconcile with the law and customs of the people' and to build a 'social constituency' which legitimised colonial rule. This social constituency was not a homogenous entity and its diverse strands were differentially situated, often in conflict with one another. Perhaps the greatest dilemma for the colonial state was to present 'a rational justification of colonial rule', particularly with regard to the differences in the practices of rule at 'home' and in the colony. In order to show that the rule of difference was commensurate with the principle of universality of Western modernity, colonial conditions were classified and slotted within the universal framework as deviations from the norm. This 'rationalised' the differences between the metropolis and colony as differences on a scale of 'social conditions' that explained why ruling the colony could not be a simple transference of the norms and practices of the modern state and economy from Britain, with the implication that an advance along the scale would justify practices closer to the norm.[6] The rational justification of the colonial state also

---

[6]Partha Chatterjee, 'Was There a Hegemonic Project of the Colonial State?', in *Contesting Colonial Hegemony*, eds. Dagmar Engels and Shula Marks (1994, 82).

required the internalisation of the rational bureaucratic norms by the colonised as indicators of 'advance along the scale'. This agency (English-educated middle class) created outside the colonial state to 'transform the indigenous tradition into universal forms of rational and scientifically ordered social life' resulted in what Partha Chatterjee calls the 'fundamental paradox' (Singh 1998, 11). This paradox manifested itself in the struggle for equality with the colonial state by the nationalist elite. The 'native' middle class was strategically situated in this contest insofar as it spoke the same language as that of the colonisers. The peasants and other subaltern classes—the mass bases of popular struggle against the colonisers—were distant as well as distanced from this contest. They were distanced from the dominant levels of discourse owing to their subalternity. The subtle nuances of the postures of the elites engaged in an intricate war of positions made the contest distant from their immediate struggles.

Owing to its precarious location at the intersection of multiple 'publics', the legitimation task of the colonial state was fraught with complexities. The British public, which was by no means an undifferentiated entity, was perhaps the primary audience to which the colonial state, as the delegate of the British parliament in the colony, had to present its reformist credentials. In the colony, the reformist agenda seems to have been split into two. One creating a 'modern' public—a replication of the public at the metropolis—and the other catering to the traditional native elite. Towards the beginning of the twentieth century, the colonial state attempted to steer clear of 'non-political' matters while bringing in piecemeal constitutional reforms, pacifying, thus, the native elite, who were seen by the government as allies, and keeping in suspended animation, from one reform to the other, the bulk of the nationalist elite struggling for enhanced civil rights that would eventually lead to 'self government'. To the majority at large—the 'subalterns' —the colonial state had to project itself as their protector against both the 'native' agencies within the colonial administration and from their immediate oppressors without disturbing, however, the traditional balance of power and the profitability of colonial (extractive/exploitative) rule.[7]

Citizenship, thus, presents a useful vantage point to explore the relationship between the colony and the metropole. It emerges as a category to which the colonised was not only external but whose exclusion was necessary for its universality and its elements of equality and rights. Subjecthood but not citizenship was the corner stone of imperial ideology, as the native was never considered adequate to be a citizen (Chakrabarty 1992, 6). While agreeing that an 'imperial state cannot function in the same way as a nation-state, nor can it create a role for its subjects that approximates that of the citizens' (Freitag 1991, 1), it must be emphasised that colonial encounters were marked by 'national-cultural/racial hierarchy and inequality' and the construction of categories such as 'race', 'nationality', and 'ethnicity', which were socially produced and 'naturalised' in various ways.[8] Narratives of feminisation and infantilisation

---

[7]Radhika Singha discusses the intricacies of the formation of the colonial state and the curdling of colonial authority in India particularly the processes by which an embryonic colonial state, epitomised by the East India Company, sought to congeal its claims to 'legitimately' (re)order the lives of its subjects by invoking a system of criminal justice which was different from past penal practices. In the discussion in the Epilogue, she shows the slenderness of the 'social constituency' of the colonial state and proposes that the claims of the colonial state to legitimately reorder the lives of its subjects was based upon the consent of a largely truncated audience. Its location at the intersection of diverse publics, often at odds with one another, made the reformist agenda of the colonial state a veneer behind which it could function only as a benevolent despot. See Radhika Singha, *A Despotism of Law: Crime and Justice in Early Colonial India* (1998).

[8]Kelvin Santiago-Valles, 'Trying to Pin Myself in History: Race, Sex and Colonialism' (1993, 73–7). In another work, Santiago-Valles points out that similar to what colonial capitalism had done and continued to do with respect to the 'Indians', 'negroes', 'the Latin race' and the 'heathen Chinee' in North America, the 'new overseas colonies' of 'Porto Rico', the Philippines, Hawaii, Guam, the Panama Canal Zone together with occupied Cuba, provided the North American coloniser 'an additional socioeconomic and textual space in which to reinscribe the discourse of Western-masculinist and cultural-national/racial superiority within a mythical sense of superclass homogeneity. But, (*contd.*)

were resorted to by the colonisers to decipher the 'nature' of the 'native' and the question of the degree of political responsibility with which they (or the various sectors of the population, for example, women) could be entrusted. The exclusionary domain of citizenship was very much conditioned in this context by the way women, slaves, workers, and subject peoples as social categories and as lived experiences were simultaneously incorporated within and omitted from national-cultural and juridicopolitical identities as citizens:

> Of course there have been many instances of brutality, cupidity and stupidity by the conquerors, but, by and large, the subject nations have benefited. To begin with, in all logic, as a rule, the conquering nation has been more civilised, certainly the more virile. During the period of its domination, it has brought the subject people into contact with knowledge they did not possess, schooled them or vitalised them.[9]

The depoliticisation of the colonised subjects took place by a hierarchical construction of masculinity. Manhood and 'solid citizenship' being seen in relation to ownership of property, it was this relationship to property and selfhood that was gradually eroded for the middle classes in the second half of the nineteenth century (Sarkar 1992, 213–35). Colonisation itself signified emasculation through denial of use of one's property.[10]

(*contd.*) the discourse of racial childhood and of feminisation of the 'lesser races' had corollary sources of formation as well. The discussion on whether to grant new Caribbean wards US citizenship or, much less, self-governance exemplifies the gender and age-graded signification practices of the new colonialists. See Kelvin Santiago-Valles, '*Subject People' and Colonial Discourses: Economic Transformation and Social Disorder in Puerto Rico, 1898–1947* (1994).

[9]Theodore Roosevelt, Jr., *Colonial Policies of the United States*, 1937 (ibid, vi).

[10]The rights of the colonised to choose their representatives were associated with the holding of property. The absence of the vote for the millions of colonised men and women made the struggle for the vote a terrain where complex ideological formulations took place, so much so that within this discursive domain, all without the vote were 'women'/emasculated/exhibiting effeminate characteristics.

Emasculation emerged also as a 'specific practice of ruling'. By what has been called the 'colonial ordering of masculinity', the coloniser privileged himself in relation to the colonised. An exploration of the historical processes that constituted the 'effiminate babu' in the late nineteenth century shows that while broad generalisations about the mild-mannered and effete nature of inhabitants of certain regions in India or believers of certain Indian religions were long part of the stock of ideas held by Europeans and even Indians themselves, this characterisation acquired a specific meaning in the political and economic context of the late nineteenth century. Over time, effiminacy had evolved from a loosely defined attribute associated with the entire population to specifically include the politically discontented middle-class 'natives' from all over India, specifically the babus or the Western-educated Indians, a large majority of whom were Bengali Hindus. The concept reflected the new development in colonial society: the political challenge posed by the Indian middle class to certain exclusive British rights and privileges in India. It was this shift in British colonial attitudes towards Western-educated Indians, from mediators between the colonial administration and the rest of the Indian population to an unrepresentative and artificial minority representing nothing but the anomalies of their own situation, that was signalled by the late nineteenth-century concept of the 'effiminate babu' (Sinha 1995, 16–17). The problem of accommodating the large numbers of Western-educated Indians, which gave rise to what Partha Chatterjee has termed the 'fundamental paradox' of colonialism, was in a major way responsible for such a construction. The colonial administration was faced with the daunting task of accommodating a growing number of these Indians within the existing colonial administrative and political structures without threatening the exclusive rights and privileges to which generations of colonial officers and nonofficials in India had grown accustomed. The only way these products of colonial rationality could be rendered unproductive was through effeminate representations. The racial exclusiveness of the colonial rulers was preserved, thus, by bringing in a gender hierarchy between manly and unmanly men.

An inherent 'lawlessness' and 'violence' was attributed to the nature of the subject populations pointing thereby to the difference in racial and civilisational time in which the coloniser and the colonised existed. This denial of co-evolution not only justified the latter's 'disciplining' and repression, but also conjured a blurring of the identity of the victim and the aggressor. The response of the home member on suggestions of the 'arbitrary nature' of 'un-British' colonial laws reveals an extraordinary inversion of the victim-oppressor positions. 'It is to us that the odious nature of an arbitrary law is more apparent. It is we who in our country enjoy the utmost liberty...that are shocked that such laws should have been made'. Their troubled minds are, however, set to rest by reconciling themselves to this necessity, however disagreeable, and the assurance that

> *our* system can never see these laws; we shall never see them in England. But England is a settled civilised country. These laws are applicable in India and the colonies where a handful of white people have to maintain themselves against lawlessness, sometimes violent people.[11]

Representing the sovereign people

Ironically, the nationalist project of assertion of equality with the colonisers took the form of displacement of their 'inadequacy' onto the peasants and workers. The language of political representation, citizenship, and citizen's rights became the prerogative of the nationalist elite as part of the project of nation building. In the crucial test of whether or not the nationalist movement and its leaders envisaged a different kind of political community, a polity of anonymous and equal citizens 'the nationalists failed miserably', avers Aloysius. While claiming the monopoly of representing the whole nation, the nationalists

---

[11]See Srinivas Shastri, *The Indian Citizen* (1948, 42–3), (emphasis added).

consistently demonstrated their Brahmanical-feudal, sectarian character.[12]

Laying claims to being the sole and legitimate representatives of the 'people' involved a 'sifting' between the political/national and social/communal concerns (Singh 1998). Aloysius points out that the political vs. social reform debate/controversy within the Congress reflects the attempt by the latter to take a (preeminent) stand with reference to other political forces. It is not surprising that what was construed as 'social' and subsequently excluded from the national-political agenda enveloped the entire gamut of radical-structural changes sought by the antifeudal, anticaste struggles against the traditional Brahmanical order. Thus, what was being 'understood' as social was in fact not 'merely social or cultural, local or regional but truly political and national' affecting the monopoly of power within the Brahmanical social order. The nationalists' preoccupation with 'the expansion of their own share in the bureaucratic and legislative power structure' involved taking care that all the power that accrued to them was absorbed by them and did not overflow their 'own narrow circle'. Since social questions were seen as divisive, it was ruled that only political questions of national importance would be relevant. This was tantamount to saying that questions relating to the transfer of power to the sole representatives, that is, the Indian national movement operating through the INC, would be the

---

[12]Political awakening in colonial India, says Aloysius, was variegated and the nationalist form was one among the several competing ones. In this framework, the question is not merely whether the dominant nationalist movement spoke for the other interests or not, but whether its leaders spoke with the other leaders to form a coalition of collaborated interests. The nationalists, however, demanded only as much power as could be absorbed among themselves. They quickly sought to turn the grinding poverty of the masses to their own advantage by prescribing increased political and administrative representation for themselves as the panacea. Replying to the charge of being a microscopic minority, R.C. Mitra had said, 'the educated community represented the brain and conscience of the country and were the legitimate spokesman of the illiterate masses, the national guardians of their interests'. R.C. Majumdar (1978, 883), cited in G. Aloysius (1997, 114–15).

sole agenda. No issue on which there was an absence of unanimity was to be discussed, an implication that national unity was to be conceived of and erected on the members present and voting. Thus, the faith of the unrepresented was of no concern to the movement. The magazine, *Bengalee*, for instance, wrote in 1887,

> who ever asked that the peasantry should participate in the government of the country and direct the affairs of the empire? Not even the most dreamy of our politicians have ever sought to compromise our cause by committing this outrage upon common cause.[13]

The INC attempted to consolidate its position through a sifting of demands construed as 'political' or 'national' from those not perceived as such. Subsequently, peasant and labour movements, as also 'communal', were defined as 'economic' and 'social' problems to be solved after the primary 'political' objective of swaraj was achieved. The 1930s have been seen as a period when Congress ascendancy was being challenged by the kisan sabhas, the communists, the Muslim League, and other communal organisations. The 'growing fear of social revolution as the doors of political office gradually gave way', Gyanendra Pandey points out, increased the compulsions for the Congress to define not only the course which the struggle for independence was to take, but also the 'responsible' people who could 'represent' the masses in terms of 'disciplining' and 'steering' them to that threshold (Pandey 1984, 15). Members and leaders of the kisan sabha, industrial labourers, and also communal organisations such as the Muslim League and Hindu Mahasabha thus fell under the purview of Congress' 'disciplining'. While the Congress as well as non-Congress ministries resisted any full-fledged reform in land tenure, at a discursive level they described the peasants with extreme condescension as 'naked', 'bewildered', 'downtrodden', 'utterly miserable', 'crushed', and 'starving'.[14] These descriptions

---

[13]S. Ghose, (1967, 25) cited in (Singh, 120).

[14]These epithets were used by Rajendra Prasad and Jawaharlal Nehru while referring to the peasants (Pandey 1984, 1–7).

not only effaced the politicisation of peasants but also obscured the vibrant struggle which the peasants had waged from the 1920s, almost independent of any Congress leadership. Sahajanand Saraswati expressed his dejection at the distorted perception of Congress leaders towards the kisan struggle. After mammoth kisan rallies in Patna, S.K. Sinha, the prime (chief) minister of Bihar, cautioned Sahajanand against the kisan 'mobs'. The allusion to peasants in agitation against the Congress ministries as 'mobs' was to deprive them of any independent political will and reason. Sahajanand wrote:

> ...there was a time when these peasants were 'masses'. They have now become mobs. They were 'mobs' earlier too but for some reason were seen as 'masses'. These leaders do not need the peasants any longer and historically the term mob has been attributed to those who become redundant in the eyes of the leaders. The government had always addressed them as such and now our ministers too have become the government.[15]

It is not surprising, therefore, that the Congress ministries in the 1930s refused to recognise peasant activists, such as Rahul Sankrityayan, as political prisoners. Peasant leaders such as Pandit Karyanand Sharma, Anil Mishra, Jagannath Prasad, and Bramhachari Ramvriksha went on hunger strikes for recognition as political prisoners. They were released by the Congress government when on the verge of death, without, however, fulfilling their demands for political prisonerhood (Singh 1998, 115). Rahul Sankrityayan, too, twice resorted to long hunger strikes in jail in order to obtain political prisoner status for the jailed kisan activists. He was released each time without any favourable decision by the ministry. Sankrityayan asserts that the Congress ministry in Bihar did not, till its last days, grant political prisoner status to kisan prisoners. Although booked on criminal charges,

---

[15]Sahajanand Saraswati, *Mera Jeevan Sangharsh* (1985, 299); Ujjwal Kumar Singh (1998, 151).

the kisans refused to be categorised as criminals.[16] Having fought for their rights over the lands they tilled, they had courted imprisonment as much as the Congress *satyagrahis* had done. The kisans in prison were asking no more than the Congress prisoners had demanded —some special facilities in jail.[17] The Congress obviously perceived the kisan struggle as an aberration from the Congress-controlled and guided struggle for swaraj.

Significantly, the notion of 'citizen' and 'citizenship' was not being expounded as only an assertion for equality and claims for rights. Citizenship as 'membership in a political community' emphasising 'institutions, habits, activities and spirit' by 'means' of which 'a man or a woman may fulfil the duties and receive the benefits of membership' was an integral part of the study of civics in colleges and universities.[18] Questions commonly asked in university and Intermediate Board Examinations (as in Calcutta University examinations of 1930 and 1927 and United Provinces Intermediate Board Examinations of 1928 and 1930) focussed on the definition, scope, and meaning of citizenship. The importance of civics as a discipline of study professedly lay in 'preparing' students for 'citizenship'. The citizen appears as the nucleus around which concentric circles of existence are woven, the closest being the family, followed by the village, the city, the country, and the outermost—the Empire. It is significant that the limits of citizenship, which the *Indian* citizen was especially subjected to, are described in terms of absence of certain (civil)

---

[16]Sankrityayan was charged after the Amwari satyagraha under CrPC sections 143 (participating in an illegal assembly) and 379 (theft of sugar cane). See for details Sankrityayan, *Meri Jeevan Yatra*, vol. II (1950, 520).

[17]During his imprisonment after the Amwari satyagraha, Sankrityayan put forward on behalf of peasant prisoners some demands pertaining to their general conditions of imprisonment including clothes, food, bedding, reading and writing material, newspapers, and a personal radio. These demands were to him and his colleagues justifiable claims accruing from their status as political prisoners and nothing more than what Congress prisoners had demanded earlier. Ujjwal Kumar Singh, (1998, 115).

[18]See for example, Mihir Kumar Sen's book *Elements of Civics*, the 14th edition of which was printed in 1946 (Sen 1946, vii & xi).

liberties. The roots of this truncated membership are, however, not seen as lying in the colonial condition; rather, there appears a tendency to explain the restrictions (away) as something specific to India, which had always been part of an empire or had empires within, and where only members of the conquering race enjoyed citizenship. The historical context of the British Empire was, however, seen as different from the earlier contexts, in the sense that the British Empire (with the exception of India and other colonies) was constituted of 'autonomous parts'. The actualisation of Indian citizenship in such a context was seen as lying in 'Dominion status'—in being 'citizen of the empire'—whereby, unlike in the ancient past, Indians would not only have Indian citizenship, but would also stand on the same footing as citizens of other parts of the Empire (Sen 1946, 83–4).

Participation in the 'defence of empire' frequently became the ground for making claims to equality within the Empire. This is borne out in a petition by V.D. Savarkar who appealed for a general release of all political prisoners in Indian jails during the First World War. The war, according to Savarkar, gave the Indian youth the opportunity to 'fight side by side with other citizens of the empire' 'against a *common* foe' and to 'share the glories and responsibilities of the Empire with perfect equality with other citizens of it'.[19] The idea of citizenship as equality within different parts of the Empire without, however, removing colonial domination, is only partially modified by legal experts like Srinivas Shastri.[20] In his exhortation for '…the education of every man [sic]…into alert citizenship and the ways of Reason, justice and dignified human relations', Shastri 'appeals' to the 'leaders' to 'build this *constructive* citizenship slowly and surely

---

[19]Petition from jail, dated 3 October 1914 by V.D.Savarkar to the chief commissioner, Andaman and Nicobar islands, file no. 245 H (P) part B, November 1914, National Archives of India, 3–5, cited in Ujjwal Kumar Singh (1998, 23).

[20]See Srinivas Shastri, *The Indian Citizen: His Rights and Duties*, (Bombay: Hind Kitab Limited, 1948). The book edited by T.N. Jagadisan carries Shastri's Kamla Lectures on the Rights and Duties of the Indian Citizen, delivered in Calcutta and Madras in 1926.

on the foundations of *ordered* progress'. While it is not immediately clear who these 'leaders' are to whom Shastri addresses himself, his scepticism of the 'nationalist' methods of change are made quite clear in the suggestions to the 'law-breaker' which follow the appeal:

> I recognise that there are situations in which one has the right to break the law, but please remember that there are others less law abiding than yourself who will see your precedent and make the extreme medicine of the constitution its daily bread (Shastri 1948, 5–6).

In a similar vein, in his lecture on 'Duties of Citizens', Shastri addresses his 'fellow-citizens, brothers [sic] in a growing citizenship' and apprises them of the 'worse alternatives' that figure 'in our inherited tendency'. This inherited tendency 'to overthrow', 'to disestablish', he is convinced, has brought about 'a state of anarchy in the country', destroying 'order and ordered government'. The 'presence of *revolutionary* and *anarchical* forces now afoot' was moreover responsible for failure 'in their duty' of 'our best men' (Shastri 1948, 86–7). For Gandhi, however, the moral right to rebel and resist an unjust government was at the core of the 'duties of citizenship'. The political culture of jail-going evolved by Gandhi in his war of positions with the colonisers in the 1920s and 1930s was premised on the moral duty to resistance which every individual possessed autonomously. This duty made it '...wrong to be free under a government [held] to be wholly bad'. Thus, Gandhi's civil resister, or satyagrahi's quest for truth and freedom lay in resisting a 'bad' government and breaking laws voluntarily, which resulted in (voluntary) imprisonment. Once imprisoned, however, Gandhi expected a satyagrahi prisoner to be 'strictly correct', 'dignified', and 'submissive', and show no disregard for prison discipline except under special circumstances of 'gross inhumanity' and 'indignity'. This adherence to prison discipline was explained by Gandhi in terms of logical rules of civil disobedience. If the person breaking laws voluntarily also violated the sanctions that follow the breach, she/he ceased to be civil (a citizen) and became anarchic (Singh 1998, 74–78).

The constitution of Indian citizenship

As pointed out earlier, the notions of equality, sameness, and sovereignty, appeared in colonial India at the interface of domination and resistance. The idea of the nation as a politico-civil society of equal rights and obligations and constitutive of a sovereign and self-determined people emerged at the broad layers of struggles against domination. The struggle against feudal and Brahmanic dominance aspired to create a political community of citizens by dismantling the structures of a society based on ascriptive inequalities and hierarchies. While seeking to break free from the strangleholds of feudal and Brahmanic domination, the anti-Brahmanic and antifeudal movements asserted inherent rights to their own culture, adopting and seeking recognition for a new identity. This identity spelt for them *equality as a group* and became at the same time the basis for *inclusion of each* of its members into the body politic as abstract citizens with equal civil, political, and socioeconomic rights. The anonymity of citizenship promised liberation from the determining role played by ascriptive hierarchies in matters of access to resources, literacy, social mobility, and political participation.[21] At the other level of resistance—against colonial domination—the nation became the

---

[21]This process involved (i) a search for a nonhierarchical religiocultural framework through a recovery of the different forms of non-Brahmanical Hinduism, (ii) expression of this new-found solidarity in associations or sabhas whose membership extended to the broadest possible understanding and definition of caste (maximum horizontal stretch) as opposed to premodern endogamous exclusivism, (iii) a new emphasis on literacy as a means of appropriating the emerging forms of power structures, occupational diversification, and upward social mobility to escape the hereditary and ascriptive fixity of occupations, (iv) a refusal to accept the view that the new politics could continue to be the monopoly of particular groups or caste and, therefore, a push for political share and representation. The ideological and philosophical scaffolding on which the collective activities and identities of lower-caste groups and their new vision of society and social-political relationship rested were offered by the likes of Phuley, Narayan Guru, Mangoo Ram, E.V. Ramaswamy Naicker, Ghasi Ram, and Ambedkar. G. Aloysius (1997, 77).

basis for the assertion of sovereignty of a people. The articulation of the nation involved carving out an exclusive national identity as a framework of sovereignty for a 'unique people'. This enunciation of the nation marked a rupture in the colonial rule of difference, where the colonised refused to accept membership in a civil society of subjects, and claimed a singular and differential identity vis-a-vis the coloniser.[22]

The political identity of citizenship in India was, thus, dependent upon the construction of the nation as a political community of equal and anonymous citizens and the articulation of a distinct collective (national) cultural identity. The Indian Constitution presents a framework of a political community, assuring horizontal camaraderie as opposed to hierarchical inequalities through its commitment to 'secure' to all its citizens, justice, liberty, equality, and fraternity. The promise of equality was premised on effacing ascriptive (hierarchical) inequalities and masking differences (of culture, caste, gender, etc.), making them irrelevant for the securities of citizenship. The integrative promise of citizenship was achieved through legal-constitutional measures that accommodated the several assertive identities into the body politic as social/cultural/minority (religious and linguistic) communities. In the Constitution this was manifested in the social/cultural rights guaranteed to the minorities with compensatory discrimination in specific cases, within the Hindu community.

---

[22]Partha Chatterjee sees the formation of the national community as part of the anticolonial national movement existing in an irreconcilable relationship with the narrative of capital and the colonial state. The forms of the modern state were imported [in the colonies] through the agency of colonial rule. The institution of civil society, in the form in which they have arisen in Europe, also make their appearance in the colonies precisely to create a public domain for the legitimation of colonial rule. This process was, however, fundamentally limited by the fact that the colonial state could confer only subjecthood on the colonised; it could not grant them citizenship. The crucial break in the history of the anticolonial struggle comes when the colonised refuse to accept membership of this civil society of subjects. They construct their national identities within a different narrative, that of community. See Partha Chatterjee (1994, 237).

The date of the enforcement of the Constitution, 26 January 1950, marked a crucial change in the status of the people of India. They were no longer British subjects, but citizens of the Republic of India and derived their status as such from the Constitution, which they, in their collective capacity as *the people* of India, enacted, adopted, and gave to themselves. While the word 'citizen' is not defined in the Indian Constitution, *Part II* of the Constitution (Articles 5 to 11), titled *Citizenship*, addresses the question, 'Who is a citizen of India?' at the time of the commencement of the Constitution on 26 November 1949, that is, the date on which the Constitution was *adopted* by the Constituent Assembly. Although the Constitution came into full force only on 26 January 1950, provisions dealing with citizenship (Articles 5 to 9) became operative on the date of its commencement. The distinction between the Indian citizen and the noncitizen (alien) thus became effective on this date. While a citizen enjoys certain rights and performs duties that distinguish him/her from an alien, the latter has certain rights of 'personhood' that she/he possesses irrespective of the fact that she/he is not a citizen. Under Articles 5 to 8 of the Constitution, the following categories of persons became the citizens of India at the date of the commencement of Constitution: (a) those domiciled and born in India; (b) those domiciled, not born in India but either of whose parents was born in India; (c) those domiciled, not born in India, but ordinarily resident in India for more than five years; (d) those resident in India, who migrated to Pakistan after 1 March 1947 and returned later on resettlement permits; (e) those resident in Pakistan, who migrated to India before 19 July 1948 or those who came afterwards but stayed on for more than 6 months and got registered; (f) those whose parents and grandparents were born in India but were residing outside India. Article 11 of the Constitution authorised the parliament to make laws pertaining to acquisition and termination of citizenship subsequent to the commencement of the Constitution. The Citizenship Act (LVII of 1955) made elaborate provisions specifying how citizenship could be acquired by birth, descent, registration, naturalisation, or through incorporation of territory. The Act was amended in 1986 to deal with migration from Bangladesh, Sri Lanka, and some African countries.[23] Unlike the United States of America (USA) where citizens have dual citizenship, national citizenship and that of the federal unit (states), Indians do not have separate citizenship of the states.

The strands of citizenship rights that Marshall sees as having evolved over the last three centuries in British constitutional tradition had a synchronous birth within the Indian Constitution. Civil, political and social rights were enumerated in the Constitution as the *Fundamental Rights* of the citizens. Part II of the Constitution read in the light of the Preamble and Part III on Fundamental Rights would indicate that citizenship was conceived, by and large, within an integrative framework of rights premised on assurances by the state to its members and by the members to one another. The notion of citizenship as prevalent in the nineteenth century and understood thereafter, we have seen, was largely a system of rights and obligations that defined the relationship between nation-states and their *individual* members. The defining parameters of this relationship were constituted by equality and freedom. Equality hinted at an identity and sameness as against iniquitous systems based on ascriptive hierarchies of race and caste. Freedom with equality would then imply a freedom to pursue individual aims and aspirations to the best of one's capacities in conditions where social differences have been negated or minimised. The citizen in liberal theory was, thus, the 'floating individual' shorn of all characteristics of his/her social context. As discussed earlier, owing to the specific historical context of the incorporation of a legal-constitutional framework of citizenship in India, the subjects of rights were both individuals and communities. Articles 14 to 24 within the chapter on Fundamental Rights give to individual citizens rights of freedom and equality. Articles 25

---

[23]See D.D.Basu, *Introduction to the Constitution of India* (1999) and Subhash Kashyap, *Citizens and the Constitution* (1997) for details on constitutional provisions.

to 30 in the same chapter, collectively termed 'cultural and educational rights', deal explicitly with the rights of religious and cultural communities and minority groups. It is this cluster of articles that forms the basis of the rights of religious communities to administer themselves in civil matters by their own 'personal laws'. These rights pertain to freedom of religion and minority rights assuring freedom of conscience, the freedom to religious communities to establish and maintain religious institutions and to 'manage their own affairs in matters of religion', to acquire and administer property, impart religious education, preserve their language, script, culture, etc.

Thus, while the masked citizen of liberal theory persists as the bearer of rights within the constitution, the community has also been included as a relevant collective unit of the social and political life of the nation. The Indian Constitution has made community membership a relevant consideration for differentiation among citizens, accommodating the notion of 'differentiated-citizenship' to assure (i) that each community has the right to be culturally different and to preserve community identity, and (ii) that communities (example, scheduled castes or dalits) victimised by social discrimination and that continue to be disadvantaged are able to compete on equal terms with the rest of society. There would thus appear to exist within the Constitution not only two subjects of rights, viz., the individual and the community, but also two languages—one catering to the individual citizen and the other to the community —one strand of the language of rights claiming to identify individual differences, and the other recognising the particular contexts of different communities (Menon 1998). For Larson, however, there is in fact no compartmentalisation in the language and subjects of rights, and some seemingly individual-catering rights are interwoven with a commitment to community rights (Larson 1997). If, for example, one looks at Articles 14 and 15, one sees that they assure equality before the law for every citizen and seek to substantiate this equality by prohibiting discrimination based on caste, religion, race, etc., and thus mitigate differences provided by social contexts. The articles, therefore, while catering to the individual, also reserve for the state a commitment to communityship, in other words, allowing for certain rights in favour of scheduled castes, scheduled tribes and other backward classes. Thus, Article 15 lays down that 'The State shall not discriminate against any citizen on grounds only of religion, race, caste, sex, place of birth or any of them' and then in clause (4) reserves for the state the right to make 'any special provision for the advancement of any socially and educationally backward classes of citizens or for the Scheduled Castes and Scheduled Tribes'. Similarly Article 16, which guarantees equality of opportunity for all citizens in matters of public employment, also provides for compensatory discrimination in favour of certain communities. Article 17 abolishes untouchability, a debilitating condition imposed on the scheduled castes.[24] Part IV of the Constitution, titled Directive Principles of State Policy, contains certain non-justiciable rights. These rights, unlike the ones in the preceding section, are not enforceable by courts, but are in the nature of reminders or directives for lawmaking to usher in conditions in which the rights enumerated in the previous section become more meaningful. Like the previous section, the rights in this section, too, show a 'simultaneous commitment' to both 'communityship' and 'citizenship', in other words, to both the community and the individual citizen. Article 38, for example, directs the state to commit itself to 'promote the welfare of the people' by promoting a 'social order' in which 'justice, social, economic and political, shall inform all the institutions of the national life'. To achieve this, the state is asked to 'strive to minimise inequalities of income' and also 'eliminate inequalities in status, facilities and opportunities'. The significant reminder, however, is that this justice and equality is to be achieved 'not only amongst individuals but also amongst groups of people residing in different areas or engaged in different vocations'. Article 46 likewise instructs the state to 'promote with special care the educational and economic interests of the

---

[24]See Gerald James Larson, *India's Agony Over Religion* (1997, 214–18).

weaker sections of the people and in particular, of the scheduled castes and tribes' and 'protect them from social injustice and all forms of exploitation'. By and large the Directive Principles envisage an active role of the state in providing a range of socially ameliorative or welfare rights ranging from access to an adequate means of livelihood, equal pay for equal work, health and strength of workers, living wage for workers, provision of just and humane conditions of work, right to work, to education, to public assistance, to equal justice and free legal aid, to adequate nutrition and health, etc. (Larson 1997, 214–18).

It may be pointed out, however, that the thrust of the commitment to communityship in Articles 14–24, and thereafter in the Directive Principles is different from that woven into Articles 25–30 promising cultural rights to linguistic and religious minorities. The rights to equality and freedom enshrined in the former set of articles make special reference to the exceptional circumstances of disadvantaged groups providing for special protective measures to overcome socioeconomic disabilities. While the subject of amelioration are indeed specific groups of people debilitated by a long history of oppression, the purpose of the provisions is ultimately to remove the debilitating conditions or, alternatively, prepare the grounds for an increasing number of persons to integrate themselves into the horizontal camaraderie of autonomous citizens.[25] The other cluster of rights (Articles 25–30), however, speaks a different language insofar as it explicitly prioritises the cultural community, concerns itself with its preservation, and is based on the assumption that

---

[25]In the context of the discussion on franchise in the previous chapter, provisions pertaining to 'elections' and 'franchise' in the Constitution are especially important in the context of the long history of deprivation of political rights under colonial rule. It is significant that the Constitution made 'universal adult franchise' the basis of elections to the Lok Sabha and the legislative assemblies of states. Article 326 of the Constitution conferred voting rights to *all citizens above the age of 21* (changed to 18 by the Constitution 61st Amendment Act of 1988, with effect from 1 April 1989). It is crucial that the Constitution did not lay down any property and education criteria.

constitutive communities are of overriding significance in shaping the needs and aspirations of the individual. A point may also be made here that the definition of community in cultural terms in this cluster means that only some individuals, that is, those belonging to these communities come under the purview of these rights, and are therefore especially and exceptionally affected by it. The section on *nation, community, and a gendered citizenship* later in the chapter will explore this point in greater detail.

The constitutional provisions of citizenship and rights discussed so far might lead one to believe that citizenship is only about legal status defining the citizens of India and the conditions in which rights might be enjoyed. A growing body of scholarship believes that such a legal-formal conceptualisation of citizenship as status is at best a passive notion, answering the question—who is a citizen—only partially. They would want us to move beyond notions of 'basic structures'—of equality and social justice—that the Constitution seeks to establish and to concentrate also on the notion of citizenship as a function of 'responsible' participation. Citizenship, then, would transcend its passive connotation to become also a measure of activity. The basis of a citizen's sense of belonging to the national community would come then from the attitudes and qualities of responsibility and virtues that distinguish her/him as a 'good' citizen. Responsible participation would manifest itself in diverse social situations, viz., how citizens view or act amidst potentially competing forms of national, regional, ethnic, or religious identities; their ability to tolerate and work together with others who are different from themselves; their desire to participate in the political process in order to promote the public good and hold political authorities accountable; their willingness to show self-restraint and exercise personal responsibility in their economic demands and personal choices which affect their health and environment, etc. Such citizenship qualities, it is said, make a democracy stable and governable. Various voluntary institutions and organisations within society including schools, environmental groups, unions, and associations are regarded as inculcating these virtues of citizenship (Walzer 1989).

The 42nd Amendment Act, 1976, has added a list of Fundamental Duties of the citizens of India in the form of Article 51A in Part IVA of the Constitution, integrating a notion of 'responsible citizenship' within the legal framework of the Constitution. The legal status of Fundamental Duties, addressed to the citizens of India, is quite like the Directive Principles, which are addressed to the state in the sense that they are not accompanied by provisions for direct enforcement. The underlying principle of Fundamental Duties appears to be that the individual while exercising her/his rights should not overlook that others have similar rights. She/he should be careful that the exercise of her/his rights do not restrict the rights of others, for example, a person cannot by what she/he says or writes injure the religious sentiments of another person and assert that she/he is protected by her/his right to freedom of expression under Article 19. Again, because the duties are not addressed to the state, a citizen cannot claim for provision of conditions for the exercise of her/his duties.[26] Similarly, the Fundamental Duties are not enforceable by *mandamus* or any other legal remedy.[27] It may be pointed out here, however, that the Supreme Court has sought to make duties effective by issuing directions to the state with regard to Article 51A(g) of the duties which enjoins the citizens to 'protect and improve the natural environment including forests, lakes, rivers and wild life, and to have compassion for living creatures'.[28] Also, the Supreme Court may also uphold as reasonable any law seeking to prohibit the violation of Fundamental Duties, even if the law restricted a Fundamental Right. This can be derived from the attitude of the

---

[26]*Head Masters v. Union of India*, A. 1983 Cal. 448 (para 27) cited in D.D. Basu, *Shorter Constitution of India* (1999, 311).

[27]*Surya v. Union of India*, A. 1982 Raj. 1 (para 19), (ibid, 310).

[28]*Rural Litigation v. State of U.P.*, A.1987 S.C. 359 (para 19): A. 1985 S.C. 652 (paras 8–12); *Sachidanand v. State of W.B.*, A. 1987 S.C. 1109 (para 4); *Mehta v. Union of India*, (1988) 1 S.C.C. 471 (paras 24–26) (ibid, 311).

court towards the implementation of provisions of Part IV of the Constitution and the belief, even before the insertion of a separate list of duties, that Part IV of the Constitution, that is, the Directives, demanded certain obligations from the citizens. Thus, the Supreme Court considered in the *Chandra Bhavan v. State of Mysore Case (1970)* that 'it [was] a fallacy to think that under our Constitution there are only rights and no duties. The provisions in Part IV enable the Legislatures to impose various duties on the citizens. The mandate of our Constitution is to build a welfare society and that object may be achieved to the extent the Directive Principles are implemented by legislation' (Basu 1999, 310). It may be said then that the inclusion of duties into the Constitution has woven an obligation into it, and although there is no provision in the Constitution for their enforcement, any law seeking to implement them may be considered 'reasonable' under the law.

The list of duties, which are 10 in number, gives an insight into what might constitute 'good' citizenship. Some of them enjoining citizens to strive towards 'excellence' and developing 'scientific temper' or safeguarding 'public property' appear generally to instil sincerity and civic responsibility. A general slant is, however, towards imbibing a sense of national commonality. Thus, it is considered a duty of every citizen of India *to respect symbols of national unity* like the national flag, the Constitution, and the National Anthem and *sources of common heritage* like the 'national struggle for freedom', and the tradition of 'composite culture'. Citizens are also expected to preserve the 'sovereignty' and 'unity' of the country not only by pledging to 'defend' the country and offer 'national service' but also by spreading a feeling of 'common brotherhood'.

Ambivalences in constitutional citizenship

Thus, given the contexts within which this legal-constitutional language of citizenship and rights evolved, with the nation equivocally defined as the dominant cultural community and as a political community of abstract citizens, citizenship in India remained ambivalently defined. The vacillation between individual and community rights has, however, resulted in ambivalences and 'tensions' within citizenship. These ambivalences have unfolded in the years after independence in a series of contradictions, conflicts, and acrimonious debates around issues concerning the rights of minority communities to manage their cultural affairs, the question of protective/ compensatory discrimination for the disadvantaged sections, the issue of uniform civil code, the question of political representation of women, etc. The collective cultural and educational rights of minority communities, for example, have come under increasing criticism from those with a radical agenda of giving individual members of religious communities the right to choose and even determine the nature and content of their membership, as well as from those who would occlude contextual difference under the mask of a hegemonically marked abstract citizen. It is indeed ironical that rights of minority communities to the preservation of their own culture was incorporated in the Constitution in the name of secular democracy at the expense of a more effective electoral system, for example, proportional representation or reserved seats in the legislatures that would have guaranteed minority communities adequate political representation and a greater say in the affairs of the polity.[29] The manner in which the terrain of minority rights has been informed by tensions played out, in particular, on issues of women's rights, is discussed in the next section. The

---

[29]In her article 'Rights versus Representation: Defending Minority Interests in the Constituent Assembly', Shefali Jha points out that this trade off between right to religion and effective political representation became apparent in the later stages of the debates. Whereas in the earlier stages not only were reservations in legislative bodies demanded for religious minorities, but the system of proportional representation was advocated over the simple majority/plurality rule in the elections. The trade off between rights and representation denied the communities the additional safeguard of better representation and gave precedence to a view of democracy as majoritarianism which would eventually prove antithetical to religious freedom (Jha 2003, 1579–83).

issue of protective discrimination including reservations for historically disadvantaged groups in public services and in representative bodies has similarly become an arena of contest in a context where citizenship tends to get marked hegemonically as upper caste and class, Hindu, and male. The long-drawn struggle against reservations in the public services in the wake of the recommendations of the Mandal Commission is illustrative of this contest.[30]

Moreover, the claim that the Preamble, Fundamental Rights, and Directive Principles embodying the values of freedom, equality, and economic and social justice have assured citizenship to individuals irrespective of their societal contexts has been questioned in some quarters. Critics point out that the nature of citizenship in the Indian Constitution and the manner in which it has unfolded over the years have shown that the values of freedom and equality have been largely elusive. Studying the nature of empowerment of citizens within the Constitution, A.R. Desai has pointed out the precarious nature of rights in the Constitution. He emphasises that not only are rights *not reserved* to the people, there is no preservation of the Fundamental Rights already guaranteed to them. The Constitution itself permits and provides the procedure for their amendment and overriding by the state. Further, the Directive Principles are not addressed to

----

[30]On the other hand, Sanjib Baruah points out that even when people may agree in principle that historically disadvantaged people deserve some form of protective discrimination or affirmative action, in concrete situations, adjudicating between competing claims of advantaged and disadvantaged groups on grounds of justice and fairness may be difficult. Baruah points at the specific contexts of the Northeast where the politics of protective discrimination for scheduled tribes is (i) predominantly an ethnic discourse of protective discrimination with the effect that the state is constantly categorising people in ethnic terms making descendants of immigrants perpetual outsiders, and, (ii) creating a two-tier system of citizenship in states like Mizoram, Arunachal Pradesh, and Nagaland where nontribals are not able to contest elections with almost all seats reserved for tribals. See Sanjib Baruah 'Protective Discrimination and Crisis of Citizenship in North-East India' (2003, 1624–26).

the people, which means that the people cannot move the courts to instruct the government to provide conditions in which their rights could be made more meaningful. Again, asserts Desai, while there does not appear to be any explicit system of accountability for the state, the people are given some fundamental duties. Desai feels that in the absence of any similar obligations for the state, the provisions relating to Fundamental Duties could be used to abridge the basic rights of citizens. Finally, the fact that certain basic rights such as the rights to work, shelter, education, and medical amenities are not Fundamental Rights indicates the class and gender biases of the Constitution-makers. Under such conditions, large sections of 'toiling' citizens, that is, the socially and economically underprivileged, including women, are forced to live in conditions in which their empowerment as citizens remains unrealised.[31] In most cases of removal of discrimination, conditions in which substantive citizenship rights can be enjoyed are listed only as Directive Principles. Article 39, for example, having significant implication for citizenship of women, provides that the state shall 'direct its policies towards securing' that the citizens, men and women equally, have the right to an adequate means of livelihood; and that there is equal pay for equal work for both men and women.

Again, the prioritisation of the community as the ossified and autonomous unit of plurality has had two important implications. It has placed the civil liberties of the individual citizen at a relative disadvantage vis-a-vis both the religious-cultural community and the political community signified by the nation-state. Owing to the limits of democratisation—social equality and social justice—being circumscribed by the boundaries of the religious-cultural community, intra-community democracy was sacrificed, and this had important implications for individual liberty, gender justice, and equality. A further implication of

---

[31]A.R. Desai, 'Empowering the Sovereign Citizens of India: Some Constitutional Obstacles', in *Social and Cultural Diversities*, ed. Abha Avasthi (1997).

recognising ascriptive identities for special consideration has been
that the significance of class—the rights of socioeconomically
disadvantaged and vulnerable groups like women and children,
the aged, and the physically challenged that cut across ascriptive
communities—has remained backstage. The relegation of civil
liberties in the interest of the national-political (community) and
social-cultural (communities) has also meant that in most
instances of violation of the rights of the individual at the hands
of the state or the authority structures of the community, it is
these vulnerable/disadvantaged classes who suffer. Although the
Constitution guaranteed political rights and civil liberties, for
example, freedom of speech, thought, association, and
movement, almost all these rights were severely circumscribed in
the interest of the (ascriptive) community on the one hand and
'national interest' on the other. The liberty to exercise all
political rights was made subject to public order and morality
allowing the legislature and the executive to regulate them in the
interests of peace, safety, and public health.[32] The fundamental
rights, as mentioned earlier, have been burdened by qualificatory
provisions, which under specific circumstances may render the
rights inoperable. This fact alone violates the fundamental
postulates of even liberal democratic philosophy, which considers

---

[32]A.R.Desai suggests that an analysis of the Constitution from the point
of view of *which* rights have been excluded, viz., the right to work, the right
to shelter, the right to education, and the right to medical and other social
amenities, would reveal the socioeconomic, class, and gender aspect of the
Constitution. A number of scholars and civil liberties activists hold that the
Constitution is not grounded in principles that could provide basic human
rights to its citizens. Desai, in particular, argues that much has been left
wanting so much so that the Constitution has an implicit 'anti-people'
grounding. The underlying assumptions with regard to the (capitalist) path of
development, he asserts, generate a situation wherein the violation of laws by
proprietary classes goes unchecked and the state resorts to coercive, illegal, and
brutal measures against the vast mass of citizens. 'Governmental lawlessness'
is explored in Upendra Baxi, *The Crisis of the Indian Legal System* (1982) and
A.R. Desai ed., *Expanding Governmental Lawlessness and Organised Resistance*
(1991).

the essence of democracy to be based on ultimate sovereignty resting in the people, and also that representatives of people in parliament have only limited powers and cannot override the 'natural rights' of the citizens. It is also significant that the specific circumstances, described in the Constitution and which would justify the withdrawal of the 'fundamental' rights of the people, have become in effect explanatory/justificatory grounds for the gross violation of the rights of the people. The fact that the Constitution reserves the right to withdraw the constitutional rights of the people with the parliament has had at different historical periods 'grave and disconcerting implications' for the rights of the citizens and a 'crippling effect on their empowerment' (Desai 1997, 40).

It may be recalled that at the core of the anticolonial struggle was the issue of equality much of which focussed on civil/political rights.[33] The deliberations on Fundamental Rights in the Constituent Assembly, however, reflect a predominant concern with law and order and the interests of the nation-state. For a nation that had faced considerable police repression, brutality, and arbitrary governmental action under the colonial regime, it is surprising that members of the Constituent Assembly showed scant regard for individual freedom and civil liberties (Mahajan 1998, 158–59). A.K. Aiyar and C. Rajagopalachari, for instance,

---

[33]Srinivasa Shastri, for instance, in a series of lectures on the Rights and Duties of the Indian Citizen delivered in Calcutta and Madras in 1926, denounces the continuance among 'our' laws of the Bengal Regulation III of 1818 which 'empowers the placing under personal restraint without any view to ultimate proceedings of a judicial nature, under orders originally of the Governor-General-in-Council and now under those of the Central or Provincial Courts' (Shastri 1948, 29). Similarly the various abrogations to 'the primary right of freedom of person' through S.126 of the Bengal Ordinance, the Criminal Law Amendment Act, 'then the whole network of Political prisoners Regulations, Bombay, Madras and Bengal…Freedom of movement restricted by passport regulations, freedom of speech and meeting by seditious meetings Act and the sections of the CrPC (127 to 132) dealing with unlawful assembly…' are denounced by him in the course of his lectures (Shastri 1948, 62–3).

maintained that the clause[34] 'The right of the people to be secure in their persons, houses, papers and effects, against unreasonable searches and seizures, shall not be violated and no warrants shall issue but upon probable cause, supported by oath or affirmation, and particularly describing the place to be searched, and the person or things to be seized' should be dropped as it was likely to encourage crime (Mahajan 1998, 173, 238–79). In another context, K.M.Panikkar argued that the right of every citizen to the secrecy of his correspondence needed to be qualified. To say that this right should be regulated only on account of public safety and tranquility was not enough. Greater power to censor and interrupt correspondence and communication needed to be given to the executive machinery for the proper administration of criminal law (Mahajan 1998, 160). The concern for law and order and security of the nation also resulted in the incorporation of the provision for preventive detention. Surveying the basic characteristics of the Indian Constitution, Upendra Baxi has pointed out how the Constitution itself has evolved within the Indian legal system two main streams of a justice system: (i) Normal Criminal Justice System, and, (ii) Preventive Detention System (PDS). It is significant that the latter has been expanding in the form of various categories of ordinances, acts and other measures, which attack the rights given to the citizens.[35]

Nation, Community, and a Gendered Citizenship

While notions of multiculturalism and minority rights have enabled the empowerment of cultural communities whereby they can lay claims to inherent rights and negotiate better terms of reference to the national culture, the conception of a community as a discrete and ossified unit can encompass the same undemocratic relations with sections of its constituents,

---

[34]Clause 11 of the Report on Fundamental Rights, 16 April 1947.

[35]See Upendra Baxi, *The Crisis of the Indian Legal System*; Ujjwal Kumar Singh (1998, 211–16) for details of the emergency provisions and preventive detention laws in independent India.

primarily women, which the community hopes to invert in its relationship with the dominant national culture. Moreover, a conceptualisation of the community in terms which underline its relative numerical disadvantage vis-a-vis the dominant community, sets the grounds for 'internal restrictions' to sustain the community as a viable and distinct cultural category. It also assumes an organic wholeness of the community, complete with symbolic boundaries and a natural cohesion among its members and which occludes differences within the community and the multifarious struggles that accompanied the recognition and appreciation of its cultural uniqueness.[36] Also, envisaging a plural society merely as a melange of groups/communities each with its discrete 'cultural identity' has a restricting effect on conceiving any kind of struggle for the ideological reconstruction of the community or the conception of a radical struggle/politics other than that which is determined by community membership and identity.[37]

The circumstances in which the language of citizenship arose in India in the struggle for self-determination against multilayered oppressive structures has been discussed in the previous section. The articulation of 'community' as the basis of a national (political) community and particular (cultural) communities, we have seen, extended to substantial issues of power and its redistribution within the nation to be (Aloysius

[36]Nira Yuval-Davis attempts to go beyond identifying citizenship in its wide social definition merely with the nation-state. On the other hand, she also resists espousing some assumptions regarding 'the community' which are, in her opinion, detrimental to a politics of 'difference'. One such assumption is the conception of the community as an organic whole, a 'natural' social unit, 'out there'. Such an assumption, she avers, restricts any dynamic construction of citizenship as the product of struggle and ideological reconstructions of communities. Nira Yuval-Davis, 'The Citizenship Debate: Women, Ethnic Processes and the State' (1991, 58–60).

[37]Chantal Mouffe proposes a radical democratic interpretation of citizenship by rethinking the way one conceptualises the political community and one's relationship with it. See Chantal Mouffe, 'Citizenship and Political Identity' (1992, 28–29).

1997, 92). A communitarian reading of equality in India made 'diversity' a veritable symbol of Indian democracy. Central to this enunciation of diversity was a notion of toleration and secularism that acknowledged the right of a community to remain (culturally) different within a unity of the national (political) community. At the same time, however, it opened up the grounds for subjecting the principle of individual equality to the specific codes of a particular community. The Indian citizen thus wore as it were a double mask—one identifying her/him to the national community and the other to the particular religious community she/he belonged to. These two identities—national-political and religious-cultural—have competed with each other for precedence, and, gender, more often than not, has provided the grounds on which this contest has been played out (Menon 1998). If the 'Hindu widow' provided the terrain on which competing versions of 'Indian tradition' were worked out in colonial India, in the 1980s, the 'divorced Muslim woman' provided a similar 'weak' link where a 'personal' matter of the Muslim community was unfolded to public scrutiny. It is not surprising that the debates in both instances made tradition, in the case of sati and secularism in the 'Shah Bano Case', the primary subject of debate. Thus, while the dignity/self-determination of the nation and community vis-a-vis the forces of domination—the colonisers and the Indian (Hindu) state respectively—came to the foreground, the prioritisation of women's rights were occluded in the process.

The twin axes of tradition and secularism have provided the limits encompassing the possible realm of activities of women. Tradition has invariably lent itself at various historical moments to bridge the contradiction in time that the nation epitomises, with women represented as the atavistic and authentic body of national tradition, inert, backward-looking, natural, and embodying nationalism's conservative principle of continuity. The Indian nationalists had conceived an 'Indian' past—a body of tradition—within which the 'new' Indian woman was inscribed as the bearer of a pristine and unsullied past. This woman was new because she was emancipated. Her emancipation emanated from her reinscribed femininity, her markers of tradition, and her capacity to purge while she herself remained untainted. While conquerors mauled the body politic, she, in her sacrosanct femininity, remained untarnished and sovereign in spirit and in her survived the nation.

Secularism would then represent the forward-looking element of the nation, of change, an aspect of the building of a modern nation. While at a basic level it is seen as the separation of religion from the public arena, secularism manifests a complex web of political and social practices and ideological formulations that determine the relationship and its forms of articulation between the state and specific communities. Read within the framework of secularism, tradition(s) would form the basis, then, of the right(s) of diverse cultural/religious communities to difference. Oscillating between the axes of tradition and secularism, the identity of 'the citizen' appears alternatively as that marked by religion and caste or masked as the abstract secular citizen (Menon 1998).

The figuration of women within this framework of ambivalent identities of citizenship has far-reaching implications for the articulation of women's citizenship. The nationalist 'construction' of the 'new woman' abstracted from the seams of history ensnared her in an elaborate set of assumptions around motherhood and other (heteronormative) familial relationships. The national movement, however, while drawing 'women' into the political arena, restricted the realm of women's politics by marginalising feminist demands/choices to the primary concern of national freedom. We saw in the chapter on women's struggles for the vote and the right to contest elections during the early part of this century how the different strands in the ensuing debate were informed by notions of 'womanhood' defined in a (dependent) relation to family, property, education, respectability, and nationalism. The various strands which conflicted and colluded in the debate on vote for women revealed at one level the tearing down of the monolith woman and at another level reinscribing the superscribed idealised woman, both of which occluded the emergence of a unified political woman. It may be noted, however, that in this resurrection of the familial nation, in the demands for political rights by women waged within the broad framework of the national movement, the class schism in the figuration of 'women' was matched by a professed unity of womanhood beyond communal divides. The conception of a womanly domain of politics was characterised by their spiritual participation in the social domain as a moral intervention for sorting out the problems of society, which domain complemented and not competed with the masculine domain of politics. The favoured slogan was universal adult franchise and fair field and no favours, and women's organisations denounced the Poona Pact and other communal awards as divisive for (Hindu and Muslim) women. In this familial nation, Hindu and Muslim women sharing common bonds of womanliness resided in a kinship relationship as Indian women.

The 'new woman' came to symbolise the public face of harmony as far as the nationalist position on gender equality was concerned. Among the first public expositions of the nationalist position was the adoption of a Fundamental Rights Resolution by the Indian National Congress at its Karachi session in 1931, where the Congress professed its commitment to equal political and civil rights for women in independent India. In 1937, when the Congress assumed responsibility of government in several provinces, a National Planning Committee was instituted with Jawaharlal Nehru as its chairman. The committee was entrusted with the task of reporting on various aspects of 'national life and work' and drawing an outline for independent India's planned development. Among the 29 sub-committees set up to report on the different facets of planned national development was the Sub-committee on Women's Role in Planned Economy (WRPE). The terms of reference of the sub-committee were comprehensive, purporting to deal with 'every aspect of women's life and work', including:

> ...consideration of her social, economic and legal status, her right to hold property, carry on any trade, profession or occupation and remove all obstacles or handicaps in the way of realising an equal status and opportunity for women... (WRPE, 27).

It focussed, in particular, on the family life and the organisation of women's work within the house; marriage and succession and laws governing these; the conditions of employment of women in various sectors; social customs and institutions which hindered women's development; and, the appropriate education and methods of education which would enable women to play their roles in household, professions, and national services. The 265-page text of the report titled 'Women's Role in Planned Economy' was divided into three main sections. Section One focussed on *the individual status* of women spread over four chapters titled 'Civic Rights', 'Economic Rights', 'Property Rights', and 'Education', respectively. Section Two on *the social status of women* covered two chapters titled 'Marriage and its Problems', and 'Family Life'. Section Three dealt with miscellaneous issues such as caste, widows, widow remarriage, widow's homes, unmarried mothers, abortion, prostitutes, etc. A summary statement of policy and policy recommendations followed the three sections (Chaudhuri 1996).

The terms of reference, and the report of the sub-committee suggest a broad tilt towards the 'hegemonic national liberal model' jostling with contesting 'visions of cultural revivalism and socialist utopias' (Chaudhuri 1996, 216). Reaffirming the shift of the paradigms of the women's question from 'upliftment' to 'equality', expressed earlier by the 1931 Fundamental Rights Resolution of the Congress, the sub-committee demanded the removal of gender disqualifications in the exercise of political rights and 'civic duties and obligations'. Thus, equal voting rights as individuals, the rights to hold public office or employment, the right to work as implied in the demand for equal access to public services and equal wages for equal work without endangering employment opportunities for women, the right to choose one's nationality, equal rights to health, leisure, and recreation, were some of the rights articulated by the sub-committee. All these rights focussed on women as individuals and expressed the notion of women as equal citizens (WRPE, 38–43). The idea that housewives were also working women runs throughout the report. The concept of fixed hours of work, adequate relief from duties in the kitchen, cooperative efforts to relieve/sharing the household duties, etc., strove to enlarge the meaning and scope of women's work. This redefinition of women's work reflected a conscious attempt by the sub-committee to break free from the gender-blindness, which characterised a liberal notion of citizenship (Chaudhuri 1996, 232–33). At the same time the stress on the right to private property—the right of the bourgeois woman 'to hold, acquire, inherit and dispose of property'—showed a general inability to dissociate from the 'unfettered individualism' of liberal citizenship. The report thus echoed the ambivalences and class dichotomies that informed women's struggle for franchise in the 1920s and 1930s.

While making recommendations which broadened the opportunities/choices available to women, the sub-committee staked claims to gender equality on the basis of the 'special' contribution women made to the nation and community as 'reproducers' and 'sustainers', 'as the guardians and trustees of future generations'. Even when it asked for 'economic liberty' and the 'right to mould her social and economic life in any way she chooses', which involved the 'reorganisation' of the 'functions which nature and society [have] imposed on her', the sub-committee declared that it did not intend to enter into a confrontation with 'traditions' which, in the past, contributed to the happiness and progress of the individual: '…We do not wish to turn women into a cheap imitation of man or to render her useless for the great tasks of motherhood and nation-building' (Chaudhuri 1996, 32–3). Here again, as in the debates on voting rights for women, the women constituting the sub-committee seem to be attempting a compromise between the liberal individualist framework of citizenship and its critique as seen in the radical redefinition of women's work by putting forth class-differentiated categories of citizenship for women. Thus, the rejection of the private/public dichotomy in rearticulating women's work is in harmony with the manner in which the citizenship of working-class women is construed. The articulation of the autonomy and economic freedom of the working-class woman sees her entirely in terms of production process, specifically as 'instruments of labour'. The subjectivities of the middle-class women are, however, firmly grounded within the dominant nationalist frameworks. While as a property-owner her economic independence is emphasised, the middle-class woman continues to be reposed with the responsibility of creating 'a cultural environment in the home for the proper nurture of the children', reaffirming, thus, womanhood's affinity with motherhood and its relationship with the improvement of the life of the nation (Chaudhuri 1996, 233).

The sub-committee thus stopped short of recommending 'drastic social changes', that is, laws relating to marriage and family and remained in consonance with the reformist ideals of the nationalist elite. Within the dominant nationalist framework, 'emancipation' and 'upliftment' of women were sought without effecting any radical changes in the social and familial structures. This can be illustrated from the anxieties and trepidation with which women's appeals to remove the 'disabilities' of Indian women in law was being received around the same period as the plan perspective for the nation was being drawn. In 1934, the All India Women's Conference (AIWC) urged the government to appoint an all-India commission to consider the promulgation of a new law that removed legal inequalities of women, especially in areas of inheritance, marriage, and the guardianship of children.[38] The question, however, as in the case of women's franchise, lingered in the shadow of matters of 'national' concern and attempts to resolve the legal status of Indian women in the 1930s proved desultory.[39] While the AIWC favoured

---

[38]Annual Report, AIWC Ninth Session, Karachi (1934, 17–31, 70–1).

[39]Among the measures introduced between 1937 and 1938 were the Hindu Woman's Right to Property Bill, an amendment to the Child Marriage Restraint Act, a bill to allow intercaste marriage, the Hindu Woman's Right to Divorce Act, the Muslim Personal Law Bill, the Prevention of Polygamy Bill, and the Muslim Women's Right to Divorce Bill. In the provincial legislatures, antidowry bills, marriage laws, and bills to allow women to inherit were introduced.

uniform laws for all women, regardless of community,[40] the discussions on the reform Bills showed that male reformers had different concepts of women's legal needs. By January 1941, when B.N. Rau was appointed chair of a committee of eminent lawyers to study Hindu law and to look at the various bills on the Hindu woman's property rights, male opinion on reforms manifested symptoms ranging from apprehensions of an impending 'havoc' in the (Hindu) household to a steadfast recourse to religious sanctity and national pride to sustain the existing system.[41] Recourse to the judiciary to set right gender biases within specific personal laws has achieved a measure of success. No changes have, however, been made which would radically alter the assumption of dependence and inferiority of women within personal laws. The Supreme Court judgment of 17 February 1999, for example, which elucidated the status of 'mother as guardian' under the Hindu Minority and Guardianship Act, 1956, and the Guardians and Wards Act, 1890, allowed the mother to act as natural guardian of her children, removing hindrances and inconveniences which were frequently encountered by 'deserted' and 'separated' women in filling up school applications or dealing with the finances of their minor children. Significantly, however, the apex court did not go all the way in removing the gender bias in the Acts insofar as it gave the mother the right to act as the natural guardian *only if* her husband was absent, indifferent, or had explicitly consented to her acting as such. It is important to note that the

---

[40]The AIWC said: 'We want no sex war'; they were demanding equality to allow women to play a role in the affairs of the country, not equality of the 'western variety'. Annual Report, AIWC, Tenth Session, 1935.

[41]If Nehru refused to negotiate/collaborate with the British for reforms in family law, for the Muslim League, reforms were fine as long as the Muslim community was not touched. Only a few Congress members agreed that women's legal rights deserved the highest priority. Some were afraid that changes might 'upset the framework on which the Hindu social system was based'. Others felt that Hindu women were not suited for public life and the women they knew were very happy with their lives and appeared to be in no need for change. (Forbes 1996, 112–15)

judgment came in response to two petitions that pleaded specifically that certain sections of the two Acts violated the fundamental rights of equality (of women in this case) given by Articles 14 and 15 of the Constitution and should, therefore, be struck down.[42]

Independence brought political rights to Indian women, with constitutional provisions removing gender disqualifications in the exercise of some basic rights. Women's rights were, however, repeatedly curtailed in the name of communal autonomy. Personal laws of the respective religious communities governed matters relating to marriage, divorce, guardianship of children, and inheritance. By and large, they limited the choices available to women with regard to economic freedom and equality by allotting them a subservient and dependent position in matters of family and finances.[43] In the 1980s, the demand that Muslim

---

[42]The disputed sections were 6(a) of the Hindu Minority and Guardianship Act, 1956 and 19(b) of the Guardians and Wards Act. The former held the contentious phrase, '...the father, and after him, the mother was the natural guardian of the child', giving the impression that the mother could act as a guardian only after the lifetime of her husband. The court, however, interpreted the phrase to mean that the word 'after' suggested 'in the absences of' which and could refer to the father's absence from the care of the child for a variety of reasons. See for details, T.K.Rajalakshmi, 'The Mother As Guardian', *Frontline* (26 March 1999, 111–12). Similarly, the Bombay High Court delivered a judgment on 4 May 1999, expanding the provisions of section 3(1)(A) of the 'iddat period maintenance' under the Muslim Women's (protection of Rights on Divorce) Act, 1986, to mean the entire lifetime of the divorced women and not merely the first three months as was being widely interpreted by the lower courts. See report by Farida Shaikh, 'Have you come here to fool me? You must be my husband's agents', *Indian Express*, Chandigarh (10 May 1999, 1).

[43]There does not exist a uniform or a 'universally' shared civil code in India. On matters of family law, Hindus, Muslims, Christians, and Parsees are all governed by separate practices or the personal law of their particular community. Personal laws, more often than not, sanction and justify differential treatment of men and women so that within the framework of personal laws, women are more likely to have a subordinate status. The terms of separation, divorce, remarriage, maintenance, etc., are weighted in favour of men with the result that polygamy, unequal rights of inheritance, (*contd.*)

women should receive alimony or property was opposed by those upholding the sanctity of the shariat (Islamic legal code). The Shahbano Case, 1985, and the Muslim Women's Bill, 1986, became rallying symbols for the protectors of the shariat and the autonomy of the Muslim community, for diverse strands of activists who opposed communalisation of women's issues and appealed for a gender-just uniform civil code, for Hindu communalists for whom the Supreme Court judgment vindicated their claims of the Muslim community being 'barbaric' and 'anti-national', and also for their Muslim counterparts for whom the reversal of the Supreme Court judgment became the ultimate source of redemption of their dignity as Muslims.[44] The similarity in the debates on sati in

---

(*contd.*) and unilateral rights of husbands to divorce are frequently upheld. The compulsions of electoral success and the procedural aspects of representative democracy have also gone against the interests of women. The dominance of (male) religious community leaders is perpetuated with their opinion receiving priority in interactions with the government and political parties. Apart from negotiating with the more conservative elements within religious communities, considerations of electoral victory have propelled political parties in the same direction. In a situation marked with communal tensions, religious minorities more than the majority have a tendency to protect and maximise their interests by taking collective decisions. Political parties have, therefore, been reluctant to take decisions that might be unacceptable to the leaders of these communities. With the prevalence of perceptions of community interests, intra-group differentiations, particularly, gender inequalities have remained unattended. (Mahajan 1998, 151–52).

[44]On 23 April 1985, the Supreme Court of India in the Mohammed Ahmed Khan vs. Shahbano Begum case gave divorced Muslim women the right to lifelong maintenance under article 125 of the Indian Criminal Procedure Code. Mohammed Khan, Shahbano's ex-husband had contested her claims for maintenance, insisting that he had, according to Muslim personal law, supported her for three months after their divorce. The Supreme Court stressed that there was no conflict between its verdict and the provisions of Muslim personal law, which in its view, also entitled women to alimony if they were unable to maintain themselves. The court further advised that the Muslim community take 'a lead in the matter of reform of their personal law' and that a uniform civil code be formulated to 'help the cause of national integration'. The decision sparked a nationwide controversy on the (*contd.*)

nineteenth-century India and the debate triggered off by the Shahbano case has been pointed out by Lata Mani to show how both of them saw the unfolding of the woman-tradition-law-scripture nexus (Mani 1985, 120). In the 1980s, the debate and demonstrations following the incident of sati in September 1987 in Deorala, a village in Rajasthan, reflected the manner in which the rights of Hindu women were imbricated with questions of religious identity, community autonomy, and eventually 'a politics of power'.[45] In both these cases what was at stake was women's economic freedom, their right to property, and the very bases on which the structures of domination within communities

---

(*contd.*) question of religious personal law and the desirability or otherwise of a uniform civil code. See Lata Mani, 'Contentious Traditions' in *Recasting Women*, eds. Kumkum Sangari and Sudesh Vaid (Kali for Women: Delhi, 1985, 1993, 119). For details of the Supreme Court decision and the circumstances in which the Muslim Women's Bill was enacted as well as the agitations which accompanied the two, see Radha Kumar, *A History of Doing* (1993, 160–71).

[45]Sudesh Vaid has shown how the tradition of sati and sati-dharma was created in the Shekhavati region (in Deorala village where the incident of sati occurred) after independence largely to regain lost authority. After independence, with the abolition of the princely states and the further abolition of the zamindari and jagirdari systems of land relations, the Kshatriyas and Banias had lost their traditional privileges. The Kshatriya Mahasabha (an organisation of ex-rulers and large landowners) and the Bhooswami Sangh (organisation of small landowners) attempted to reclaim their lost privileges by invoking a chivalric 'Rajput' tradition in which men defended the Hindu tradition on battlefields and women defended it at home by self-sacrifice through jauhar and sati. Sati came to be projected as exemplifying the true Rajput identity. Sudesh Vaid, 'Politics of Widow Immolation' (1988). Radha Kumar shows how despite a High Court order against holding the ritual of *chunari mahotsava* (veil festival) ten days after Roop Kanwar's death, the mahotsava was performed. From an act of mourning, it transformed itself into a show of strength, a victory celebration, with the male marchers, traditionally dressed, waving their fists aloft in triumph and shouting slogans. The site of sati was transformed into a political rallying ground: a highly charged state-of-siege atmosphere was created with sword-wielding youth who surrounded the *sati-sthal* and instead of devotional songs, shouted slogans modelled on mainstream political slogans (Kumar 1993: 176–77).

were organised. Wives and widows claiming the right to property threatened to destabilise more than just economic structures. They aimed to transform radically the multifarious whorls of domination that informed their lives as women. Yet, in both cases the (male) religious leaders and fundamentalists were able to raise the alarm of 'community in danger' and reaffirm their claims to representing the community. In both cases, the government sacrificed women's rights to strike a balancing act with the two communities, aiming eventually at strengthening its electoral prospects with both.[46] The then government thus brought a highly retrograde legislation, the Muslim Women's (Protection of Rights on Divorce) Bill, 1986, which freed Muslim men from the obligation put by Section 125 towards abandoned or divorced wives.[47] Similarly, while the state government in Rajasthan took no action against the ideologues and profiteers of sati in Deorala, all major centrist and right-wing parties visited the site not to enquire into what had happened, but to stake their own claim to 'tradition' and via this to the Rajput and Hindu vote (Kumar 1993, 177).

With Government inactivity in the Ramjanmabhumi issue, the resurgence of a jingoist Hindu nationalism and the relative invisibility of (Hindu) public opposition to these, the Muslim community closed it ranks, preferring reforms from within the community rather than opening its boundaries for uniform laws.[48]

---

[46]The government sought to compensate its inactivity towards the Ramjanmabhumi agitations by conceding to Muslim fundamentalist demands for allowing personal law to cut into the application of uniform laws such as Section 125 (Ibid, 169).

[47]The Muslim Women's (Protection of Rights on Divorce) Bill, 1986, excluded Muslim women from the purview of Section 125, stating that the obligation of their husband to maintain them ended with the three-month *iddat* period, after which their families would have to support them, failing this the local *waqf* board.

[48]Many Muslims who had earlier supported change in personal laws, now started to support them. The Committee for the Protection of the Rights of Muslim Women, which was formed to oppose the bill, limited its membership to Muslims.

The period also saw a vehement and vociferous rise in upper-caste opposition to caste-based reservations in jobs. The Hindu right wing, in particular, waged a tirade against the state for eroding unmarked abstract citizenship by promoting caste- and community-based privileges and 'pampering' religious minorities and scheduled castes and tribes. Thus, in the context of the 1980s, the framework of the discourse on rights was inverted with the (upper caste, Hindu, male) 'oppressors' presenting themselves as 'victims' 'pleading' for abstract citizenship unmarked by 'privileges' of caste and community.[49] At this historical juncture, points out Aditya Nigam, the 'subaltern' and the 'victim' were not what was being excluded from hegemonic narratives, but, rather, being produced by them.[50]

The hegemonic discourses on citizenship of the period, as epitomised by the anti-Mandal struggle and *Hindutva*, by occluding the markings of caste, gender, class, and community,

---

[49]Nivedita Menon shows how upper-caste opposition to the Mandal Commission reservations in jobs for the scheduled castes and tribes and the backward castes came from both left-wing secularists as well as from the Hindu right wing. The latter is usually understood to be asserting particularity rather than the universal, for they appear to be asserting religious identity in the realm of the state. A closer analysis shows, however, that the claims are rather that the state has not adequately protected the abstract, unmarked citizen. In other words the argument is that the state has not delivered on its promise of abstract citizenship—minorities have retained their personal laws, and the only Muslim majority state, Kashmir, has a special status within the framework of the Constitution. See Nivedita Menon (1998).

[50]Aditya Nigam sees a 'discursive break' occurring in the period 1990–92 in India. He identifies three events as marking this rupture: (i) the inauguration of structural adjustment policies, (ii) the violent upper-caste agitations against implementing the Mandal Commsssion report which made job reservations for backward castes, and, (iii) the demolition of the Babri Masjid by Hindu right-wing forces. He sees these events as 'symbolically overturning the discourse of privilege and oppression'—the first transformed the organised worker into being privileged by 'socialist tyranny' which oppressed the entrepreneur/capitalist; the second demanded justice for the dispossessed upper castes; the third created the besieged victim in the Hindu majority, outflanked by the oppressive minority. Aditya Nigam, 'Nation, Locality and Representation: India after the 1996 Elections' (1996).

continued to mark the citizen as upper-caste, Hindu, and male. A similar structuring of the feminist subject is also revealed within the hegemonic culture of the period.[51] The political subjectivities of women in both the above-stated movements expressed itself in claims to equality and freedom not as 'women' but as 'citizens'. The rallying point for these active 'political subjects was not the deprivation women experienced as women, but the deprivation they suffered along with their men on account of the failure of successive governments to keep their constitutional promise of protecting the universal abstract citizen. Moved with the ideal of saving the 'nation' from descending into 'mediocrity', the anti-Mandal women 'took to the streets', claiming deprivation and injustice not as women but as citizens. The claims to equality were not grounded in gender terms, for to do that would have meant pitting themselves against their men. The alignment of their claims to citizenship with similar claims by men put them against both lower-caste men and women. In this quest for equality and freedom, not only were gender issues effaced, the 'universal citizen' was produced through a 'secularising' of the middle-class sphere. The process of secularisation involved an othering of caste and community from the middle-class sphere, and the subsequent abstraction and universalisation of the 'residual' citizen—upper caste, Hindu, male.[52] Not only was the citizen marked hegemonically, quite

---

[51]Susie Tharu and Tejaswini Niranjana, 'Problems for a Contemporary Theory of Gender' in *Subaltern Studies* vol. IX, eds., Shahid Amin and Dipesh Chakrabarty (1996, 237).

[52]Susie Tharu and Tejaswini Niranjana point out that the anti-Mandal struggle saw young middle-class women foregrounded as assertive, nonsubmissive, jointly protesting with men the erosion of their rights as citizens. These women declared that they were against reservation for women in jobs and in public transport as reservations would make them soft and dependent. The nearly unanimous media celebration of the upper-caste students suggests that the authors framed them within a nonsectarian nationalism and humanism: as truly egalitarian and therefore anti-Mandal, whereas the pro-Mandal groups were accused of supporting casteism. Like the anti-Mandal agitations, Hindutva, too, seems to inculcate an articulate, fighting individualism (*contd.*)

like the days of the national struggle, 'women' were marked upper-caste and Hindu. Susie Tharu and Tejaswini Niranjana assert that the 'category' of woman and, therefore, in a very important sense, the field of feminism as well as the female subject emerge in this context by obscuring the dalit women and marking the lower caste as the predatory male who becomes the legitimate object of feminist rage.[53] Similarly, women of the Rashtrasevika Sangh, in an ironic inversion of the traditional invisibility of middle-class, upper-caste women, played an active role in communal rioting in the wake of the Ramjanmabhumi movement.[54] Quite like the anti-Mandal movement, this movement too contributed towards women's political self-activisation and self-actualisation insofar as these women stepped

---

(*contd.*) for women and men, inciting its subjects to speak and act as independent, agentive citizens. Though the new Hindu self is projected as discriminated and embattled, it presents itself as occupying a 'neutral ground' not only vis-a-vis other religious communities but also on issues of gender. Members of the Rashtrasevika Sangh would, for example, distance/distinguish themselves from other women's organisations in that they did not always take the woman's side while arbitrating: 'We are neutral...*hum ghar torne wale nahin hain* (we do not break houses)' (Ibid, 237–39, 251).

[53]The resurgence of women in the public sphere as claimants to the nation and citizenship results in a masculinisation of the lower caste (the lower caste women not being women) and all women being upper-caste. (Ibid, 239–45).

[54]The Rashtrasevika Sangh was set up in 1936 by Lakshmibai Kelkar as a parallel (women's) wing of the RSS (Rashtriya Swayamsevak Sangh). Tanika Sarkar asserts that Karsevikas (women who had pledged to build the temple with their own hands) have been mobilised from traditionally the most conservative backgrounds—upper class, middle-ranking service sector and trading sector. These women have played a visible and active role in expanding the scale and range of the aggressiveness and violence of the Hindu-right wing. Pictures of women sporting the saffron band symbolising sacrifice and martyrdom have appeared in VHP fortnightly magazines as a symbol of the 'rise of Mother Power'. Rural women in Bhagalpur in 1989 and upper middle-class women in Ahmedabad in 1990 played an active role in rioting. According to VHP, an estimated 20,000 karsevikas courted arrest at Ayodhya on 4 January 1991 and a total of 50,000 were involved in the entire December 1990–January 1991 round of nonviolent agitation (satyagrahas). Tanika Sarkar, 'Hindu Women: Politicisation Through Communalisation', in *Internal Conflict in South Asia*, eds. Kumar Rupesinghe and Khawar Mumtaz (London: Sage 131).

out of their iconic images, where anti-Muslim tirades were woven around the figure of the endlessly raped or threatened Hindu woman, to a new empowering self-image. The karsevika, in a reversal of the epic narrative of *Ramayana* where Rama and his army save Sita from the demon king, is now entrusted with the task of rescuing the birthplace of Rama from unscrupulous politicians and the Muslims: 'We have come here to shed blood....the meaning of temple building is that *mullahs* (Muslim religious leaders) should be hanged.[55] Mulayam Singh Yadav and V.P. Singh should be hanged'. Their identity as women is grounded in the 'awakening of Hindutva' to be realised in citizenship in a Hindu State.[56] Their identity as citizen is grounded not merely in equality with men, but in the inculcation of a woman-citizen who is fearless, responsible, and strong. Interestingly, unlike the middle-class Hindu woman of the nationalist period, strength here refers not to any inner, spiritual, strength, but physical courage and strength emanating from the trained, hardened, invincible female body.[57] The Muslim woman like the lower-caste Hindu woman is caught in a curious no-win situation. She cannot really be woman anymore than she can be Indian. As woman and as Indian, she cannot really be Muslim. The Hindu women on the Right are empowered by these new movements, but in a way that sets up the feminist project as one that endorses caste/class hierarchies and the othering of Islam (Tharu and Niranjana 1996, 252).

---

[55]A karsevika from Aligarh. (Ibid, 132).

[56]The official history of the Samiti explains that the Samiti was founded with the '...primary aim of the awakening of *Hindutva*...'. (Ibid, 137).

[57]The implication is that the female body is trained in a 'patriotic' war against the Muslim aggressor, allowing considerable space thereby to the myth of Muslim lust within the general mythology of Hindu communalism. Within the Samiti, the etiology of this thrust on physical strength is traced to a train incident witnessed by Mrs. Kelkar where a young woman on a train was raped by (Hindu) 'ruffians' in her husband's presence. Sarkar points out, however, the usefulness of this emphasis on self-reliance, in the public and mixed-gender spaces where women encounter overt and daily sexual harassment and threats as well as in situations at home of domestic violence and dowry-related violence and murders. (Ibid, 138).

The struggles of feminists against the Muslim Women's Bill and sati confronted them with issues that were to become increasingly important for the definition/delimitation of 'women's politics'. The contending definitions of secularism, churned out by the debates, ranged by and large between a classic liberal-democratic view of secularism by opponents of the Bill, which distrusted religious definitions of the rights of the individual, to official enunciations which not only allowed the right of communities to make their own laws but also legitimised the subversion of individual rights to the dictates of particular communities. Moreover, the reaffirmation of community boundaries in the course of these debates undermined feminist demands through 'authoritative' contentions that there was no such thing as a 'common', 'unified' category of women, distinguished as they were by caste, class, and community, with differing experiences, needs, and interests. Almost logically, as it were, the question of representativeness assumed significance, and the symbol of the 'real woman' posited in opposition to the 'feminist', began to be used widely. Feminist demands for a uniform civil code, for instance, were countered by assertions that they did not represent the 'real' desires of 'real' women.[58] This spectre of the 'real woman' can, however, be seen as having sprung roots in the early part of the twentieth century. If the latter half of the nineteenth century saw both the colonialists and the nationalists rival each other in identifying 'women' as 'objects' to be saved from the effects of a heathen civilisation or,

[58]Radha Kumar refers to two specific instances where this was brought out in this context. For some years prior to the agitation against the Muslim Women's Bill, feminists had revived demands for a uniform civil code to replace religion-based and differentiated personal laws. Two initiatives in this regard by Mary Roy against Christian personal law and Shahnaz Sheikh against Muslim personal law received wide publicity and support from feminists all over the country. These initiatives, however, were confronted by questions of representation or representativeness, and whereas both Mary and Shahnaz were demanding reforms in the personal laws which affected them directly, it was argued that none of them represented the 'real' desires of 'real' Christian/ Muslim women (Kumar 1993, 171).

as in the case of the nationalists, retrieve them as emblems and bearers of the national tradition, the twentieth century saw the colonialists define their 'civilising mission' differently. As in the construction of the Bengali babu (the product of colonial modernity) as a 'deviant' form of masculinity, the new Indian woman (the product of nationalist modernity) was no longer seen as representing real women. The quintessential Indian woman needing the coloniser's protection was now replaced by the 'poor woman' who came to represent the millions of 'ignorant' Indians who lived in villages, callously scorned by the Indian middle class. The question of representativeness of women activists and that 'real women' were poor, rural, and, significantly, 'traditional' emerged also in the nationalist reluctance to effect changes in personal laws. Gandhi, for example, while agreeing with the need for improvement in women's status, disagreed with their tactics and urged women activists to spend their time in the villages and learn about local customs. In doing so they would, he thought, understand that legal changes were irrelevant for most rural women. Congressmen opposed to the reforms were convinced that the demands for change were not 'real' since the women they knew were very happy with their lives and appeared to be in no need for change. The 'new woman', who in the late nineteenth century became the epitome of a 'reformed' national tradition, can be seen in this period to be wielding power to embarrass the nationalist male before the colonising outsider by asking for changes in *their* family laws.[59] It was, as we mentioned in an earlier chapter, this threat perception that the women activists demanding franchise hoped to ease and thereby elicit male support. They achieved this by persisting with the late nineteenth-century constructions of Indian womanhood and underlining complicity with Indian men by stressing their own difference from the Western women.

---

[59]While the All India Women's Conference favoured uniform laws for all women regardless of community, male reformers seemed to have different views on women's needs. For details see Geraldine Forbes (1996, 112–15).

In the context of the 1980s mentioned above, the longstanding demand for a uniform civil code by women's groups seeking to unburden women through liberatory, abstract citizenship underwent a rethinking. Women's groups, which had consistently struggled for citizenship rights for women, focussing on uniform laws irrespective of community membership, faced the danger of the appropriation of their demands by hegemonic discourses on citizenship. Though constituted of various strands, women's groups modified their stance and looked for ways to make women's rights as citizens commensurate with their membership within particular communities. In order to carve out maximum possible spaces for women as individuals, they looked for possible exits that enabled individual constituents of communities to opt out of and reassess their terms of belonging to a community and also assure the availability of alternatives in terms of a gender-just framework of rights and laws.[60]

Conclusion

Citizenship, as a legal status and as the organising principle for a sovereign nation and democratic political society, was

---

[60]Women's groups drew consensus on three possible ways: (i) support for and initiation of attempts to bring about reform within personal laws; (ii) bringing about legislation in areas which are not covered either by secular or personal laws—such as domestic violence and right to the matrimonial home—thus avoiding a direct confrontation with communities and the wider communal politics; (iii) working on setting up a comprehensive gender-just framework of rights covering areas not merely covered by personal laws but also the 'public' domain of work (creches, equal wages, maternity benefits, etc.) which should be available to all citizens. Where these laws do not conflict with personal laws, they should be automatically applicable, and where they do conflict, it should be open to individual citizens to make the choice (Menon 1998, PE-3). For an exploration of the dilemmas before women's groups at this historical conjuncture and a mapping of the shifts in the trajectory of feminist thinking on the Uniform Civil Code at different levels to re-engage with notions of citizenship, nation and gender, see Nivedita Menon, 'Women and Citizenship' in *Wages of Freedom*, ed. Partha Chatterjee (1998, 242–65).

incorporated in the Indian Constitution in the context of the struggles for self-determination waged against multilayered oppressive structures and discursive constructions of racial and caste superiority. Within this context, the cultural/religious community on the one hand and the national-political community on the other acquired equivocal primacy, leading to tensions in citizenship as it has unfolded over the years after independence. Nowhere is this tension more manifest than in the citizenship of women. The articulation of women as citizens in India was imbricated within a web of discourses of liberation and equality, which made the national-political and religious-cultural communities the primary and often contesting sources of a person's identity as citizen. The primacy given to community membership and the manner in which women were implicated into it has had important ramifications on voicing women as citizens and on carving out a space for women's politics.

The articulation of the category 'woman' has historically been done in a manner which makes her the medium through which a community—religious/national-political/caste—is bound together. Women's lived experiences have had, therefore, to contend with various superscriptions and circumscriptions. The idealised superscribed *woman*—pure, chaste, with superhuman qualities of purging the body politic—ensnares women within normative forms of behaviour. A unified category of women—a collective body of women, as agents and subjects of liberatory change—proves elusive as it attempts to homogenise disparate entities, ironically within an abstracted category of woman. Within the confines of a plural society and differential life experiences of women, spaces for women's politics emerge in dispersed ways and locations. I have in mind here what Kumkum Sangari calls 'a politics of the possible' and a rather revealing explication of it in the anti-arrack movements in Andhra Pradesh in the last decade. A unique feature of this movement was the steadfast refusal of women to take the initiative beyond the confines of their own village: the refrain 'Are the women of the other villages dead? Why should we go there to fight against *sara*?'. By confining their initiative to their own local conditions, the women were in fact demarcating in precise terms the domain over which they could usher in change and exercise control, demonstrating thereby a 'politics of the possible'.[61] Again, women as common components of various social movements, peasant, tribal, dalit, environment and, not the least, the women's movement itself could form the bridges within movements urging radical social change to usher in a society which is equitable and gender-just.[62]

---

[61]The phrase is the title of Kumkum Sangari's article 'The Politics of the Possible', in *Interrogating Modernity: Culture and Colonialism in India*, eds. Tejaswini Niranjana, P. Sudhir and Vivek Dhareshwar (1993). The example is taken from Susie Tharu and Tejaswini Niranjana (1996, 260).

[62]Omvedt points out that the emergence of new women's organisations after 1985 has been linked largely to mass organisations of the new social movements unleashing a new dynamic, giving scope to both middle-class women and rural women to act autonomously. New issues began to be raised, new theoretical formulations made, new campaigns begun that involved not only women but the deepening of other social movements as well. The women's movement, says Omvedt, was in many ways the weakest of the new social movements, yet the recovery of the social movements after 1985 was associated with women's participation and the issues raised by women. See Gail Omvedt, *Reinventing Revolution: New Social Movements and the Socialist Tradition in India* (1993, 200).

6

Rethinking Citizenship in an Age of Globalisation

As seen in the earlier chapters, the notion of citizenship has historically connoted membership in a political community. The form of this political community and the nature of membership it invokes have, however, always been in flux. Nonetheless, the quest for an ideal membership and the political community in which it can best unfold has persistently provoked struggles and debates, making citizenship a contested terrain. In this chapter, an attempt will be made to map the contours of this contest since the late 1980s. As noted in the first chapter, there has been an unprecedented upsurge in the writings on citizenship in the last fifteen years. Almost all these writings profess that the context of globalisation has produced changes that demand that the notion of citizenship be reconceptualised. The changed circumstances of globalisation, they suggest, have brought about a displacement of two categories that had hitherto been the core of citizenship theory, viz., the *individual* as the bearer of rights and the *nation-state* as the unit of citizenship identity. These displacements, they claim, have made it necessary to talk of human rights and world citizenship in place of national citizenship and cultural and community rights instead of individual rights. This chapter proposes that the emphasis on human rights and cultural communities have brought into conflict existing ideological strands within the theory of citizenship. It further proposes that the arguments put forward to support the redefinition of citizenship are ambivalent and fraught with contradictions, and, quite like the dominant orthodoxy on citizenship, they work within the framework of exclusion and difference-deferral.

The relevance of human rights and community rights under conditions described as 'specifically' late twentieth century, viz., the globalisation of economies, the unprecedented scale of transnational movement of workers and refugees, the displacement of class politics by identity politics, the changing position of women, the cataclysmic effects of technological and economic expansion, etc., cannot be denied. At the same time, however, it must be emphasised that the claims for human rights and community rights are ridden by contradictions, especially as they continue to place themselves within the exclusionary discourse of difference-deferral.[1] Moreover, alongside the apotheosis of the world citizen and the individual-in-community, there coexists an anxiety over a *crisis* in citizenship. More significant, however, is the manner in which it informs state practices, which, perhaps more vehemently than ever before, have striven to reinforce national boundaries and which restrict the inflow of foreigners,

---

[1] The idea of the world as a unified and hierarchised whole was central to colonial practices of rule. The colonial state, while presenting a 'rational' basis for colonial rule, relied on this notion whereby the differences in the social conditions which prevailed in the colonies and the metropole were seen as fundamental. The colonial strategy of rule justified the deferral or postponement of self-rule and democracy, which characterised the political structures in the metropoles, by classifying colonial conditions within the universal framework in terms of differences from the norm. This rationalised the differences between metropolis and colony as differences on a scale of social conditions, with the implication that an advance along the scale would justify practices closer to the norm (Chatterjee 1994, 82).

immigrants, and refugees. Again, a growing preoccupation with hegemonically articulated notions of 'global risks', notably 'terrorism', have rendered certain communities 'suspect'. These suspicions make themselves manifest in extraordinary laws, for example, antiterrorism laws as the Prevention Of Terrorism Act (2002) in India, Patriot Act (2002) in the USA, that target specific communities. The proliferation of political conservatism in most countries has seen the intensification of an exclusionary nationalism, where 'immigrants' are seen outside the ties that constitute a nation. Closer, at home, the humiliating tirade against non-Hindus, violence perpetrated against Muslims, Christians, and dalits and intermittent debates on the 'foreign origins' and 'citizenship' of the president of the Indian National Congress (I), Sonia Gandhi, have sought to enforce a hegemonic national identity which thrives on exclusion, coercion, violence, and extermination.

In this context, it becomes imperative to examine the contours of the present debate to show the contradictions and ambivalences which inform it. It is important to see the manner in which the strands in the debate seek to change the existing idea of citizenship and also to examine how these ideas of change have influenced the theory of citizenship. As mentioned before, the perceptions of displacement of the core elements of citizenship have brought a range of issues and ideological strands into conflict. Moreover, the arguments that are based on the assumptions of displacement are inconsistent, so much so that the justification in the reconceptualisation of citizenship on the basis of one leads to a dismantling of the other. This chapter proposes that there is a pressing need to rethink the existing frameworks of citizenship; but the paradigms suggested by the writings under review are inadequate and exclusionary. The need, therefore, is to look beyond them and work out a framework that offers the analytical tools for understanding the present complexities and retains at the same time the idea of citizenship as constitutive of equality and identity.

New Contexts and Changing Concerns: World Citizenship and Multiculturalism

The idea and practice of citizenship was, till recently, determined by the liberal formulation that placed the rights-bearing individual at its core, and citizenship was seen as a legal status indicating the possession of rights which an individual held equally with others. Towards the late twentieth century, amidst a plethora of Western writings on citizenship, two influential strands appeared and attempted to redefine the manner in which citizenship has so far been understood. Rooted within the globalisation framework, they claim that the rapid, inexorable, and cataclysmic changes experienced in the late twentieth century have made it necessary that citizenship be reconceptualised. They suggest in particular that the two categories that had hitherto been integral to the notion of modern citizenship, viz., the *individual* as the bearer of rights, and the *nation-state* as the unit of citizenship identity, be displaced by cultural and community rights and human rights and world citizenship, respectively.

The growing interconnectedness of the world, the writings propose, has made national boundaries porous. As a result, notions of bounded political communities and national sovereignty as well as the identity between national culture and political membership, have become redundant. Bryan Turner (1986), Ursula Vogel (1991), Jurgen Habermas (1992) and Yasemin Soysal (1994), for example, have suggested that there exists a tension between traditional forms of social and political membership and the interdependence that contemporary world developments have brought about. In this context, they argue, citizenship has to part company with the nation-state and the accompanying notions of nation-state sovereignty. The restrictive rights of citizenship confined within the boundaries of the nation-state have to be given up in favour of membership in the world community and the universal human rights that this community upholds.

The other strand has made it acceptable to talk of differential rights and differentiated citizenship for members of cultural communities, their rights depending on their membership of the community and the special needs that accrue from it. The majority of the present writings, almost predictably, take off with a critique of the British sociologist, T.H. Marshall (1950). While accepting Marshall's definition of citizenship as 'full and equal membership in a political community' (Marshall and Bottomore 1992, 50–51) encapsulating the two promises of citizenship, viz., 'horizontal camaraderie' or equality among members of the political community and 'integration as equals' into the political community with a share in a common (national) culture and social heritage quite like the Marxist and feminist critiques of liberal citizenship, they question the basis on which this equality is sought to be assured. Within the framework of liberal democracy, which formed the context of Marshall's exposition, citizenship constitutes an overwhelming identity masking all other identities to produce masked/unmarked (and therefore) 'equal' citizens of the nation. This promise of equality is premised on effacing ascriptive (hierarchical) inequalities and masking differences (of culture, caste, gender, etc.) to make them irrelevant for the exercise and enjoyment of the rights of citizenship. Thus, the notion of citizenship, working within the framework of the Enlightenment and modernity, places the rational self-actualising and self-determining individual at the core of the theory and practice of citizenship. It seeks to establish free and equal citizens by effacing ascriptive inequalities and differences of culture, caste, gender, race, and ethnicity.

Marshall's analysis of the emergence of the constitutive elements of citizenship in England over the last three centuries is primarily a study of the growth of citizenship in a relationship of conflict and collusion with capitalism. It focusses on citizenship as the gradual extension of equality in what is seen primarily as a class-differentiated society. The current scholarship seeks to deflect attention to cultural communities. Questioning the idea that the citizen can enjoy rights independent of the contexts to which she/he belongs, this strand opens up a significant terrain of contestation by making plurality, diversity, and difference significant terms of reference for retheorising citizenship. This contest pertains to the unmasking of those differences that were earlier seen as irrelevant to citizenship. The writings assert that modern societies are multicultural and that the specific contexts of individuals—cultural, religious, ethnic, linguistic, etc.—determine citizenship in significant ways. In most Western societies, the ethnic, religious, and racial communities have pressed for rights that would look at their special needs and would thereby substantiate the formal equality of citizenship. There is a growing effort to redefine citizenship by giving due importance to cultural differences among individuals and strike a balance between the numerous religious, ethnic, linguistic identities while constructing a common political identity of the citizen. The notion of 'differentiated citizenship' has been advanced by some theorists who felt that the common rights of citizenship, originally defined by (and for) white men in a class-differentiated society, could not accommodate the needs of specific cultural groups. The concept advocates the incorporation of members of certain (cultural) groups not only as individuals but also as members of groups, their rights depending in part on this group membership catering to their special needs (Young 1989). A substantial bulk of the present debate on the nature and scope of citizenship, therefore, concerns itself with the so-called 'universalism' (of Western constitutional democracies) vs. 'particularism' (claims of specific communities to preserve their ways of life) debate—issues of individual entitlement vs. attachment to a particular community—issues, in other words, critical to the debate between the liberals and the communitarians. There is also a growing impulse to find a meeting ground between the two, seeking to make cultural rights relevant and admissible in societies where a 'universal' culture of 'liberal' values (respect for individual rights, a rule of law, etc.) already exists (Kymlicka 1996; Mahajan 1998, 2002).

Historical Trends and Emerging Contests

Two distinct strands/traditions may be identified in the historical evolution of the concept of citizenship, viz., the classical tradition or civic republicanism characterised by ideas of the common good, public spirit, political participation, and civic virtue, and the modern liberal tradition of citizenship with its emphasis on individual rights and private interests. The two strands have almost divergent conceptions of citizenship. In the republican tradition, the manner in which citizenship is understood flows primarily from the primacy of the political in human life. As such, it envisages the political community as the primary unit of membership and conceptualises it as a closely-knit body of citizens. The citizen is primarily conceived as a political actor who bears the responsibility of citizenship proudly, for not only is political participation a primary virtue, it is at the very core of a human being's life, binding citizens together in a common commitment and duty towards civic life. On the other hand, the liberal tradition posits the citizen as an unencumbered self, an individual who seeks his/her actualisation not through political activity, but through a range of other commitments and activities, which take place in a diverse and loosely connected body. Unlike the republican tradition that makes political participation a duty and a citizen's core activity, the liberal tradition would rather see it as a status and entitlement giving access to a set of rights. The liberal theory, while removing impediments towards the assumption of the status of a citizen, visualises citizenship as an outer frame of a person's life, as encompassing activities that are often seen as more fulfilling than political participation. If republicanism makes the citizen the primary political actor, liberalism sees political activity as impersonal. The citizen is a private person with the autonomy to choose when or how to enter the public domain unlike republicanism's stern adherence to the citizen's duties towards civic life (Walzer 1989).

While the two strands synchronised in the early modern period, they parted company as the liberal strand became predominant. The frameworks of political participation put forward in the republican tradition remained, however, a subterranean current around which notions of empowerment, political participation, and 'political' community wove themselves. Since the 1980s, with the emergence of multiculturalism as a democratic value, the dividing lines between the liberal and republican notions of citizenship have resonated. The forms in which the divisions have manifested themselves, have, however, been different. The main areas of contention continue to lie as in the case of the former divide, around issues of the primacy of individual as opposed to the community and, again, the primacy of rights as opposed to duty.

The notion of citizenship as integration and horizontal camaraderie, enunciated within the liberal framework, is based on a specific notion of equality that has been seen as both its *achievement* and its *limitation*. The notion of equal membership in the liberal framework involves the uniform generalisation of citizenship across social structures, implying equal application of the law and the promise that no person or group is legally privileged. The idea of the citizen as a masked individual, while facilitating uniform application, is problematic because it overlooks the faultlines in society and the differential positioning of individuals in it. Further, the process of masking, which requires the dissociation of the individual from social, economic and cultural contexts, may in most cases constitute a disadvantage and injustice. The power of dissociation may not be equally available to all, and the (debilitating) identities of caste, race, and gender may continue to determine an individual's participation in the public-political as citizens. The requirement of dissociation is moreover, hegemonic, since the political community in which the members enter after shedding their ascriptive identities, is already marked as male, upper class, upper caste, Hindu, or white. In these circumstances formal citizenship rights cannot influence the conditions that render the possession of citizenship ineffective, if not worthless.

It is this primacy of the masked, rights-bearing individual that has been questioned by multiculturalists. They point, in particular, to the fact that the existing frameworks within which liberal citizenship unfolds puts at a disadvantage those who belong to minority communities. We have seen that within liberal theory, citizenship is a legal status which enables citizens to enjoy rights equally with other citizens, the conditions for equal enjoyment being laid out by making irrelevant the particular contexts of individuals, that is, their special circumstances defined by birth, race, caste, culture, ethnicity, gender, etc. This view is counterposed by the multiculturalists who, in the civic republican tradition, assert the significance of the particular contexts of individuals for determining the extent to which rights can be enjoyed equally. These theorists emphasise that instead of masking these differences in the allocation of rights, efforts must be made to take account of the specificity of the different circumstances of citizens. An increasing number of theorists argue that large numbers of ethnic, religious, and linguistic groups feel excluded from the 'common' rights to citizenship. These groups can be accommodated into common citizenship only by adopting what Iris Marion Young calls 'differentiated citizenship', which means that members of certain groups should be accommodated not only as individuals but also through their group, and their rights would depend partially upon their group membership. According to Young, the attempt to create a universal conception of citizenship transcending group differences is fundamentally unjust because it oppresses historically marginalised groups:

> In a society where some groups are privileged while others are oppressed, insisting that as citizens persons should leave behind their particular affiliations and experiences, and adopt a general point of view, serves only to reinforce the privileged, for the perspective and interests of the privileged will tend to dominate this unified public, marginalising or silencing those of other groups (Young 1989, 257).

While addressing issues of equality and discrimination in plural societies, theorists of multiculturalism relocate the individual within the community. The notion of the community, however, differs from the civic republican insofar as it is primarily cultural and ascriptive. Yet, in significant ways, this relocation alters the notion of the individual, and also brings back commitment to the sustenance of the community as a core duty of the individual-in-community. The arguments made in favour of multiculturalism are, thus, not only for the correction of 'historical wrongs' or even the alleviation of discrimination; the commitment to sustain the community is primarily rooted in the belief that communities have much of value to offer to the political community (Mahajan 2002). The investment in diversity is also based on the assumption that every culture has valuable elements that can be shared and learned. This assumption immediately opens up possibilities of conceiving the political community as a shared public space where equality is a significant norm. An important contribution of multiculturalism to the theory of citizenship has thus been that it has altered the way in which the political community has been thought of. Far from being a homogenous whole, the political community is seen as heterogeneous. Moreover, this heterogeneity is seen as valuable for a democratic public space. Yet, in its enthusiasm to establish the primacy of the community and the idea of individual-in-community, multiculturalism denies the individual the right of critical and creative membership in the community. Significantly, this is the right that the community itself claims for redefining the terms of its membership within the political community.

Alongside the recognition of the community as the bearer of rights, the republican ideas of 'civic virtue' and 'good citizenship' have also been revived within different ideological strands. The idea of good citizenship defined by civic virtue, patriotism, and participatory citizenship emerged in classical antiquity and was revived as an ideal in Renaissance Italy and eighteenth-century America and France. The revival of these principles in the last two decades has drawn a second set of dividing lines between those who see some basic rights as the defining principle of citizenship and those who regard rights as conditions which follow the exercise of a citizen's duty to participate in the political process. This faultline, however, assumes different forms depending on the specific ideological tradition in which it is placed. Civic virtue and participation have acquired as much significance as measures of active citizenship among theorists of the Left as among the civil society theorists and the communitarians. The idea of citizenship as activity in all these theories may be seen as a reaction to the political passivity which liberal citizenship is seen to have generated, leading to the degeneration of liberal democracies. While Left theorists would like to 'empower' citizens through democratic participation (Phillips 1991; Pierson 1991), radical pluralists such as Chantal Mouffe believe that a relation of 'democratic equivalence' may be established through participation and the articulation of difference (Mouffe 1992). Theorists such as Michael Walzer, too, acknowledge the plurality of social life and propose that a common forum or a common binding principle to social diversity can be accorded by political citizenship. It is in public life, the common forum of participation of diverse groups, that individuals think of a common good beyond their own conceptions of the good life. For Walzer, while citizenship is the basis of social unity, it is the civil society, 'the setting of settings', which provides the forum where individuals as part of diverse social groups are trained in civility and self-restraint. While critical of the growing numbers of people who are radically disengaged—passive clients of the state—Walzer is equally uncomfortable with political participation as the only form of active citizenship. He places faith in the idea of 'critical associationalism', which is based in the belief that in the modern world the density of associational life and the activities and understandings that go with it need to be recaptured and relearned and proposes that participation in voluntary organisations of civil society—churches, families, ethnic associations, voluntary groups, schools—inculcate civic virtues, which bind citizens in mutual obligation (Walzer 1992). At the other extreme, communitarian theorists such as Alisdair MacIntyre and Michael Sandel, while dismissing the idea of the 'unencumbered self', reject all forms of pluralities and argue that the 'politics of right' should be replaced by a 'politics of common good'.[2] In this view,

---

[2]A significant intervention in the ongoing debate on competing notions of good and what constitutes good citizenship comes from a liberal, (*contd.*)

liberal individualism by treating citizenship as a status investing individuals with rights and entitlements has resulted in the disintegration of social bonds and the rise in anomie and alienation which characterise modern societies (MacIntyre 1981; Sandel 1982). MacIntyre and Sandel represent the growing strand of social and political conservatism. This 'new right' has developed within the broad spectrum of communitarianism and is distinguished by its stress on a substantive notion of common good and the rejection of political and cultural plurality. We may recall that in Marshall's formulation, social rights constituted the third phase of the evolution of rights, coinciding with the development of the welfare state and instrumental in integrating the poor, the migrants, and racial minorities into the fold of citizenship. Theorists of the 'new right', however, see social rights as promoting passive citizenship and a culture of dependency among the poor. Working within a framework of common good and common obligation of all citizens, they argue for a workfare programme instead of a welfare programme, cutting back the safety net of the poor and tying welfare benefits to work responsibilities. Unlike the civil society theorists who argue for the enhancement of responsible citizenship through participation in institutions of civil society, the 'new right' sees the 'market' characterised by free trade, deregulation, tax-cuts, the weakening of trade unions, and the tightening of unemployment benefits, as the 'school' where citizenship

---

(*contd.*) Stephen Macedo. Macedo argues that liberal citizenship possesses its own virtues, which enable a citizen to justify and accept conceptions of the good only when they are reasonable. Freedom, which is the essence of liberalism, requires vital moral qualities of citizenship which include tolerance, self-criticism, moderation, and a reasonable degree of engagements in the activities of citizenship. Good citizenship, however, is not merely a citizen acting as a civically moral individual. Beyond individual morality is a morality of the community that is founded on the twin principles of impersonal justice and reasonableness, which require that the citizen not only be eternally vigilant of the government, but also engage in activities of protest including civil disobedience if constitutional channels fail to ensure efficient and just running of the political system (Macedo 1990, 2, 29–35, 50–64, 278).

'virtues' of initiative, self-reliance, and self-sufficiency are learned (Kymlicka and Norman 1994).

Ambivalences in Contemporary Citizenship Theory

Apart from the contests that the new circumstances have generated, ambivalences can also be detected in the contemporary theorisations. The changing contexts of late twentieth century we are told have necessitated a delinking of the relationship between citizenship and the nation-state and dislodging the individual as the core of citizenship theory. It has become acceptable, therefore, to talk of global/world citizenship, with its basis in human rights, and a differentiated citizenship, with its emphasis on group/cultural rights. Yasemin Soysal, for example, argues that globalisation has brought in a 'new and more universal' concept of citizenship that has 'universal personhood' rather than 'national belonging' as its core principle. Soysal sees the idea of universal personhood delinking legal rights from citizenship status and national belonging reflected in the status of guest workers in Europe, who have lived in Europe for years without ever acquiring citizenship, primarily because the countries of residence assured their legal and social rights. These assurances, feels Soysal, are further augmented by the global system of human rights law, the United Nations network, regional governance, etc., that have ushered in the idea of a global civil society (Soysal 1994). The assurances guaranteed by membership of this global civil society apparently make the securities of nation-state membership redundant. Much of this assurance emerges from the 'high degree of agreement' on the need for human rights and the creation of a common interest and awareness of the 'frailty of human existence' (Turner 1993, 184). The agreement on the need for human rights and recognition of human frailty has emerged alongside a growing preoccupation with the idea of 'global risks'. Again, the 'rhetoric' of 'global risks' has the implicit connotation that problems of 'security' and 'social order' are no longer the concern of a single nation and cannot, therefore, be determined or safeguarded by one. All such concerns require and must be tackled with a global approach.

Attempts at affirming the 'universality' of human rights have indeed been augmented with the adoption of the Right to Development by the General Assembly on 4 December 1986 and the statement supported by 171 governments at the World Conference on Human Rights held in 1993 in Vienna. Both the documents attempted to go beyond the universalism-relativism divide by emphasising that human rights were 'universal, indivisible, interdependent and interrelated'. However, despite the increased role envisaged for a transnational network of nongovernmental organisations in promoting these rights, human rights by themselves are not able to ensure the development of participatory networks essential for safeguarding the rights of individuals. In the case of Soysal's guest workers, for example, the denial of political rights, even when social and civil rights are assured, deprives them of a right to participate in the formulation and implementation of policies, which may impact their social entitlements and civil liberties. Noncitizens are thus objects of particular state policies rather than active participants (Faulks 2000). The latter, it may be emphasised, was at the core of the 1986 Declaration of the Right to Development (Baxi 1998). Again, Turner's formulation of human frailty as the basis for a consensus on a global approach to human needs and rights also enters shaky grounds when one examines the manner in which consensus is arrived at in a hierarchised world. The contemporary 'global consensus' on international cooperation to end terrorism, for example, has not only made Muslims a 'suspect community' the world over, it has turned countries not in tune with the United States policies into 'an axis of evil' which needs to be crushed and annihilated.

Again, it may be worthwhile to ask whether the circumstances described as 'specifically' late twentieth century, are entirely 'new'. The assumption that these new developments have brought in a more democratic form of citizenship transcending national boundaries also needs serious questioning. The circumstances purportedly conditioning the redefinition of citizenship may well be seen as persisting from older contexts of globalisation.[3] It was largely in the context of the expansion of modern Europe marked by the slave trade, imperial domination, and the production of the 'West' and 'the colonies' or the 'third world' as sociohistorical realities that mutually, though hierarchically, constituted each other that the discursive formulation of the 'universal citizen' took place. The exclusionary domain of citizenship was very much conditioned in this context. This is manifested in the manner in which the universal categories of 'man' and 'citizen' were formulated, and women, slaves, workers, and subject peoples as social categories and as lived experiences were simultaneously incorporated and omitted from national-cultural and juridicopolitical identities as citizens.[4] There appears to be discursive continuity from the

---

[3]Arjun Appadurai points out, for instance, that globalisation, closely linked to the current workings of capital on a global basis, extends, in this regard, the earlier logics of empire, trade, and political dominion in many parts of the world. Its most striking feature, however, is the runway quality of global finance, which appears remarkably independent of traditional constraints of information transfer, national regulation, industrial productivity, or 'real' wealth in any particular society, country or region (Appadurai 2001, 4).

[4]Research into the extension of political rights in the late nineteenth and twentieth centuries has shown that women, slaves, workers, and the colonised were considered incompetent and lacking the rational capacity to exercise the rights of citizenship. Often, the debate on the question of their inclusion as citizens focussed on the effect this would have on the fabric of the nation. Thus, the debates surrounding the 1864 Reforms Act which gave political rights to 35–40 per cent of adult male workers in Britain seemed to concur that this extension of citizenship to heads of households will not make Britain any less British. In the case of women, however, it was felt that their inclusion would subvert women's 'natural' roles and undermine the nation (Hall 1994). Through much of the nineteenth century, the debate over franchise for women and the working class in Britain saw the vote being defined increasingly in national imperialist, class, and gender terms. Opponents of universal franchise compared the working class to colonial 'natives', both requiring firm, unflinching, and unsentimental control (Hall 1992, 285). The constant reiteration of this authority was important for continued subjection of these sections of the population by the white, propertied male.

older forms of citizenship and the present reformulation emerging from these changed circumstances.

The talk of human rights and the world citizen directed towards a supposedly more humane 'world order' where respect for human dignity goes beyond the confines of national boundaries, for example, is more than counterbalanced by a simultaneous lament of a 'crisis in citizenship'. In this chant of crisis, citizenship gets reaffirmed and reinscribed in exclusionist terms, emerging yet again as the bastion on which the nation-state asserts its sovereignty and fortifies itself against the 'hordes of starving people'. Consider, thus, the dissonant notes that persist alongside the apotheosis of the 'world citizen' and 'human rights' in a work on 'global constitutionalism'—this work suggests that human rights, with the exception of political ones, were always proclaimed to be universal, from the declaration of the Rights of Man of 1789 onwards. These rights were, however, proclaimed universal, it points out, 'when the distinction between man and citizen did not create any problems, it being neither likely or foreseeable that the men and women of the third world would arrive in Europe and these statements of principle might be taken literally' (Ferrajoli 1996, 151–54). That the 'universalism' of human rights is put to test by the pressures placed on 'our' borders by 'hoards of starving people', and the assertion of their 'difference' by minority groups, which puts into 'crisis' citizenship, is a sentiment which resonates in other writings as well.[5] It is not surprising then that this 'crisis in citizenship' has been addressed by invoking stringent immigration laws and the fortification/reinforcement of Western national and regional boundaries which emphasise 'descent' and 'blood ties' in consideration for citizenship while devaluing permanent legal resident status. Thus, in a bizarre situation, following the collapse of communist rule across Eastern Europe, many 'ethnic' Germans, linguistically and culturally different from the present Germans, were welcomed into Germany as

---

[5]See for example, John Porter, *The Measure of Canadian Society* (1987).

citizens. In contrast two million Turkish guest workers living in Germany and contributing to its economy were denied citizenship (Faulks 2000, 45–6). Similarly, changes in welfare legislation in the United States in 1996 limited the eligibility of immigrants to virtually all cash benefits (Faulks 2000, 144).

Similar fortification of national boundaries is seen in the manner in which the international refugee law has unfolded to, reveal a 'growing tension between its language of protection and the ground reality of rejection' (Chimni 2000, xiv). The industrialised world has in practice taken a series of 'restrictive administrative and legal measures' that ensure that refugees do not come to their doorsteps. If one were to examine then the contention made about the relationship between globalisation, human rights, and world citizenship, one would be compelled to conclude that far from making boundaries permeable, a direct outcome of movement of populations has been the fortification of national boundaries. Moreover, the international legal regime pertaining to refugees has historically been selective and discriminatory and has addressed itself inadequately to all contexts within which the flight of refugees takes place. The manner of the application of the legal regime also gives rise to a duality where, in some cases, the application of legal principles allows the retention of the connection between sovereignty, national-boundaries, and citizenship, while in others the displacement of the legal language with that of welfare and humanitarianism makes the connection permeable by subjecting it to international scrutiny and inspection.[6]

Moreover, human rights, like 'citizens', are almost always articulated in abstract and universalistic, that is, context-free terms masking the diversity and historicity of citizenship and

---

[6]B.S. Chimni shows how this duality comes into play owing to the neglect in international instruments for the protection of refugees and neglect of the particular contexts in which refugees are produced in the non-Western world. Even existing frameworks of protection are amenable to selective and subjective interpretations that work to the detriment of the protection of the rights of refugees from the third world (Chimni 2000).

rights.[7] The idea of human rights as the replacement for citizenship rights can be retained only when citizenship is construed in passive terms, and rights themselves are detached and distanced from the social and political structures that sustain them and the specific struggles which produce them (Faulks 2000, 145). Advocates of a new theory of citizenship, who plead for global and world citizenship based on human rights, fall into the trap of not only upholding certain universal elements of human rights, that is, equal protection, free speech, freedom of religion and association, etc., they also seem to be specifying a normative framework within which these rights can function or apply.[8] These prescriptive-normative and restrictive-exclusionist sentiments are reflected in the writings of some advocates of global citizenship who believe that certain parts of the world do not have the conditions in which such 'universal' values as human rights and natural rights can find legitimate place. Some of the most prolific Western theorists of citizenship see it as 'specifically western' in their origins and growth and doubt very much if the notion of citizenship can be applied to Muslim societies of the Middle-East or other countries of the

---

[7]In an interesting analogy, alluding to the generally ahistorical terms of articulation of the category of a citizen and the abstraction of citizenship in 'universal' terms, Roberto Alejandro (1993) has referred to citizens as particular individuals wearing universal masks.

[8]This position is associated with the universalist arguments in the universal vs. relative debate in human rights. A relativist position to universalist claims stresses that rights and rules about morality and human behaviour are encoded in and depend upon cultural contexts. A substantive relativist position goes beyond the empirical position to say that (i) there is a diversity of cultures and subsequently a great diversity of ideas on rights; (ii) therefore, there cannot be one transcendental or transcultural notion of rights; and, (iii) therefore, no culture (whether or not in the garb of enforcing international rights) is justified in imposing on others what are essentially its own ideas; (iv) international human rights instruments are associated with Western cultural imperialism, imposing liberal political ideas and Christian ideals; (v) these covenants seek to make the Western ideals as universal and attempt to universalise it; (vi) these attempts at 'homogenisation' would destroy the diversity of cultures and tradition (Steiner and Alston, 1996).

'developing' world where 'premodern' forms of social relations persist.[9] Though non-Western countries as a result of political conquest or modernisation have adopted Western constitutions and constitutional principles and terms such as citizenship and civil society, it is suggested that the idea of citizenship cannot be a universal concept (as in applicability) because of its development out of a particular conjuncture of structural and cultural conditions peculiar to the West and its experiences with modernity (Turner 1993). The nonapplicability of this manifestation of Western rationality to non-Western societies is reminiscent of colonial practices, which rationalised imperial domination in terms of an inadequacy and incapacity on the part of the colonised. The talk of human rights and the world citizen is therefore more than counterbalanced by the manner in which these rights become contingent for their realisation on the domain of citizenship defined in exclusionary terms.

Quite like the discourse on human rights, the multicultural strand seeking to redefine citizenship has not been able to extricate itself from the difference-deferral framework. This influential strand within citizenship theory has sought to invest in multiculturalism as the core element of democratic citizenship that 'cherishes cultural diversity' and 'envisages a society in which different communities forge a common identity while retaining their cultural provenance' (Mahajan 1999, 12). While posing 'the problem' in the journal *Seminar*, Gurpreet Mahajan discusses five elements of multiculturalism and their implications for democratic citizenship: (i) multiculturalism embodies not merely a statement of fact but also a value, so that when modern democratic societies embrace multiculturalism, they demonstrate a more profound egalitarian impulse than the mere presence of plural cultures; (ii) it accords a positive value to the collective identities of all ethnic communities by picturing a society which is characterised not by multiple cultural solitudes or endemic

---

[9]Jack Donnelly argues that the concept of individual rights (which inhere in modern liberal citizenship) is fundamentally foreign to Indian society since the latter is based upon a radical inequality of persons (Donnelly 1989).

cultural strife, but by communities living together and participating as equal partners in national political life; (iii) it represents a new kind of universalism, one where integration of individuals into the state is not predicated on a total disengagement from particularistic community ties. People are included into the nation-state as members of diverse but equal ethnic groups, and the state recognises that the dignity of the individuals is linked to the collective dignity of the community to which they belong; (iv) this radical redefinition of a democratic polity makes multiculturalism a normative value that is applicable as much to the modern liberal democracies of the West as it is to modernising polities like India; and, (v) the democratic citizen in this multicultural society remains simultaneously embedded in a variety of particularistic ties. Given this reality, multiculturalism endeavours to initiate policies that allow citizens to maintain their cultural distinctiveness (Mahajan 1999).

In her later work, however, Mahajan draws an important distinction between policies that aim merely to enhance cultural diversity and those that aim to prevent homogenisation and discrimination of particular cultures. Rather, than concentrating on enhancing cultural diversity, which involves the dangers of conceptualising communities as ossified units and subjecting individuals to the authoritative structures of the community, Mahajan argues for multicultural policies that aim at checking discrimination. The latter, she suggests, require the presence of options that allow individuals to have access to their culture. What needs to be valued and promoted, therefore, is a 'non-conformist' membership, which while meeting the multicultural aim of preventing cultural homogenisation, also protects the individual from loss of choices (Mahajan 2002). In most Western formulations, however, multiculturalism remains part of the normative framework where democratic values are seen as exclusive to specific cultures. Even those strands that strive to find a meeting ground between individual and cultural rights, find cultural rights and multiculturalism relevant and admissible only in societies where a 'universal culture of liberal values' already exists. While seeking to redefine the principle of equality, and the relationship between individual liberty and 'societal culture', for example, Will Kymlicka invokes a 'historical obligation' to invest in the 'multicultural present'.[10] At the same time, however, the allusion to a different trajectory of development of rights in the West, and the specific (normative) conditions in which these rights can be expected to operate, makes this formulation susceptible to charges of exclusion. Thus, the proposition that the addition of collective community rights on the democratic agenda in the West has come after a uniform structure of social and civil laws was already established and the liberal ethic of regard for equality and individual liberty firmly entrenched so that they would find expression in intra-group practices needs to be interrogated. Similarly, the suggestion that the specific circumstances of the development of rights in the West would ensure that community rights may not 'frequently' conflict with the principle of individual equality, again, needs to be contested for the following reasons: (i) because it leads to the conclusion that such discord is more likely to be experienced in societies where the (Western) 'historical sequence' of the development of rights was not replicated, (ii) because it seems to propose that the multicultural path in the West has adequately addressed group discrimination and inequality, and, (iii) because by focussing disproportionately on the preservation of the community, it leads to arguments favouring not only the protection of the community from external constraints, but also the acknowledgement of its right to apply internal restraints. It may, moreover, be pointed out that the discord between individual and community rights is built into this formulation of multiculturalism. By empowering the community to apply

---

[10]While reiterating the liberal faith in individual choices, Kymlicka (1996) emphasises the importance of the 'contexts' which fashion such choices, especially what he calls 'societal culture', referring to 'practices and institutions' that are territorially and linguistically concentrated and provide individuals with 'meaningful ways of life across the full range of human activities, including social, educational, religious, recreational and economic life, encompassing both public and private spheres'.

internal restraints it preserves structures of authority that work to the detriment of individual freedom. Moreover, by acknowledging the community's power to apply internal restraints, it seems to subscribe to the notion that the rights and freedoms of *all* individuals do not matter. In other words, within such a framework, the rights of individuals who belong to minority communities, appear to be dispensable.

The Search for Alternatives

Resisting globalisation and transcending multiculturalism: feminists rethink citizenship

The changed contexts of citizenship have compelled feminists to rethink citizenship, especially in response to some of the changes that threaten to roll back feminist gains after prolonged struggles of over a century. Recent works on citizenship, as mentioned earlier, are distinguished by their emphasis on the cataclysmic changes that have come in the wake of globalisation—changes that have unsettled and displaced some of the core elements of citizenship. Feminists have attempted to think of a notion of citizenship appropriate to feminist politics in globalising times. In response to writings that attribute extraordinary transformative qualities to globalisation, feminists have rejected the contention that globalisation is an irresistible and irreversible natural force that has no alternative and will result in homogenisation/equalisation. They argue that globalisation is not a uniform, unilinear, and inevitable process, and impacts unequally and differentially different regions, classes, and people. Again, the imputation of natural, even 'magical' self-propelling qualities to the market, feminists assert, depoliticises it, distracting from the myriad political and economic decisions and practices that propel it and the hierarchies and inequalities that it produces (Pettman 1999). While critical globalisation literature[11]

---

[11]Primarily associated with journals like *New Political Economy, New Left Review,* and *Monthly Review.*

has stressed the importance of recovering agency, often around class, as spaces of resistance to globalisation, such literature does not take into account the gendered effects of globalisation. For feminists this is of utmost importance, since the transformed nature of the state under the influence of neoliberal ideology and global interests seeking to facilitate global competition have sought to cut-back on 'unproductive social expenditure', which are precisely those areas where feminists struggled hard to push the state into action. The shift in the language of citizenship from social rights to competition, productivity, and efficiency, and from the public to the private and individual responsibility have reduced the political space for citizenship and its component of social rights (Pettman 1999). Apart from introducing a field of tension in the domain of social citizenship by launching an attack on the welfare role of the modern state, these changes are particularly inimical to women's citizenship, as they withdraw the resources which make substantive citizenship possible.

The rise in exclusivist identity politics has threatened to roll back feminist gains on both equal citizenship and the politicisation of the personal. As has been discussed in an earlier chapter, notions of multiculturalism and minority rights have enabled the empowerment of cultural communities whereby they can lay claims to inherent rights and negotiate better terms of reference to the national culture. The stress on preservation of the community as a discrete and ossified unit, however, encompasses the same undemocratic relations with sections of its constituents, primarily women, which the community hopes to invert in its relationship with the dominant national culture. Thus, the idea of differentiated citizenship read with multiculturalism has produced a situation where cultural communities are empowered to sustain themselves by imposing internal restrictions on members of the community that work towards a loss of women's agency in particular.[12] The assumption that the community is

---

[12]The problem of restrictive ossification informs the conceptualisation of 'community' in several formulations which make a case for community rights, including that by Partha Chatterjee, who while defining toleration (*contd.*)

an organic whole, a 'natural' social unit, 'out there', hampers any dynamic conceptualisation of citizenship as the product of struggle, and also precludes ideological reconstructions of communities (Yuval-Davis 1991, 58–60).

A Dialogical Citizenship

Feminist formulations of citizenship in the 1980s have had to take into account the challenges posed by both globalisation and multiculturalism. Both globalisation and multiculturalism have, as discussed earlier, inhibited women's citizenship, and have served a blow to the gains made by women's struggles for equal rights over the last hundred years. Feminists have criticised the prioritisation of cultural rights for their articulation of the community as a set of inward-looking ossified relationships, for essentialising women, thwarting democratic dialogue, restricting the public-political, and enunciating a thin and passive notion of citizenship for women. Similarly, the imperatives of globalisation leading to the erosion of social rights and a gradual abdication by the state of its social responsibility has meant that women, especially those belonging to the marginalised sections, have been deprived of the resources which create conditions for substantive citizenship.

Feminist responses to these challenges have been two pronged. While not rejecting the importance of cultural contexts in shaping the needs and rights claims of an individual, they take care to distance themselves from any notion of community which fixes an individual inextricably within such a community. While stressing the importance of paying heed to multicultural questions pertaining to discrimination and diversity, they warn against sliding into a theoretical position that endorses watertight compartments founded on notions of 'deep' diversity (Mahajan 2002). The rejection of this idea of the community is entwined

---

(*contd.*) suggests 'a collective cultural right' 'not to offer a reason to be different', provided, however, that the cultural groups 'explains itself adequately to its own chosen forum' (Chatterjee 1994: 1774–76).

with the articulation of a feminist politics directed towards reclaiming and reforming the political as a dialogical space that nurtures equality, individual and associational freedom and autonomy, and a self-conscious respect for otherness. This idea of a dialogical political space is informed primarily by a pressing need to resist the passivity imposed by the prioritisation of cultural communities and also to create transnational linkages that enable women to counter their marginalisation and oppression. Most of these theoretical formulations display an abstract notion of global community, grounded in complex interactive relationships and a dynamic notion of citizenship.

In perhaps the most expansive framework of citizenship and feminist politics, Nira Yuval-Davis and Pnina Werbner place the idea of 'feminist transversal practice' at the core of the 'transnational resistance' to globalisation. The idea of the *transverse* is significant, in that it shows both the *direction* and the aspired *scale* of resistance to transnational power. The notion of the transverse connotes, as in a wave motion, a movement or disturbance at right angles, or cross wise, rather than parallel, or in the same direction as wave propagation. A notion of resistance as transversal denotes the determination to obstruct and inhibit the forces of domination at right angles. At the same time, the embeddedness of this transversal practice in a set of interactive relationships and the fact that there are multiple points of resistance produces almost a grid of relationships of resistance across and in opposition to the global forces of domination.[13]

The idea of feminist politics as transversal practice, enables the conceptualisation of citizenship as a set of intersecting relationships which are dialogical and continually evolving. The fact that transversal relationships evolve in the course of

[13]Feminist transnational resistance involves evolving extensive networks, conversations, organisations, and alliances within international fora, in international NGOs, and international conversations, conferences, and campaigns. See Nira Yuval-Davis, 'Women, Citizenship and Difference' (1997, 4–27).

resistance in specific contexts of domination gives an idea of relationships that are not stagnant. On the other hand, the recognition that these relationships are historically inflected and emerge within specific cultural and social context makes transversal resistance sensitive to ideas of similarity and difference. The negotiation of these differences and specificities of contexts may generate at different times and places quite different sets of practices, institutional arrangements, modes of social interaction and future orientations (Yuval-Davis and Werbner 1999). At the same time, the fact that transnational resistance focusses on global imbalances of power makes citizenship a transcendental notion, both temporally and spatially. Thus, citizenship signifies a set of relationships which are not only historically determined, they also go beyond notions of circumscribed territoriality, so that national and transnational citizenships constitute two interrelated and coexisting modalities of citizenship. Thus, at any given point in time and space, citizenship may be conceived as an encompassing set of intersecting relationships that are also 'multi-layered'. This notion allows Yuval-Davis and Werbner to recognise that political subjects are often involved in more than one political community—whose boundaries may be local, ethnic, national, or global, and may extend within, across, or beyond state lines, with membership in one collectivity having crucial implications for citizenship in others. It is important to note that the notion of a widening scale of membership responds to a need to comprehend the transformations in contemporary notions of citizenship. At the same time, the conception of citizenship as a set of 'intersecting' and 'multilayered' relationships vindicates the feminist position that essentialised and naturalised assumptions of citizenship boundaries ought to be revised.

The relationship which Yuval-Davis and Werbner see in their encompassing, intersecting, and multilayered notion of citizenship is dialogical. This adds to the complexity as well as the explanatory potential of the relational model they offer against the communitarian and liberal models. The notion that citizenship is multilayered and dialogical not only recognises multiple political subjectivities and simultaneous membership in several political communities, it also identifies the sites of 'exclusions'. The insertion of the variable, exclusionary citizenship concentrates on the way the different positionings of women affect their citizenship in policy areas such as education, planning, welfare etc., and how these various positionings contribute to the construction of boundaries—between national collectivities and between the private and public. The inclusion of a broad canvas and intersecting-dialogical layers of membership also allow them to examine how these intersections and their different/discrepant positionings give rise to 'ambivalences' or 'ambivalent citizens' on the 'borders' of citizenship, viz., refugees and asylum seekers, and stateless persons (Yuval-Davis and Werbner 1999). Thus, feminist transversal politics is seen as paving the way out from an exclusivist identity politics and forces of globalisation. Transversal politics differs from 'identity' politics in the sense that it rejects the communitarian claim that a social positioning can automatically be conflated with personal values. It is not only premised on dialogues across communities, it also proposes that social differences in positionings must be grasped in all their complex intersections, rather than in terms of a single prioritised identity. Such a politics aims to use dialogue to reach closer to a shared reality (Nira Yuval-Davis 1997).

From Constitutive Community to Epistemic Community

Endorsing active, participatory, and emancipatory citizenship, Alison Assiter puts forward a framework of citizenship based on two premises: (i) that there are no constitutive communities or, in other words, no fixed moral ground or unitary value which a community shares, and, (ii) citizenship is a continuous process of expanding emancipatory politics. A person may be born in a moral community, yet in the course of a lifetime, the citizen's moral journey continues as she/he comes dialogically to experience other perspectives and other moralities. A participatory, active citizenship is thus seen as continually evolving in a dialogic relationship with unlike 'others'. While engaging with the 'other', the need is to sift out those discourses that are restrictive, and recover those narratives which lead to more inclusive socialities and ultimately to human rights as a global discourse.

Assiter makes several propositions that form the grounds for rejecting the notion of constitutive communities and lead her to the epistemic community as the basis of active and emancipatory citizenship. She posits, first of all, that there are different kinds of communities, in some of which, such as the family, nation, and the ethnic community, a person may just find oneself on account of birth. This membership does not reflect an exercise of choice by the individual; rather, it manifests the 'constraints of necessity', which one has to accept. There are, however, other communities such as the workplace that are not bound by such constraints and reflect a degree of choice. Whether reflecting constraint or choice, communities do not share a unitary value system in the sense that membership of the community may hold radically different meanings for its members. Even if there were a degree of shared meaning in a collectivity, it may not automatically mean a shared value system. It would be doubtful, therefore, says Assiter, to expect two persons belonging to the same ethnic community, viz., Jewish, Hindu, or Muslim, who have not grown up in the same country nor have had comparable life experiences to share the same political and moral outlook. To describe a person's Jewishness as being formative of his or her value system seems to Assiter arbitrary and possibly even pernicious. Again, while communities may, to an extent, determine personalities and the aims or ends persons attach themselves to, this does not mean that individuals are 'constitutively' attached to particular ends and the ends are immune from criticisms. Also, even if certain types of community constitutively form people, it does not automatically follow that people continue throughout their lives to uphold the specific values of those particular communities. They may choose to opt for a different kind of community or they may find themselves in a new kind of situation that incorporates radically different kinds of values. Again, if one says that the ends to which one is constitutively tied may be open to criticisms, it does not imply that the person is not constitutively attached to anything or that he or she is detached with no commitments (Assiter 1999, 44–5).

Thus, the notion that there are no constitutive communities, which tie a person inextricably to the ends of the community precluding a right to critical association, enables Assiter to talk of an *epistemic community as the basis of citizenship* (Assiter 1996). An epistemic community recognises the existence of a plurality of voices and is at the same time committed to certain ends or values that allow persons to make value judgments. It is formed in the process of negotiating with radical otherness, that is, when conditions are created where marginal voices can speak, are heard, and are *listened* to. At the same time, all voices and expressions of identity are amenable to questioning and rejection on moral and political grounds. While listening is a vital corrective, listening without judgment would allow one to listen to all kinds of voices including the fascist, whose ends are counter to the interests of some people. A vital aspect of the formation of the epistemic community is not only questioning and challenging parts of our own identities on moral and political grounds, but also looking for some common shared grounds on the basis of which such questions may be raised. An epistemic community is constituted precisely when people in an interrelated process of listening and questioning also start looking for the right answers and are interested, in other words, in knowing the truth of their views and providing evidence for their truth. Thus, an epistemic community may be characterised as a group of individuals who *share* (they may or may not come together) certain interests, values, and beliefs in common, (example, untouchability is wrong, racism is wrong, sexism is wrong). Members of one epistemic community may be members of diverse other social, cultural, and political groupings, they may contain people unequal in power and status and may never communicate with each other (Assiter 1999, 41–53). What binds the epistemic community is, therefore, a belief in a set of values which are emancipatory, that is, they contribute towards removing oppressive power relations. These values are, however, not absolute and will be emancipatory only relative to others (thus liberal values may be emancipatory relative to the Nazi, but not relative to the feminist). Assiter then makes a case for a universal humanity and scale of types of emancipatory values, with the preservation of life as the ultimate value. Arguing that there may be at any particular moment a set of values more emancipatory than the others, each set of values may be judged on the basis of the degree of freedom and well-being it is able to impart and uphold. The components of such well-being fall into a hierarchy of goods, ranging from life and physical integrity to self-esteem and education. Rather than globalisation leading us back into the constitutive communities of our childhood and our history, as the communitarian would have it, Assiter would have global thinking and culture extend the horizons of the epistemic community. Following this perspective, then, there is neither a value nor a set of values that would be adhered to by disembedded, disembodied selves, nor are there values that are integrally connected with the traditional identity of groups of individuals. Rather, the significant values are those that emancipate some groups from particular kinds of oppression (Assiter 1999).

Conclusion

Since the late 1980s, the idea that citizenship needs to be redefined to reflect the realities of a globalised world has been put forth with great zeal. It has become acceptable to talk of a global/world citizenship, with its basis in human rights, delinking, thereby, the relationship between citizenship and the nation-state. The idea of differentiated citizenship, based on the notion of differential rights, has similarly gained credence. In this chapter I have argued that these two influential strands are based on assumptions that are irreconcilable with one another. Moreover, while they do mark a rupture in the dominant liberal notion of citizenship that places the masked individual at its core and prioritises the nation-state as the primary unit of membership, the manner in which they are formulated places them within an exclusionary formulation of difference-deferral. While the idea of human rights acknowledges the porousness of national borders, the global/world citizen, which the discourse produces, continues to be circumscribed by privileges of class, gender, caste, and race. Thus, while the increase in the volume of transnational migration is recognised, the human rights discourse seems to be riddled by state practices that fortify national and regional boundaries. The international human rights covenants also appear to be inadequately reflecting the contexts and claims of those forced to leave their homes in the non-Western world. A similar exclusion seems to be at work in the notion of multicultural citizenship, which while seeking to articulate democratic citizenship based on the equality of cultural communities, preserves oppressive structures of authority. The notion of citizenship it brings into play, then, is based on the principle that individual freedom and choice do not matter for those who want to have an identity different from the masked citizen of the nation-state.

It would be pertinent to recall here that the idea of the 'community' emerged within the national liberation discourse in India as the basis of a 'national' identity distinct from and opposed to Western modernity. Located in the cultural domain, it resisted interaction with the institutions of civil society (of subjections) in the public domain, where a battle of sameness and equality was waged with the colonial rulers. In the postcolonial nation-state, however, the idea of the community as the basis of a sovereign identity becomes anomalous and even contradictory in a context where the only permissible political identity is that of the masked citizen of the nation-state. While the colonial context occluded this contradiction by precluding any relationship between the political and the cultural domains, their articulation with the public domain in the nation-state has been seen, given the communalised nature of realpolitik, as 'violent, divisive, fearsome, irrational', illuminating the fragmented state of citizenship in India (Bharucha 1998, 99). Elsewhere, Partha Chatterjee, while defining toleration, suggests 'a collective cultural right' 'not to offer a reason to be different' provided, however, that the cultural groups 'explains itself adequately to its own chosen forum' (Chatterjee 1994, 1774–76). The problems with such a right to silence is that it becomes a convenient alibi for the inability of the communities to interact with the larger political community of which it is a part or to resist their deliberate exclusion from the hegemonic discourses of masked citizenship.

On the other hand, mere apotheosis of the masked individual —the citizen—is no guarantee for equality and freedom. Often, equality and freedom become facades behind which intolerance of difference (cultural, religious, racial, gender, etc.) flourish. With the rise of political conservatism and neoliberal ideology worldwide, Hannah Arendt's rendering of Western democracies around the period of the Second World War as 'mass society', begins to look familiar and relevant yet again. For Arendt, the advent of modernity was marked by the decline of the public sphere of politics, the emergence of bureaucratic rule or the 'rule by nobody', and the rise of an amorphous, anonymous, uniformising reality that she calls the 'social'—a realm characterised by the predominance of economic contractual relationships. The realm of the social compelled conformity, producing not a society based on egalitarian relations but a 'mass society' that discouraged difference through enforced behavioural norms and even elimination and annihilation of differences as in the case of the Jews. Equality in such a society was 'only the political and legal recognition of the fact that society has conquered the public realm and that distinction and difference have become private matters of the individual' (Arendt 1958, 41). It was this perversion of equality from a political into a social concept that brought about a tension between political equality and social/cultural difference, making special groups and individuals all the more conspicuous by leaving them little space in the public/political. For Arendt, it was the public sphere— 'that sphere of appearance where freedom and equality reign, and where individuals as citizens interact through the medium of speech and persuasion, disclose their unique identities, and decide through collective deliberation about matters of common concern'—that is the only repository and guarantee of equality. The political community, which referred to a group of people who come together and are bound by shared citizenship regardless of their culture, ethnic, and other loyalties, is the best possible form of the public sphere (Arendt 1958).

At the same time, quite like Assiter's notion of epistemic community as well as Yuval-Davis' dialogic community, Arendt's nostalgia for the political community presents what may be called a hyper-energised participatory framework which may eventually fail to provide a basis for democratic citizenship. If the liberal framework can be faulted for masking the differences that are crucial to substantive citizenship, the participatory model while endorsing active citizenship, also fails to take into account the constraints that most people normally face in life that impede any kind of public participation. Even if a dialogical community were to bring in conditions in which participatory citizenship becomes possibile, such a community, too, may run the risk of promoting an exclusionary dialogue. Second, an emphasis on participatory citizenship when coupled with the epistemic basis of the community works on several assumptions: (i) that people are willing to communicate their differences even if they fear suppression, (ii) that the means and tools of communication exist both in terms of a language as well as its transmission, (iii) that there is a shared understanding of oppression and everyday experiences of oppression at the local level, (iv) that the dialogue among the oppressed will be able to influence the forces of domination, etc.

What has been experienced, on the other hand, is that the discourses on globalisation and epistemic communities have gradually become far removed from the life-world of the poor and the manner in which they experience globalisation or oppression at the hands of the everyday structures of domination. In place of a grid of transversal resistance that Yuval-Davis and Werbner propose, hierarchised layers of debates, anxieties, and resistance have unfolded, each layer of the hierarchy separated from the other by a communication and intelligibility barrier. Each layer in this hierarchy envelopes a progressively narrower space, so much so, that the aggregate picture is that of an inverted pyramid rather than an interconnected and powerful grid of relationships. Arjun Appadurai sees this hierarchy in terms of an evolving 'double apartheid' characterised by a growing divorce between debates in the academia, which has found in globalisation an 'object around which to conduct its special internal quarrels' about such issues as representation, recognition, the 'end' of history, the spectres of capital etc., and the debates that characterise vernacular discourses about the global that are concerned with how to plausibly protect cultural autonomy and economic survival in some local, national, or regional sphere in the era of 'reform' and 'openness'. The second form of apartheid is the separation of the poor and their advocates from the anxieties of their own national discourses about globalisation as in the intricacies of the debates in global policy discourses surrounding trade, labour, environment, disease and warfare. (Appadurai 2001, 2–3).

The purpose of the arguments in this chapter, however, is not to give up altogether the bases on which citizenship has been sought to be reformulated in the discourses on human rights and multiculturalism. The importance of the contextualised self, for example, is crucial to building a substantive notion of citizenship. The idea of the individual as a part of the community, bound to other individuals not by necessity or private interest, but by community or social concerns, is a significant part of such a formulation. At the same time, the notion of community and social concern is to be worked out continually through intersecting sets of dialogical relationships which surround an individual as member of several overlapping communities. It is perhaps a concerted effort at the retrieval of the political as an interactive public space that can congeal collective energies into shared bonds of citizenship. What is required, therefore, is not the essentialisation of community/cultural identities into compartments that exclude dialogue, but to see how economic, social, and political factors constitute the life experiences of people within and across communities. Thus, the notion of democratic citizenship will have the idea of the practice of citizenship at its core. The practice of citizenship produces a community of citizens, which holds together because of a shared commitment to fundamental emancipatory values. The unit of this membership, then, would depend on the scale of the shared commitment. The viability of the community would depend on the extent to which it holds together through dialogue and adheres to the commitment of resisting and rolling back structures of domination. At the same time, however, even when the forces of domination are embedded in structures of transnational power, it is in the contexts of struggles in specific locations that the citizen emerges and reclaims the political. It is in these struggles that the citizen can preclude abstraction and appear as part of specific socioeconomic contexts. Citizenship, then, may be seen as a mosaic of struggles linked together by a shared language and commitment to democracy and equality.

Bibliography

I. Books and Articles

A. Books

Agnew, Vijay. 1979. *Elite Women in Indian Politics*. New Delhi: Vikas Publishing House.

Alloula, Malek. 1986. *The Colonial Harem*. Translated by M. and W. Godzich. Manchester: Manchester University Press.

Aloysius, G. 1997. *Nationalism Without a Nation in India*. Delhi: Oxford University Press.

Amin, Shahid, and Dipesh Chakrabarty, eds. 1996. *Subaltern Studies* vol. IX. Delhi: Oxford University Press.

Anderson, Benedict. 1991. *Imagined Communities*. Revised edition. London: Verso.

Appadurai, Arjun. 2001. *Globalization*. Durham & London: Duke University Press.

Arnold, David, and David Hardiman, eds. 1994. *Subaltern Studies* vol. VIII. Delhi: Oxford University Press.

Assiter, Allison. 1996. *Enlightened Women*. London: Routledge.

Avasthi, Abha, ed. 1997. *Social and Cultural Diversities: D.P. Mukerji in Memorium*. Jaipur: Rawat Publications.

Baig, Tara Ali, ed. 1958. *Women in India*. Delhi: Manager Publication.

Ball, Terence, James Farr, and Russell L. Hanson, eds. 1989. *Political*

Innovation and Conceptual Change. Cambridge: Cambridge University Press.

Barbalet, J.M. 1998. *Citizenship: Rights, Struggles and Class Inequalities.* Open University Press, Milton Keynes.

Barker, Francis, ed. 1985. *Europe and its Others.* Colchester: University of Essex Press.

Basu, D.D. 1999. *Introduction to the Constitution of India.* Nagpur: Wadhawa and Wadhawa.

Baxi, Upendra. 1982. *The Crisis of the Indian Legal System.* Delhi: Vikas.

Bharucha, Rustom. 1998. *In the Name of the Secular: Contemporary Cultural Activism in India.* Delhi: Oxford University Press.

Book, Gisela, and Susan James, ed. 1992. *Beyond Equality and Difference.* London: Routledge.

Borthwick, Meredith. 1984. *The Changing Role of Women in Bengal 1849–1905.* Princeton,.

Bowles, Samuel, and Herbert Gintis. 1986. *Democracy and Capitalism: Property, Community and the Contradiction of Modern Social Thought.* New York: Basic Books.

Brubaker, Rogers. 1992. *Citizenship and Nationhood in France and Germany.* Cambridge: Harvard University Press.

Buchanan, Allen. 1989. *Marx and Justice: The Radical Critique of Liberalism.* New Jersey.

Callaway, Helen. 1987. *Gender, Culture and Empire: European Women in Colonial Nigeria.* Urbana: University of Illinois Press.

Carby, Hazel. 1987. *Reconstructing Womanhood: The Emergence of the Afro-American Woman Novelist.* New York: Oxford University Press.

Cesaire, Aime. 1972. *Discourse on Colonialism.* Translated by Joan Pinkham. New York, MR.

Chatterjee, Partha. 1994. *The Nation and its Fragments: Colonial and Postcolonial Histories.* Delhi: Oxford University Press.

—. ed. 1998. *Wages of Freedom: Fifty Years of the Indian Nation-State.* Delhi: Oxford University Press.

Chaudhuri, Nupur, and Margaret Strobel, eds. 1992. *Western Women and Imperialism.* Bloomington: Indiana University Press.

Chimni, B.S. 2000. *International Refugee Law: A Reader.* Delhi: Sage.

Collins, Patricia Hill. 1991. *Black Feminist Thought.* New York and London: Routledge.

Cousins, Margaret. 1941. *Indian Womanhood Today.* Allahabad.

Dallmayr, F., ed. 1978. *From Contract to Community.* New York: Marcel Decker.

Davies, Miranda. ed. 1983. *Third World/Second Sex: Women's Struggles and National Liberation*. London: Zed Books.

Desai, A.R., ed. 1991. *Expanding Governmental Lawlessness and Organised Resistance*. Delhi: Popular Prakashan.

Donaldson, Laura. 1992. *Decolonizing Feminism: Race, Gender and Empire Building*. London: University of North Carolina Press.

DuBois, W.E.B. 1968. *The Souls of Black Folk, Essays and Sketches*. Chicago: A.C. McClurg.

Ehrenreich, B., and D. English. 1979. *For Her Own Good: 150 Years of Experts' Advice to Women*. London: Pluto.

Elshtain, Jean Bethke. 1981. *Public Man, Private Woman: Women in Social and Political Thought*. Princeton: Princeton University Press.

Engels, Dagmar, and Shula Marks, eds. 1994. *Contesting Colonial Hegemony*. London: Academic Press.

Enloe, Cynthia. 1989. *Bananas, Beaches and Bases: Making Feminist Sense of International Politics*. Berkeley: University of California Press.

Fanon, Frantz. 1965. *The Wretched of the Earth*. New York: Penguin.

—. 1967. *A Dying Colonialism*. New York: Grove Press.

Faulks, Keith. 2000. *Citizenship*. London & New York: Routledge.

Finer, S.E. 1999. *The History of Government III: Empires, Monarchies and the Modern State*. Oxford: Oxford University Press.

Forbes, Geraldine. 1989. *Shudha Mazumdar: Memoirs of an Indian Woman*. New York: Sharpe.

—. 1998. *Women in Modern India*. South Asian paperback edition. Cambridge: Cambridge University Press.

Gellner, Ernest. 1964. *Thought and Change*. London: Weidenfeld and Nicolson.

—. 1983. *Nations and Nationalism*. Oxford: Blackwell Publishers.

Giddens, Anthony. 1984. *The Constitution of Society: Outline of the Theory of Structuration*. Berkeley and Los Angeles: University of California Press.

Gilligan, Carol. 1982. *In a Different Voice: Psychological Theory and Moral Development*. Cambridge: Harvard University Press.

Greenfeld, Liah. 2001. 'Etymology, Definitions, Types'. In *Encyclopedia of Nationalism*. London: Academic Press.

Guha, Ranajit, ed. 1982. *Subaltern Studies* vol. I. Delhi: Oxford University Press.

Hall, Catherine. 1992. *White, Male and Middle Class: Explorations of Feminism and History*. Cambridge: Routledge.

Hashmi, Safdar. 1989. *The Right to Perform*. New Delhi: SAHMAT.

Heater, Derek. 1990. *Citizenship: The Civic Ideal in World History, Politics and Education*. London: Orient Longman.

—. 1999. *What is Citizenship?*. Cambridge: Polity.

Jayawardena, Kumari. 1982. *Feminism and Nationalism in the Third World*. Institute of Social Studies, The Hague.

Karlekar, Malvika. 1991. *Voices From Within*. Delhi: Oxford University Press.

Kashyap Subhash. 1997. *Citizens and the Constitution*. Delhi: Publications Division, Government of India.

Keddie, Nikkie, and Beth Baron, eds. 1992. *Women in Middle-Eastern History*. New Haven: Yale University Press.

King, Desmond S. 1987. *The New Right: Politics, Markets and Citizenship*. London: Macmillan.

Kumar, Radha. 1993. *History of Doing*. Delhi: Kali for Women.

Kymlicka, Will. 1996. *Multicultural Citizenship: A Liberal Theory of Minority Rights*. Oxford: Clarendon Press.

Larson, Gerald James. 1997. *India's Agony Over Religion*. Delhi: Oxford University Press.

Lister, Ruth. 1997. *Citizenship: Feminist Perspectives*. London: Macmillan.

Lukes, Steven. 1987. *Marxism and Morality*. Oxford: Oxford University Press.

Macedo, Stephen. 1990. *Liberal Virtues: Citizenship, Virtue, and Community in Liberal Constitutionalism*. Oxford: Clarendon.

Mahajan, Gurpreet. 1998. *Identities and Rights: Aspects of Liberal Democracy in India*. Delhi: Oxford University Press.

—. 2002. *The Multicultural Path: Issues of Diversity and Discrimination*. New Delhi: Sage.

Marshall, T.H. 1950. *Citizenship and Social Class and Other Essays*. Cambridge: Cambridge University Press.

Marshall, T.H., and Tom Bottomore. eds. 1992. *Citizenship and Social Class*. London: Pluto Press.

Marx, Karl. 1975. *Early Writings*. Harmondsworth: Penguin.

Mazumdar, Vina, ed. 1979. *Symbols of Power*. Bombay: Allied Publishers.

Merchant, Carolyn. 1983. *The Death of Nature: Women, Ecology and the Scientific Revolution*. San Francisco: Harper and Row.

Mies, Maria. 1986. *Patriarchy and Accumulation on a World Scale: Women in the International Division of Labour*. London: Zed.

Miliband, Ralph, and Leo Panitch, eds. 1990. *Socialist Register*. London: Merlin Press.

Mills, Sara. 1991. *Discourses of Difference*. London: Routledge.

Minh-ha, Trinh T. 1989. *Women, Native, Other: Writing Postcoloniality and Feminism*. Bloomington: Indiana University Press.

Mouffe, Chantal, ed. 1992. *Dimensions of Radical Democracy*. London: Verso.

Nairn, Tom. 1977. *The Break up of Britain: Crisis and Neo-Nationalism*. London: New Left Books.

Nehru, Shyam Kumari, ed. n.d. *Our Cause*. Allahabad: Kitabistan.

Niranjana, Tejaswini, P. Sudhir, and Vivek Dhareshwar, eds. 1993. *Interrogating Modernity: Culture and Colonialism in India*. Calcutta: Seagull Books.

Omvedt, Gail. 1993. *Reinventing Revolution: New Social Movements and the Socialist Tradition in India*. London: Sharpe.

Pandey, Gyanendra. 1994. 'The Prose of Otherness'. In *Subaltern Studies* vol. VIII. Delhi: Oxford University Press.

Pateman, Carole. 1988. *The Sexual Contract*. Cambridge: The Polity Press.

Prakash, Gyan. 2000. *Another Reason*. New Delhi: Oxford University Press.

Qidwai, Anees. 1990. *Azadi ki Chhaon Mein* (Hindi translation), p. 151. New Delhi.

Reddy, Muthulakshmi. 1956. *Margaret Cousins and Her Work in India*. Madras: WIA.

Riley, Denise. 1988. *'Am I That Name': Feminism and the Category of Women in History*. London: Macmillan Press.

Rubinstein, David. 1986. *Before the Suffragettes: Women's Emancipation in the 1890s*. Sussex: The Harvester Press.

Sankrityayan, Rahul. 1950. *Meri Jeevan Yatra* vol. II. Allahabad.

Saraswati, Sahajanand. 1985. *Mera Jeevan Sangharsh*. Delhi.

Said, Edward. 1978. *Orientalism*. New York: Vintage Books.

Sangari, Kumkum, and Sudesh Vaid, eds. 1989. *Recasting Women: Essays in Colonial History*. Delhi: Kali for Women.

Sarkar, Sumit. 1985. *The Critique of Colonial India*. Calcutta: Papyrus.

Scott, Joan Wallach. 1988. *Gender and the Politics of History*. New York: Columbia University Press.

Sen, Indrani. 2002. *Woman and Empire: Representations in the Writings of British India (1858–1900)*. New Delhi: Orient Longman.

Sen, Mihir Kumar. 1946. *Elements of Civics*. 14th edition. Hindustan Publications.

Shafir, Gershon. 1998. *The Citizenship Debates: A Reader*. Minneapolis: University of Minnesota Press.

Sharpe, Jenny. 1993. *Allegories of Empire: The Figure of Women in the Colonial Text*. London: University of Minnesota Press.

Shastri, Srinivas. 1948. *The Indian Citizen: His Rights and Duties*. Bombay: Hind Kitab Limited.

Singh, Ujjwal Kumar. 1998. *Political Prisoners in India*. Delhi: Oxford University Press.

Singha, Radhika. 1998. *A Despotism of Law: Crime and Justice in Early Colonial India*. Delhi: Oxford University Press.

Sinha, Mrinalini. 1995. *Colonial Masculinity: The Manly Englishman and the Effiminate Bengali*. Manchester: Manchester University Press.

Smith, Anthony D. 1983. *Theories of Nationalism*. 2nd edition. London: Duckworth.

Smith, Dorothy. 1987. *The Everyday World as Problematic: A Feminist Sociology*. Northeastern University, Boston.

Smith, Vincent A. 1919. *Indian Constitutional Reforms Viewed in the Light of History*. London: Humphrey Milford.

Southard, Barbara. 1995. *The Women's Movement and Colonial Politics in Bengal*. Delhi: Manohar.

Soysal, Yasemin. 1994. *Limits of Citizenship*. Chicago: University of Chicago Press.

Steiner, Henry J., and Philip Alston, eds. 1996. *International Human Rights in Context*. Oxford: Clarendon Press.

Stromquist, Nelly, ed. 1998. *Women in the Third World*. New York: Garland.

Tagore, Rabindranath. 1917. *Nationalism*. Macmillan.

Thorner, Alice, and Maithreyi Krishnaraj, eds. 2000. *Ideals, Images and Real Lives: Women in Literature and History*. Delhi: Orient Longman.

Turner, Bryan. 1986. *Citizenship and Capitalism: The Debate Over Reformism*. London: Allen and Unwin.

—. 1990. *Theories of Modernity and Post Modernity*. London: Sage.

—. 1993. *Citizenship and Social Theory*. London: Sage.

Valles-Santiago, Kelvin. 1994. *Subject People and Colonial Discourses: Economic Transformation and Social Disorder in Puerto Rico, 1898–1947*. Albany: SUNY Press.

Vogel, Ursula, and Michael Moran. 1991. *The Frontiers of Citizenship*. New York: St. Martin's Press.

West, Lois A., ed. 1997. *Feminist Nationalism*. New York: Routledge.

Woolf, Virginia. 1938. *Three Guineas*. New York: Harbinger Book.

Yuval-Davis, Nira, and Flora Anthias, eds. 1989. *Women-Nation-State*. Basingstoke: Macmillan.

Yuval-Davis, Nira. 1997. *Gender and Nation*. London: Sage.

Yuval-Davis, Nira, and Pnina Werbner, eds. 1999. *Women, Citizenship and Difference*. London: Zed.

B. Articles

Alexander, Alexander. 1958. 'Sarojini Naidu: Romanticism and Resistance'. *Economic and Political Weekly* (26 October).

Ali, Aruna Asaf. n.d. 'Women Suffrage in India'. In *Our Cause*. Edited by Shyam Kumari Nehru. Allahabad: Kitabistan.

Antonius, Soraya. 1983. 'Fighting on Two Fronts: Conversations with Palestinian Women'. In *Third World/Second Sex*. Edited by Miranda Davies. London: Zed Books.

Assiter, Alison. 1999. 'Citizenship Revisited'. In *Women, Citizenship and Difference*. Edited by Nira Yuval-Davis and Pnina Werbner. London: Zed.

Bagchi, Jasodhara. 1985. 'Positivism and Nationalism: Womanhood and Crisis in Nationalist Fiction-Bankimchandra's Anandmath'. *Economic and Political Weekly* (26 October).

Banerjee, Nirmala. 1989. 'Working Women in Colonial Bengal: Modernisation and Marginalisation'. In *Recasting Women*. Edited by Kumkum Sangari and Sudesh Vaid. Delhi: Kali for Women.

Bartholomew, Amy. 1990. 'Should a Marxist Believe in Marx on Rights?'. In *Socialist Register*. Edited by Ralph Miliband and Leo Panitch. London: Merlin Press.

Baruah, Sanjib. 2003. 'Protective Discrimination and Crisis of Citizenship in North-East India'. *Economic and Political Weekly* 38, no. 17 (26 April).

Bottomore, Tom. 1992. 'Citizenship and Social Class: Forty Years On'. In *Citizenship and Social Class*. Edited by T.H. Marshall and Tom Bottomore. London: Pluto Press.

Chakrabarty, Dipesh. 1992. 'Postcoloniality and the Artifice of History: Who Speaks for the Indian Past'. *Representations* no. 37 (winter).

—. 1993. 'The Difference-Deferral of (A) Colonial Modernity: Public Debates on Modernity in British Bengal'. *History Workshop Journal* no. 36.

—. 1995. 'Modernity and Ethnicity in India: A History for the Present'. *Economic and Political Weekly* (30 December).

—. 1995. 'Radical Histories and Question of Enlightenment Rationality'. *Economic and Political Weekly* 30, no. 14.

Chatterjee, Partha. 1989a. 'Colonialism, Nationalism and Colonialised Women: The Contest in India'. *American Ethnologist* 16, no. 4 (November).

—. 1989b. 'The Nationalist Resolution of the Women's Question'. In *Recasting Women*. Edited by Kumkum Sangari and Sudesh Vaid. Delhi: Kali For Women.

—. 1994. 'Secularism and Toleration'. *Economic and Political Weekly* (9 July).

Chaudhuri, Maitrayee. 1996. 'Citizens, Workers and Emblems of Culture'. In *Social Reform, Sexuality and the State*. Edited by Patricia Uberoi. New Delhi: Sage.

Clark, Anna. 1996. 'Gender, Class and the Nation: Franchise Reform in England, 1832–1928'. In *Re-reading the Constitution*. Edited by James Vernon. Cambridge: Cambridge University Press.

Cornell, Drucilla. 1984. 'Should a Marxist Believe in Rights'. *Praxis International* no. 45.

Cohn, Bernard S., and Nicholas B. Dirks. 1988. 'Beyond the Fringe: The Nation-State, Colonialism and Technologies of Power'. *Journal of Historical Sociology* 1, no. 2 (June).

de Groot, Joanna. 1995. 'The Dialectics of Gender: Women, Men and Political Discourses in Iran c.1890–1930'. *Gender and History* 5 (summer).

Desai, A.R. 1997. 'Empowering the Sovereign Citizens in India: Some Constitutional Obstacles'. In *Social and Cultural Diversities: D.P. Mukerji in Memorium*. Edited by Abha Avasthi. Jaipur: Rawat Publications.

Dietz, Mary. 1992. 'Context is All'. In *Dimensions of Radical Democracy*. Edited by Chantal Mouffe. London: Verso.

Ferrajoli, Luigi. 1996. 'Beyond Sovereignty and Citizenship': A Global Constitutionalism'. In *Constitutionalism, Democracy and Sovereignty: American and European Perspectives*. Edited by Richard Bellamy. Avebury.

Forbes, Geraldine. 1979. 'Caged Tigers: First Wave Feminists in India'. *Women's Studies InternationalQuarterly* 5, no. 6.

—. 1979. 'Votes for Women'. In *Symbols of Power*. Edited by Vina Mazumdar. Bombay: Allied Publishers.

Freitag, Sandria B. 1991. 'Introduction'. *South Asia* 14, no. 1.

Ghosh, Srabashi. 1986. 'Birds in a Cage: Changes in Bengal Social Life as Recorded in Autobiographies by Women'. *Economic and Political Weekly* (25 October).

Guha, Ranajit. 1982. 'On Some Aspects of Historiography of Colonial India'. In *Subaltern Studies* vol. I. Edited by Ranajit Guha. Delhi: Oxford University Press.

Haggis, Jane. 1990. 'Gendering Colonialism or Colonising Gender? Recent Women's Studies Approaches to White Women and the History of British Colonialism'. *Women's Studies International Forum* 13.

Habermas, Jurgen. 1992. 'Citizenship and National Identity: Some Reflections on the Future of Europe'. *Praxis International* 12, no. 1 (April).

Hansen, Kathryn. 1988. 'The Virangana in North Indian History: Myth and Popular Culture'. *Economicand Political Weekly* (30 April).

Inden Ronald. 1986. 'Orientalist Constructions of India'. *Modern Asian Studies* 20 (July).

Jha, Shefali. 2003. 'Rights versus Representation: Defending Minority Interests in the Constituent Aseembly'. *Economic and Political Weekly* 38, no. 16 (19 April).

Kandiyoti, Deniz. 1992. 'Islam and Patriarchy: A Comparative Perspective'. In *Women in Middle-Eastern History*. Edited by Nikkie Keddie and Beth Baron. New Haven: Yale University Press.

Kaviraj, Sudipta. 1994. 'On the Construction of Colonial Power: Structure, Discourse, Hegemony'. In *Contesting Colonial Hegemony*. Edited by Dagmar Engels and Shula Marks. London: Academic Press.

Klein, Lawrence E. 1995. 'Gender and the Public/Private Distinction in the 18th Century: Some Questions About Evidence and Analytic Procedure'. *Eighteenth Century Studies* 29, no. 1.

Kymlicka, Will, and Wayne Norman. 1994. 'The Return of the Citizen'. *Ethics* no. 104 (January).

Leonard, Virginia W. 1998. 'Women in Anticolonial Movements'. In *Women in the Third World*. Edited by Nelly P. Stromquist. New York: Garland.

Liddle, Joana, and Rama Joshi. 1985. 'Women's Organization under the Raj'. *Women's Studies International Forum* 8.

Lister, Ruth. 1997. 'Towards a Feminist Synthesis'. *Feminist Review*, special issue on *Citizenship: Pushing the Boundaries* no. 57 (autumn).

Lukes, Steven. 1982. 'Can a Marxist Believe in Rights'. *Praxis International* no. 334.

Mahajan, Gurpreet. 1999. 'Multiculturalism'. *Seminar* no. 484.

Mani, Lata. 1985. 'The Production of an Official Discourse on Sati'. In

Europe and its Others. Edited by Francis Barker. Colchester: University of Essex Press.

—. 1989. 'Contentious Traditions: The Debate on sati in Colonial India'. In *Recasting Women: Essays in Colonial History*. Edited by Kumkum Sangari and Sudesh Vaid. Delhi: Kali for Women.

Mayaram, Shail. 1991. 'Criminality or Community? Alternative Constructions of the Mev Narrative of Darya Khan'. *Contributions to Indian Sociology (n.s.)* 25, no. 1.

Mazumdar, Sucheta. 1992. 'Women, Culture and Politics: Engendering the Hindu Nation'. *South Asia Bulletin* 12, no. 2 (fall).

McBride, William. 1984. 'Rights in the Marxian Tradition'. *Praxis International* no. 57.

McClintock, Anne. 1993. 'Family Feuds: Gender, Nationalism and the Family'. *Feminist Review* no. 44 (summer).

Menon, Nivedita. 1998. 'State/Gender/Community, Citizenship in Contemporary India'. *Economic and Political Weekly* (31 January).

—. 1998. 'Women and Citizenship'. In *Wages of Freedom*. Edited by Partha Chatterjee. Delhi: Oxford University Press.

Mies, Maria. 1998. 'World Economy, Patriarchy and Accumulation'. In *Women in the Third World*. Edited by Nelly Stromquist. New York: Garland.

Moraes, Frank. 1958. 'In Political Life'. In *Women in India*. Edited by Tara Ali Baig. Delhi: Manager Publication.

Mouffe, Chantal. 1992. 'Citizenship and Political Identity'. *October* no. 60 (summer).

Nash, Catherine. 1993. 'Remapping and Renaming: New Cartographies of Identity, Gender and Landscape in Ireland'. *Feminist Review* no. 44 (summer).

Nigam, Aditya. 1996. 'Nation, Locality and Representation: India After the 1996 Elections'. *Asian Survey* (December).

Oommen, T.K. 1998. 'Unpacking Identities: Notions of Citizenship and Nationality'. *Times of India* (16 December).

Pandey, Gyanendra. 1998. 'The Prose of Otherness'. In *Subaltern Studies* vol. VIII. Edited by David Arnold and David Hardiman. Delhi: Oxford University Press.

—. 1984. 'The Congress and the Nation, c.1917–1947'. *Centre for the Study of Social Sciences*, Calcutta.

Patel, Sujata. 1988. 'Construction and Reconstruction of Women in Gandhi'. *Economic and Political Weekly* (20 February).

Pateman, Carole. 1992. 'Equality, Difference, Subordination: The Politics of Motherhood and Women's Citizenship'. In *Beyond Equality and Difference*. Edited by Gisela Book and Susan James. London: Routledge.

Pearson, Gail. 1983. 'Reserved Seats: Women and the Vote in Bombay'. *The Indian Economic and Social History Review* 20, no. 1.

Pettman, Jan-Jindy. 1999. 'Globalisation and the Gendered Politics of Citizenship'. In *Women, Citizenship and Difference*. Edited by Nira Yuval-Davis and Pnina Werbner. London: Zed.

Phillips, Anne. 1992. 'Must Feminists Give up on Liberal Democracy'. *Political Studies* 40, special issue.

Prokhovnik, Raisa. 1998. 'Public and Private Citizenship'. *Feminist Review*, special issue on Feminist Ethics and the Politics of Love no. 60 (autumn).

Said, Edward. 1990. 'Third World Intellectuals and Metropolitan Culture'. *Raritan* 9 (winter).

—. 1991. 'The Politic of Knowledge'. *Raritan* 11 (summer).

Sangari, Kumkum. 1993. 'The Politics of the Possible'. In *Interrogating Modernity: Culture and Colonialism in India*. Edited by Tejaswini Niranjana, P. Sudhir, and Vivek Dhareshwar. Calcutta: Seagull Books.

Santiago-Valles, Kelvin. 1993. 'Trying to Pin Myself in History: Race Sex and Colonialism'. *Border/Lines* no. 29/30 (December).

Sarkar, Tanika. 1987. 'Nationalist Iconography: Images of Women in the 19th Century Bengali Literature'. *Economic and Political Weekly* (21 November).

—. 1992. 'The Hindu Wife and the Hindu Nation: Domesticity and Nationalism in Nineteenth Century Bengal'. *Studies in History* 8, no. 2.

Scott, Joan Wallach. 1991. 'The Evidence of Experience'. *Critical Inquiry* no. 17.

Sen, Samita. 1993. 'Motherhood and Mothercraft: Gender and Nationalism in Bengal'. *Gender and History* 5, no. 2.

Sinha, Mrinalini. 1992. 'Chatham, Pitts and Gladstone in Petticoats': The Politics of Gender and Race in the Ilbert Bill Controversy, 1883–1884'. In *Western Women and Imperialism*. Edited by Nupur Chaudhuri and Margaret Strobel. Bloomington: Indiana University Press.

Somers, Margaret R. 1993. 'Citizenship and the Place of the Public Sphere, Law, Community and the Political Culture in the Transition to Democracy'. *American Sociological Review* no. 58.

Tharu, Susie, and Tejaswini Niranjana. 1996. 'Problems for a Contemporary Theory of Gender'. In *Subaltern Studies* IX. Edited by Shahid Amin and Dipesh Chakrabarty. Delhi: Oxford University Press.

Turner, Bryan. 1993. 'Outline of a Theory of Human Rights'. In *Citizenship and Social Theory*. Edited by Bryan Turner. London: Sage.

van Gunstern, Herman. 1978. 'Notes Towards a Theory of Citizenship'. In *From Contract to Community*. Edited by F. Dallmayr. New York: Marcel Decker.

Uberoi, Patricia. 1990. 'Feminine Identity and National Ethos in Indian Calendar Art'. *Economic and Political Weekly* (28 April).

Vaid, Sudesh. 1988. 'Politics of Widow Immolation'. *Seminar* no. 342 (February).

Valles-Santiago, Kelvin. 1993. 'Trying to Pin Myself in History: Race, Sex and Colonialism'. *Border/Lines* no. 29/30.

Vogel, Ursula. 1991. 'Is Citizenship Gender Specific?'. In *The Frontiers of Citizenship*. Edited by Ursula Vogel and Michael Moran. New York: St. Martin's Press.

Walzer, Michael. 1989. 'Citizenship'. In *Political Innovation and Conceptual Change*. Edited by Terence Ball, James Farr, and Russell L. Hanson. Cambridge: Cambridge University Press.

—. 1992. 'The Civil Society Argument'. In *Dimensions of Radical Democracy*. Edited by Chantal Mouffe. London: Verso.

Yang, Anand. 1990. 'Gender and Colonialism'. In *Women's Studies International Forum* 13.

Young, Iris Marion. 1989. 'Polity and Group Difference: A Critique of the Ideal of Universal Citizenship'. *Ethics* no. 99.

Yuval-Davis, Nira. 1991. 'The Citizenship Debate: Women, Ethnic Processes and the State'. *Feminist Review* no. 39 (winter).

—. 1997. 'Women, Citizenship and Difference'. *Feminist Review* no. 57 (autumn).

II. Hindi Sources

Chhedalal, Babu. 1915. *Grihalakshmi Granthamala: Abalonnati Padyamala*. Prayag: Grihalakshmi Karyalaya.

Das, Shayamsundar. 1906. *Vanita Vinod*. Kashi: Nagari Pracharini Sabha.

Devi, Yashoda. 1924. *Grihini Kartavyashastra, Arogyashastra Arthat Pakshastra*. 3rd edition. Prayag: Vanita Hitaishini Press.

—. 1925. *Pati Prem Patrika*. Prayag: Vanita Hitaishini Press.

—. 1934. *Pativratadharma Mala—Nari Dharma Shiksha*. Allahabad: Vanita Hitaishini Press.

—. sam.1982. *Nitigyan*. Prayag: Vanita Hitaishini Press.

Devi, Manavrata. 1942. *Nari Dharma Shiksha*. 7th edition. Kashi Pustak Bhandar.
Garg, Mahendralal. 1900. *Stri Shiksha*. Nai Sarak, Delhi: Govindram Hasanand.
Goyandeka, Jayadayal. sam.2002. *Nari Dharma*. 8th edition. Gorakhpur: Geeta Press.
Hardevi, Shrimati. 1892. *Striyon Pe Samajik Atyachar*. Allahabad.
Mishra, Baldevprasad. sam.1965. *Nariratnamala*. Bombay: Shri Venkateshwara Steam Yantralaya.
Srivastava, Shaligram. 1937. *Prayag Pradeep*. Allahabad: Hindustani Academy.

III. Official Reports

Annual Report of the All India Women's Conference, 1933–34.
Indian Statutory Commission, *Survey Report*, Government of India, 1930.
Report of the Joint Committee on Indian Constitutional Reform, Session 1933–34, vol. I.
Report of the Franchise Committee on Division of Functions, 1918–1919.
Report of the Franchise Sub-Committee of the Round Table Conference, 1931.
Indian Round Table Conference 12 November 1930 to 19 January 1931, Proceedings of Sub-Committees, Part II.

IV. Unpublished Sources

Jimenez-Munoz, Gladys. 1993. 'A Storm Dressed in Skirts: Ambivalences in the Debate on Women's Suffrage in Puerto Rico'. Ph.D. dissertation, State University of New York, Binghamton.
Nigam, Sanjay. 1987. 'A Social History of a Colonial Stereotype: the Criminal Tribes and Castes of Uttar Pradesh 1871–1930'. Ph.D. thesis, University of London.
Sainsbury, Alison. 1995. 'Domesticity and Empire'. Ph.D. dissertation, Cornell University.
Visweswaran, Kamala. 1990. 'Family Subjects: An Ethnography of the 'Women's Question' in Indian Nationalism'. Ph.D. dissertation, Stanford University.

Index